Theological Turning Points

Theological
Turning Points

Major Issues in Christian Thought

DONALD K. McKIM

Westminster John Knox Press
Louisville, Kentucky

Library of Congress Cataloging-in-Publication Data
McKim, Donald K.
    Theological turning points.

    Bibliography: p.
    Includes index.
    1. Theology, Doctrinal–History. I. Title.
BT21.M19   1988   230'.09   88–45432
ISBN 0–8042–0702–X

©copyright John Knox Press, 1988
10 9 8
Printed in the United States of America
Westminster John Knox Press
Louisville, Kentucky

Preface

Nearly twenty years ago I purchased a small book by R. A. Finlayson entitled *The Story of Theology* (London: Tyndale, 1963). Six of its chapters were lectures for lay people on the history of Christian doctrine. Through this book I first became aware of an inner logic in the development of doctrine. Following James Orr's major work, *The Progress of Dogma* (1901), Finlayson spoke of the historical development of Christian doctrine, which Orr says follows a "logical order that renders it scientific as well as historical." Finlayson's chapters showed me how the church had progressed first through the doctrine of the Trinity, then Christology, then the doctrine of humanity, and so on, each solidifying some aspect of Christian faith, then raising new questions and issues for later generations. Further studies acquainted me with a number of the important controversies in the history of Christian thought. These were turning points in the development of Christian doctrine that helped put subsequent discussions on new footings.

In the present volume I attempt to give an account of some of these turning points and to trace the development of major Christian doctrines in their formative stages. As such, the work is both historical and systematic in approach. The book is written for three groups of people. College and theological students will find it a useful guide in capsulizing what they read in other books and study in their classes. I have tried to provide ample documentation in the notes, so that topics can be explored further. Though the secondary literature is extensive, I have made direct quotations in the text only from primary sources, that is, from the theologians and documents being studied. Unfortunately it has not been possible to alter all these citations to reflect more inclusive language.

Second, lay people in churches will find this book a helpful way to gain a broad picture of some of the significant theological issues the church has faced and some of the important formulations that have shaped our understanding of these issues. I feel keenly the need for a one-volume work that introduces the history of Christian theology to people with little or no theological background. My purpose in working on these doctrines is to focus attention on how they developed and to make it easier to study specific issues. The book can be read most naturally chapter by chapter as each traces doctrinal development. Or it can be approached by historical periods or by theologians, in order to get a picture of what the early church or a particular theologian said on the doctrine being covered.

Third, I hope that pastors as well will turn to this book and that a few apt quotations may find their way into Sunday sermons. Beyond this I hope the book will reawaken interest—perhaps submerged since seminary—in how the church has done its theology, and that in teaching and preaching this may be a convenient place to turn to find out who has said what and to be stimulated to think about the implications and ongoing relevance of Christian doctrine.

Numerous people and resources have contributed to the preparation of this book. Those who write on the history of Christian thought find the works of scholars like J. N. D. Kelly, Jaroslav Pelikan, Reinhold Seeberg, Justo González, Otto Heick, and Bernhard Lohse indispensable. Behind them all stands the great historian of dogma, Adolf von Harnack, who, though not cited directly, has added immensely to theological understanding.

Most of all, however, I am grateful to the teachers who helped me learn and love the history of Christian doctrine. Dr. Jack B. Rogers, Dr. Robert S. Paul, and Dr. Arthur C. Cochrane have all been close friends and superb teachers. And the late Dr. Ford Lewis Battles, an incomparable historian of the church and its theology, left a lasting imprint upon me from our studies together at Pittsburgh Seminary.

Also to be thanked are LindaJo, Stephen, and Karl McKim—the teachers who show me daily what Christian doctrine and life together really mean.

This book is dedicated to the memory of my friend and former pastor, the Reverend John E. Karnes, who introduced me to Christian theology. Through preaching, conversation, and caring he helped me develop a love for the history of Christian thought. For him I will always be deeply grateful.

Donald K. McKim

To the memory of John E. Karnes
preacher, teacher, and friend
with gratitude and appreciation
for introducing me to the joys
of Christian doctrine
and the Christian life

Contents

Introduction

The following chapters focus on some of the major theological issues the church has faced through the centuries. They are studies in historical theology: the development of Christian doctrine and the history of Christian thought. The eight so-called controversies presented here are chosen because they represent major sources of contention among Christian theologians. What follows is obviously not a complete history—even of the doctrines considered. It is, rather, a basic discussion—at times somewhat narrowly focused—of those areas where the church has considered a variety of viewpoints.

The key rubric used in the controversies is *turning point*. At some junctures turning points have been quite sharp: for example, when Athanasius countered Arius or Augustine engaged Pelagius. Yet in a broader sense, as doctrines have taken shape in the church, the view of each theologian is a turning point in itself. As new proposals are made, older ones are discarded, modified, or reemphasized in a different context. Each new formulation of a theological issue introduces new questions and concerns, and perhaps brings new conclusions. Each proposal is thus a new turning point. The history of Christian doctrine involves change and development, as the church studies, dialogues, debates, and perhaps at

some points—by means of a church council—declares a certain understanding to be normative or binding. In other instances the church has
issued no official pronouncement but lived instead with multiple theological options.

The present work concentrates on the development of doctrine in the
early church period. These were the centuries in which the most fundamental and crucial understandings developed as the church's theological
foundation. Each chapter begins with the biblical basis of the issue and
tracks the development of the doctrine—or at times of one or two aspects
of the doctrine—through the early centuries and then (with varying
amounts of detail) through the Middle Ages to the Reformation and
Counter-Reformation. This has led to greater weight on the earlier period
and in some instances to a definite slighting of other important emerging
views.

The Reformation and post-Reformation period provides the necessary
stopping point for several of the discussions. There are, of course, significant later turning points, and some of these are considered briefly in the
final chapter. This stopping point, however, recognizes that by the end of
the sixteenth century, many of the classic issues had been joined, and
future discussions would find their sources—both positive and negative in
the insights of previous centuries. Thus the following chapters are not
meant to be comprehensive but instead to pinpoint key directions and
show the broad contours of how various understandings developed.

The problem of how doctrines *develop* is a complicated one. How does
the church explain, for example, that centuries elapsed before some of its
beliefs were fully stated? By the time of the Reformation, the usual answer
was that the earlier generations did not find it necessary to make all the
logical connections between the scriptural data, church teachings, and
certain issues. If a controversy had not raised the issue, the church just did
not fully realize what was involved.[1]

A related question is the problem of doctrinal change. How could the
unchanging truth of Christianity develop and grow? The well-known
maxim of St. Vincent of Lérins that "one must take the greatest possible
care to believe what has been believed everywhere, ever, by everyone"
meant by implication that theological truth does not change and has not
changed from one part of the church to another, regardless of time, culture,
and location.[2] The history of doctrine, however, seems to indicate other-
wise.

Questions related to the issue of whether and how doctrines can
develop stand behind all attempts to describe how, in fact, various viewpoints have emerged. A number of historians of doctrine, beginning with
John Henry Newman's *Essay on the Development of Christian Doctrine* in

1845, have wrestled with the issues, and the accounts of these complex struggles are fascinating.

In the preface mention was made of James Orr's view that there has been real development and progress in the church's doctrines through the centuries. Orr believed the historical order in which Christian doctrines were debated and clarified was also the most logical order. "The development is not arbitrary, but shaped by the inner reason and necessity of the case. The simple precedes the more complex; fundamental doctrines those which need the former as their basis; problems in the order in which they naturally and inevitably arise in the evolution of thought."[3]

Orr's views have been criticized both theologically and historically, and the most logical way of dealing with Christian doctrines has been variously assessed. The fact that theologians and Christian confessions of faith treat doctrines in various orders shows that no one logical sequence has been agreed upon. Historically, it has been claimed that Orr's presentation requires a "selective reading and ordering of the way in which dogma emerged."[4] For example, his book does not deal with the doctrine of the church, the ministry, or the sacraments.[5] Despite these strictures, it is still possible to maintain a historical approach that broadly recognizes an inner logic, but it cannot be pressed too far; not every doctrine can be brought within its scope.

Some doctrines are more central to the faith than others, and they are the focus of the following chapters. The progression from Trinity to Christology to salvation to authority seems clear as the general path of historical development. Inserted into this progression are chapters on the doctrines of the church and of humanity; and then, after authority, we move on to the sacraments and the kingdom of God. I have not included a direct discussion of atonement, which is part of the doctrine of salvation, nor of Christian ethics or the ministry.[6] Also, some doctrines are considered in only one of their many aspects. Instead of propounding a "developmental theory" that neatly weds history and logic, I want only to show, within the limits of energy and space, that many of the major theological turning points did follow a broad pattern. They moved on to each question after another, more basic one had been more or less answered. The point is that there was a certain trajectory of thought within the church, and that it did not emerge haphazardly.

1

Trinitarian Controversy

Who Is God?

The early church began in a Jewish environment, and many of the first Christians were converts from the Judaism in which they had been born and raised. The emerging church also took from Judaism its holy writings, the Old Testament. Indeed, until Christianity unmistakably established its own identity in the middle of the second century, it was considered a variation of Judaism.

Yet the influence of Jewish faith on the church was accompanied by the increasing influence of Greek thought. For in the first century A.D. the Mediterranean basin experienced a powerful political and cultural unity. This unity was provided by Alexander the Great, who from 334 to 323 B.C. conquered vast areas, which were then infused with the teachings of the great philosophers of Greece, Plato and Aristotle. This hellenistic culture, with its heavy emphasis on philosophy and logical thinking, was the larger context in which early Christians lived, worked, and thought, as the church spread throughout the Roman Empire during the first centuries after Christ.

Biblical Basis

In this environment the Christian church tried to express its faith and understand its God. Through both words and actions Christians sought to obey the God they worshiped. To say precisely who God is and what God is like, however, is no easy task. For contemporaries to understand its message, the church had to confess its faith intelligibly and describe it accurately on the basis of the church's sacred literature, which eventually became the Old and New Testaments.

The church also faced a variety of groups and sects that sought the religious allegiance of people in the first and second centuries. A number of mystery religions, with their origins in ancient fertility rites, as well as various philosophical systems, such as Platonism and Stoicism, all vied for attention. In this context the church saw the necessity of defining the content of its beliefs. It felt the need to sharpen its articulation of the elements it considered essential to the faith. Among the most important issues was the question Who is God?

God Is One

(In common with Judaism, the early Christian church confessed its belief in one God, which is mentioned and summarized often throughout the Old Testament.)The *Shema*, which became the confession of faith for Judaism, is the affirmation, "Hear, O Israel: The LORD our God is one LORD" (Deut. 6:4). "The LORD" (*Yahweh*) is the only and unique God, who has been revealed in human history. For the people of Israel—and against the polytheism of their neighbors—"the LORD is God; there is no other besides him" (Deut. 4:35; see 4:32–39). Numerous passages in Isaiah affirm belief in one unique God, who is unmatched in wisdom, majesty, and power, who is the Lord of all human history, and who is the creator of heaven and earth (see 41:28–29; 42:17; 43:10–11; 44:7–8; 45:5–6, 14–17, 21–22; 46:1–2, 8–11). This affirmation of the uniqueness of God was an inheritance the Christian church also confessed.

The God of Israel, who is to be worshiped above all other gods, is variously described in the Old Testament. God is addressed by many names, such as *Yahweh* (Exod. 34:5; 33:19) and *Elohim* (Gen. 1:26; Exod. 22:9) and described in many images and actions. God is hidden and must be revealed (1 Sam. 3:21); God is personal and is revealed to people like Abraham, Isaac, and Jacob (Gen. 12:1; 26:24; 28:13). Beginning with the covenant with Abraham (Gen. 12) and then with Israel, God chooses a people to be God's own people (Exod. 6:7; Jer. 31:33; Ezek. 37:27; Hos. 2:23; cf. Isa. 40:1). God is present with God's people and is revealed to them in various ways: by theophanies (Exod. 19; 20:18–22), in the ark and tent of meeting (Exod. 33:7–11), by the *angel* of the Lord (Gen. 21:17; Exod. 3:2–5), by the *face* of the Lord (Exod. 23:15, 17; Ps. 24:6; Isa. 1:12), by the *glory* of the Lord (Ps. 29:9; Isa. 6:3; Ezek. 28:22), and by the *name* of the Lord (Deut. 12:5; 1 Kings 11:36).

In addition to these descriptions, the Old Testament has other important ways of saying who God is and what God does. These cluster around
certain terms and descriptions that point to the personality of God and the
personal means of God's activities. God has a parental relationship with
the people of Israel (Exod. 4:22; Isa. 49:15; Jer. 31:9). God acts in the world
through God's *word* (Heb. *dābār*), a powerful way of indicating the outward
expression of the person who speaks, an extension of the speaker's self
(Gen. 1:3; Isa. 55:11). The *Spirit* (Heb. *rūaḥ*, "wind" or "breath") of God in
the Old Testament is a means through which God acts in the world (Judg.
6:34; 1 Sam. 10:10) as God's creative force (Job 33:4), saving power (Zech.
4:6), and all-pervading presence (Ps. 139:7). God works through *wisdom* as
an agent of creation and guide for the world (Job 28; Prov. 8:22–31). God is
also seen in the Old Testament as ultimately coming to establish a kingdom
on earth through a *messiah* (anointed one), who will establish the glorious
reign of God marked by peace and blessedness (Isa. 11:6–9; Jer. 23:5–6; Mic.
5:4).

In all of this, the Old Testament pictures a God who stands alone as the
Creator of the world, who excludes all other deities, and yet who is also
personal and enters into relationships with humans. Although this God is
"one," God's Word, Spirit, and wisdom are often personified expressions of
how God works and what God does (Gen. 1:2; Pss. 33:6; 104:24; Prov. 3:19;
8:22–31; Isa. 40:13). As the early Christian church appropriated the Old
Testament writings as its holy Scripture, it also received the God who is one
yet acts in the world in these particular ways.

God Is Three

As the church developed and a New Testament canon took shape,
other dimensions of the question Who is God? became prominent. The
realities described by various New Testament writers are further ascriptions to the God whom they knew especially and particularly in Jesus
Christ.

As the church studied its Scriptures, the variety of its witness to the
living God became apparent. While the church shared with Judaism its
monotheistic faith in one God, it also recognized the reality of God in Jesus
Christ as well as the work of God's Spirit in specific and vital ways. What
emerged from reflection on the New Testament as a whole was a growing
realization of the relationships between God, Jesus Christ, and the Holy
Spirit; how these three are related was a source of discussion and debate for
many years. From the New Testament comes the strong sense that to
answer who God is requires Christians to affirm God not only as one but
also three.

The actions of God, Jesus Christ, and the Holy Spirit provide the focus of the New Testament. In the different groups of writings, the three are portrayed with a variety of special emphases. In the Synoptic Gospels of Matthew, Mark, and Luke, as well as in the book of Acts, there is a clear affirmation of the oneness of God (Mark 12:29), as in the Old Testament, and God is seen in a parental relationship of love (Matt. 6:9); but the Evangelists also agree that this relationship with God was seen uniquely in Jesus Christ. This is expressed in the titles ascribed to Jesus, such as *Son of God* (Luke 10:22; Matt. 3:17), *Son of Man* (Matt. 9:6; Mark 10:45), and *Lord* (Acts 10:36; 7:59–60). In Paul's writings, the titles *Son of God* (Rom. 1:4; Gal. 2:20; Eph. 4:13) and *Lord* (1 Cor. 11:23; 2 Cor. 4:5; Phil. 2:9) are frequently applied to Jesus, while in the writings of John, he is the *Word* (*Logos*; see John 1) and the *Son of God* (John 3:16; 20:31), and *God the Father* is God's most frequent designation (John 1:14; 10:38; 14:6).

(In these writings the Holy Spirit also plays an important role, and the implication is strong that the Spirit is also a person. This is true particularly in Acts, where the Spirit is said to speak (1:16; 8:29), send (13:4), bear witness (5:32), prevent (16:7), and appoint (20:28). In the Gospel of John, the Holy Spirit is often associated directly with Jesus (1:32; 3:5; 7:39), and in the Paraclete passages, the Gospel writer explicitly portrays the Holy Spirit as a person distinct from the Father and the Son (14:16, 17, 26; 15:26; 16:7–15). In Paul's writings the Spirit is treated even more fully and especially as active in the ordinary life of the Christian (Rom. 8:29; Eph. 1:17; Gal. 6:1). Many passages in Paul also point to the personality of the Holy Spirit (Rom. 8:14, 16; Gal. 4:6; Eph. 4:30; 1 Cor. 2:11).

In addition to these descriptions of God, Jesus Christ, and the Holy Spirit, early Christian theologians point to a number of New Testament passages that show a triadic pattern, in which there is a grouping of Father, Son, and Holy Spirit. The pattern occurs in God's announcement to Mary through an angel that she would have a child by the power of the Holy Spirit. "The angel said to her, 'The Holy Spirit will come upon you, and the power of the Most High will overshadow you; therefore the child to be born will be called holy, the Son of God'" (Luke 1:35). Likewise, in Luke's account of Jesus' baptism, God is portrayed as speaking in conjunction with the Holy Spirit: "And the Holy Spirit descended upon him in bodily form, as a dove, and a voice came from heaven, 'Thou art my beloved Son; with thee I am well pleased'" (3:22). In the temptation narrative also, Jesus is said to have been "full of the Holy Spirit" (4:1) and to have quoted Scripture: "You shall not tempt the Lord your God" (4:12). In the opening of Acts, Jesus, the Father, and the Holy Spirit are mentioned together (1:1–6). Traces of such a pattern appear elsewhere in Acts (2:33, 38–39; 9:17–20; 10:38).

In the writings of Paul, triadic formulas occur often. They name Father, Son, and Spirit together and thus indicate some kind of relationship in the mind of Paul. One such verse is the concluding benediction of 2 Corinthians 13:14: "The grace of the Lord Jesus Christ and the love of God and the fellowship of the Holy Spirit be with you all" (cf. Gal. 4:4–6; Titus 3:4–6; 1 Cor. 12:4–6). While Ephesians 4:4–6 refers to the Spirit, Son, and Father, it is the oneness that is emphasized: "There is . . . one Spirit . . . one Lord . . . one God and Father of us all."(Paul also saw this parallelism of God, Christ, and Spirit in the work of redemption: God sent Christ, who was crucified, was raised, and ascended, so that "we might receive the promise of the Spirit through faith" (Gal. 3:14; cf. 4:4–6).[1])

Such passages indicated to early church theologians a uniqueness in the relationship of God the Father to Jesus the Son and suggested that the Holy Spirit, though portrayed as a divine power or force, may also possess a distinct personal existence. Thus, to the question Who is God? early Christians, on the basis of the Old and New Testaments, had to answer that while God is Father, Son, and Holy Spirit, God is somehow also one God. Such a confession needed a much fuller elaboration, and this was the task of Christian theologians for the next several centuries.

Backgrounds to Nicaea

Such a complicated and important theological problem as God's identity obviously requires careful thought and expression. It is not surprising, therefore, that the church took a long time to clarify its understanding of God as Father, Son, and Holy Spirit. At some points the wrong road was followed and steps had to be retraced while the right road was sought. At times, answering this question seemed an impossible task. From the start, however, certain basic tenets were accepted: (1) God is one and not two or three gods as in pagan religions; (2) God is revealed in three ways as Father, Son, and Holy Spirit; (3) the Father and the Son are distinct from each other and thus should not be equated so as to erase differences between them. Yet discovering how to hold these tenets and express them clearly and succinctly while finding concepts that were adequate to that task was a major undertaking indeed.

The difficulty of this problem was further heightened when the second-century church increasingly faced the necessity of translating its faith into forms of expression intelligible to the Greek mind. As the church grew beyond the limits of Palestine and its Jewish backgrounds and moved into the arena of Greek thought, the Christian message spread throughout the Roman world, which was permeated by hellenistic culture. This resulted in the need to express the faith in philosophical concepts in addition to the concrete forms of biblical expression. Whereas the scriptural accounts spoke of the actions of God in history, Greek philosophy centered attention on the question of metaphysical being—what is "real." This fundamental shift in thought pattern and expression challenged the church to greater clarity in answering the question Who is God?]

Apostolic Fathers and Apologists

The early Christian writers of the first and second centuries, called the *Apostolic Fathers*, mostly echoed the teachings of later biblical writers. In the writings of Clement of Rome, Ignatius of Antioch, Hermas, Polycarp, and Papias, as well as in the *Letter of Barnabas*, the *Letter to Diognetus*, *2 Clement*, and the *Didache*, there are references to one God who is the Creator, and Christ is referred to as "our God." The Holy Spirit is the inspirer of the prophets (*1 Clem.* 45:2; cf. 13.1; 16.2), and there are instances of the triadic formula; for example, Ignatius writes, "Like the stones of a temple, cut from a building of God the Father, you have been lifted up to the top by the crane of Jesus Christ, which is the cross, and the rope of the Holy Spirit" (*Epistle to the Ephesians* 9.1). But no developed answer to the question Who is God? is to be found.

Those who took seriously the task of trying to communicate with the Greek-speaking world in the late second century are called the apologists. These writers sought to vindicate Christianity and extend its influence by establishing a point of contact between Christians and philosophers. Their goal was to show that the Christian faith was a form of wisdom but was greatly superior to the speculations of Greek philosophy. These theologians included Justin Martyr, Tatian, Athenagoras, and Theophilus of Antioch.

Justin Martyr (d. 165) uses both biblical and philosophical language to describe God. He adopts the Greek concept of *logos* (thought, word, reason) as a way to explain how the great gulf between God and humanity was bridged. In accord with Greek thought, Justin says that humans are united with God by reason and know God through reason. Prior to the coming of Christ, humans had "seeds of the Logos" (*logos spermatikos*) and could thus gain fragmentary truths about God. These were actually "Christians before Christ." In Jesus Christ, however, the divine Logos "assumed shape and became a man," thus becoming entirely incarnate in him. Jesus as the Logos is distinct from the Father not only in name but also in number. The function of the Logos is to be the Father's agent, creating and ordering the universe, and to reveal truth to humanity.[2]

The next important question for Justin is how the Logos and the Spirit are related to God the Father. Is the Logos an eternally distinct divine person or only a power in God that became a divine person shortly before creation? This question was to arise again and again, and in Justin the answer is not plain. For him the Holy Spirit is the inspirer of prophets and the power of God who, along with the Son, should be worshiped. Yet

Justin also ranks the three beings, saying that the Son is in "the second place" and the Spirit in "the third rank" after God the Father.[3] While this indicates a certain subordination of two of the three, it also safeguards the inherited monotheistic faith.

Justin's disciple Tatian speaks explicitly of two states of the Logos. The *immanent* Logos existed when God was alone in creation. The *expressed* Logos came into being at the moment of creation, leaping forth from God. Creation marked the beginning of a personal existence for the Word.[4] Theophilus of Antioch distinguishes the "immanent" and "uttered" Logos. "God, having His Word immanent in His bowels, engendered Him along with His wisdom, emitting Him before the universe. He used this Word as His assistant in His creative work, and by Him He has made all things. This Word is called First Principle because He is the principle and Lord of all things fashioned by Him."[5]

The apologists thus tried to speak of God in a way that recognized the distinctions between Father, Son, and Holy Spirit. They lacked the technical vocabulary to go much beyond this, and they focused mostly on the question of the relation of the Logos to the Father. In God there is a unity of power or rule as well as a trinity of persons, writes Theophilus.[6] While little attention is given to the place of the Spirit, the threefold pattern is used by Justin and Athenagoras.[7] These writers helped provide a framework for future consideration of the question Who is God? and also helped Christian theology take seriously its relationship to Greek philosophy.

Irenaeus

Irenaeus, Bishop of Lyon at the end of the second century, forms a bridge between the Eastern and Western churches in their thought about God. Irenaeus has a strong doctrine of creation: he speaks of God alone as Father, Creator, and Lord. He too speaks of the Logos and identifies it with the Son. Yet Irenaeus does not speculate on how the Logos came into being, and he identifies it with the Son even prior to creation. Irenaeus's approach is to speak first of God when God existed solely as God and then when God was revealed to humanity. This is the divine *economy*, God's ordered process of self-disclosure in history. For Irenaeus the Son was eternally with God and continues thus after creation.[8] God is one, existing in eternity with both God's Word and wisdom. The Logos and the Spirit are linked in the creative process, and Irenaeus calls them "God's hands." For him "the Father is God, and the Son is God, for whatever is begotten of God is God." The Logos displays God's true image, and the Spirit makes it possible to receive this knowledge of God. Hence both the Son and the Spirit are fully divine.[9]

Thus Irenaeus gives a greater place to the Spirit than did his predecessors. He strongly affirms God as one but also recognizes distinctions between Father, Son, and Spirit. God is known in history through the Son and the Spirit. Yet these distinctions have been there through all eternity. By stressing the Father as the One who is above all, the Word as through all, and the Spirit in all, Irenaeus led some later theologians to draw the conclusion that the Son and the Spirit are subordinate and somehow less than the Father. Irenaeus's great contribution, however, is his *economic trinitarianism,* his description of how God was disclosed in history and how the three members of the Godhead may be described as distinct and equally divine.

Tertullian

By the third century the Western church began to experience a reaction to the apologists' doctrine of the Logos and to Irenaeus's economic trinitarianism. The concern was that both of these descriptions imperiled the unity, the oneness of God. To do justice to biblical (especially Old Testament) teaching, some theologians began to urge that God be seen as a *divine monad* with no distinctions within the unity of God's own self. This movement became known as *Monarchianism,* because it stressed one divine source or principle (Gr. *monarchia*) for all things. In the Eastern church, on the other hand, a movement was underway to stress the reality of the three *persons* of the Godhead. These theologians did not intend to sacrifice the oneness of God, but rather to do justice to the full divinity of both the Son and the Spirit as well as the Father.[10]

In this context, one of the leading Western theologians, Tertullian (d. 220), helped to clarify the church's expression of who God is. Called "the father of Latin theology," Tertullian wanted to show that the "threeness" of God is not contradictory to God's essential oneness and unity.

Tertullian began with God the Father, who with the Word and the Spirit is part of the divine triad. He used Irenaeus's *economy* to describe God's work of creation and redemption in history. But the key to Tertullian's teaching was in his use of the Latin terms *substantia* (substance) and *persona* (person).

For Tertullian the three members of the Trinity (he was the first to use the Latin *trinitas*) are distinct numerically. They have different roles to play in God's economy, but the three persons are *essentially* united. That is, they are united in their *essence*: they share the same underlying reality, the same capacity for action, the same *substance,* which literally means "that which stands under." In this way there is a *unity* in God as well as *trinity.* The members of the Godhead may be distinct from each other but are not fundamentally separated or divided from each other. Tertullian describes this unity with analogies to a root and its shoot, a source and its river, the sun and its ray. "Even when the ray is shot from the sun, it is still part of the parent mass; the sun will be in the ray, because it is a ray of the sun—there is no division of substance, but merely an extension. Thus Christ is Spirit of Spirit, and God of God, as light of light is kindled."[11] In Tertullian's characteristic expression the Godhead comprises one substance and three persons.

This stress on unity of substance and distinction of persons was a helpful way for the church to move further in saying who God is. What was at stake for Tertullian was to maintain the history of God's salvation as the work of three persons instead of one. This was different from the Monarchians, who blurred distinctions between Father, Son, and Spirit. Tertullian also stresses the sharing of the same divine nature or essence among the Father, Son, and Spirit: the Godhead is indivisible and shares the same essential being. Tertullian uses the term *person* in a relational way. For him the Father cannot be the Father without the Son, and the Son cannot be the Son without the Father. Although the two are distinct, they are inseparable. The Holy Spirit likewise shares this divine essence or substance.[12] Thus the three members of the Godhead share both an interrelatedness and a distinctiveness.

Origen See EHEMAU p 211

Tertullian's framework has helped shape the Western church's understanding of the Trinity to the present time, but the most influential theologian in the East was Origen (d. 254?). Heavily influenced by the philosophy of Plato as it was taught in his time,[13] Origen stresses God alone as Creator, Sustainer, and Ruler of the universe. Even Jesus, says Origen, spoke of the Father as "the only true God" (John 17:3). The mediator between God and all beings in the created universe is the Son, who is the image of the Father. Since this relationship between Father and Son is eternal, Origen rejects the two-stage process of the apologists.[14] The emerging of the Son from the Father is like the emerging of the will from the mind, says Origen, and is a continuing generation. Among his analogies for the generation of the Son are the reflection of a mirror and the union of husband and wife.[15] Origen sees the union of Father and Son as a union of love and action. He also describes the Son and the Father as *homoousios*, a Greek word meaning "of the same substance (*ousia*)" or "of one substance with."[16] This term became an important theological turning point in the next century. Yet Origen does not spell out in detail exactly what he means by it. Because the relation of Father and Son is eternal, Origen says, one cannot say of the Son, "There was [a time] when he was not." This slogan was also to be disputed in the Arian controversy of the following century.

Origen's statements about the Holy Spirit, however, are unclear. He speaks of Father, Son, and Spirit as "three persons" (or "three individuals"—Gr. *treis hypostaseis*), but in speaking of the Son and the Spirit, Origen occasionally says that they are excelled by the Father and that the Spirit is "inferior" to the Son. In this sense Origen begins with the divinity of God the Father and derives from it the divinity of the Son and the Spirit. Hence, while the three are different persons, or hypostases, they share a unity of will or harmony of will, which Origen calls *homoousios*.[17]

The ambiguities of Origen's teachings led to further difficulties. While he indicates the differences between the members of the Trinity, he is not as clear on how they are united. Origen could speak of the Son both as a *creature* of the Father and thus subordinate to the Father, while also saying that Father and Son are of the same substance. Despite their unity, the Son holds a lower rank in the hierarchy of divine Beings; he is described as a "secondary God" to whom prayer should not be directed, since he is not absolute goodness and truth but only reflects the image of the Father's goodness and truth.[18] Because Origen wrote so widely and did not fully work out all his insights, some theologians could appeal to Origen's stress on the eternal nature of the Son with the Father, while others looked to his subordination of the Son to the Father. A number of features in Origen's thought were later rejected when the church had worked out its doctrine more fully, and this led to the condemnation of his theology as heretical at the Second Council of Constantinople in 553.

Summary

The early church seriously wrestled with the question Who is God? during its first three centuries. The number of religious opinions that surfaced during these years made it imperative for theologians to say what they thought the church should believe. In the midst of the Roman Empire, these theologians—including the apologists, Irenaeus, Tertullian, and Origen—tried to show the world that the Christian faith was an intellectually satisfying way to believe and that it was not a threat to the empire itself.

In answering the question of God's identity, it was crucial for the church to formulate its response on the basis of biblical teachings and in thought forms that could be understood and communicated. As the church expanded, with some of its members in the East speaking Greek while Western Christians spoke Latin, the church itself faced problems of communication. The terms *person* and *substance* were particularly problematic.

Yet there was more, for as the churches developed, different emphases developed too. In the Western church, the stress was on the monarchy and sole rule of God. This led Western theologians to be interested primarily in the unity of God. They recognized distinctions, but they wished to preserve the essential oneness of the God who acts in history. Eastern theologians, on the other hand, stressed the pluralistic nature of God and focused on the distinct persons of the Godhead. They recognized the unity of God but also wanted to preserve the status of the other distinct members of the Godhead in relation to God the Father.

By the year 300 it was obvious that further thought was needed. The question Who is God? concerned not only the nature of God and God's characteristics, but also how the members of the Godhead were related to each other. The church needed to clarify its understanding and communicate it in ways that were compelling to contemporary people.

Turning Point: The Nicene Crisis

Arius

The major crisis of the fourth century in terms of the church's understanding of God centered upon two theologians, Arius and Athanasius. This struggle represented a new phase in doctrinal development and led to the Council of Nicaea in 325 and the church's first official statement of its understanding of the Trinity.

The tensions in Origen's doctrine of God became more clearly focused in the teachings of Arius (d. 336), a presbyter of Alexandria. Arius forced the church to define its understanding of the divine nature of the Son and to say how the Son and the Father are related. For Arius the basic principle is that God must be understood absolutely as uncreated, unbegotten, and unoriginated. There is only one God, who cannot share or communicate divine being or substance with any other being or person. To do so would imply that God is divisible and subject to change.

Around 318 Arius began to preach that this eternal God decided to create the world by first creating a being superior to the rest of creation. This was the *Logos*, the Son, who was created by God out of nothing but had a beginning. The Son was God's helper, or agent, in creating the world and thus stands in an intermediate position between God the Father and the created order. The Son is neither a part of God nor of the world system. The Logos existed before all creatures as the instrument of their creation, but the Son is not eternal and does not share in the divine nature of the Father. Since the Logos is a created being, Arius's slogan became "There was [a time] when he was not."[19]

Arius turns to Scripture and to the writings of the early church theologians to justify his position. He sees biblical passages such as Deuteronomy 6:4, 32:39, John 17:3, and 1 Corinthians 8:6 as speaking of God's unity, while John 14:28 and 1 Corinthians 15:28 teach the Son's subordination and Mark 13:32 stresses the limited character of his knowledge. Arius acknowledges three distinct persons in the Godhead, but he believes that they are three different beings who do not share a common nature or essence. Each is "of another substance" (*heteroousios*). The Holy Spirit, he thinks, is probably a creature of the Son.[20]

Though his views were condemned, Arius did serve the church by advancing the discussion of the question Who is God? He raised an important issue: how is the Son related to the Father? Arius frames his answer in philosophical terms and ontological categories. He speaks of the relation of Son and Father in terms of being and substance, and he also uses the Hebrew categories of *Creator* and *creature*. The question is, Is the Son God or not? Is the Son a participant in creation as God, or does he belong to the order of creatures, who are not God? Arius's answer is that the Son is *not* God: the Son is a creature.

Council of Nicaea

Arius's teachings roused the opposition of his bishop, Alexander of Alexandria, who, through letters to bishops of the church, sought to defend his own position against the attacks of Arius.[21] But Arius's position was gaining support and causing controversy in the churches and even riots in the streets. A tavern song promoted his views:

> Arius of Alexandria, I'm the talk of all the town,
> Friend of saints, elect of heaven, filled with learning and renown;
> If you want the Logos doctrine, I can serve it hot and hot:
> God begat him and before he was begotten, He was not.[22]

Constantine was then the sole emperor of the Roman Empire. In this situation he saw the danger that Christianity would split over a theological issue that he found hard to understand. In an attempt to gain control, the emperor convened a universal council of the church to put the controversy to rest. In June 325 Constantine opened the council, which was held at Nicaea in Asia Minor with nearly three hundred bishops present, the vast majority of whom were from the East. Arius was present, along with his theological consultant, Eusebius of Caesarea. Bishop Alexander took with him Athanasius, the future bishop of Alexandria.

The creed adopted at Nicaea stated:

> We believe in one God, Father, all-sovereign, maker of all things seen and unseen; and in one Lord Jesus Christ, the Son of God, begotten from the Father as only-begotten, that is, from the substance of the Father, God from God, light from light, true God from true God, begotten, not made, *homoousios* [of the same substance] with the Father, through whom all things came into existence, the things in heaven and the things on the earth, who because of us [human] and our salvation came down and was incarnated, made [human], suffered, and arose on the third day, ascended

into heaven, comes to judge the living and the dead; and in one Holy Spirit. And those who say "there was once when he was not" or "he was not before he was begotten" or "he came into existence from nothing" or who affirm that the Son of God is of another *hypostasis* or substance, or a creature, or mutable or subject to change, such ones the catholic and apostolic church pronounces accursed and separated from the church.[23]

IMPORTANCE OF CREED The stress of this creed is on the Son and the Son's status in relation to the Father. Instead of *Logos* it uses the term *Son*, which is more personal and implies that the Son is not created but begotten from the Father, that there is a real and essential relationship between the two, and that the Son is not called into being out of nothing. The term *homoousios* was suggested by the Emperor Constantine himself (probably at the urging of his theological consultant, Hosius of Cordova) and was meant to counter directly Arius's view that the Son is a creature. While it is unclear precisely what the term included at the time, it clearly established a real relationship between the Son and the Father, who share the same divine nature. The Son is a different person from the Father but is also God. This view prevailed at Nicaea against the Arians and against views that subordinate the Son to the Father. The Holy Spirit, mentioned in the creed with the Father and the Son, received no further attention; but Nicaea did settle the issue of the Son's coeternity with the Father. Important as it was, however, the Council of Nicaea still did not fully answer the question Who is God?

Post-Nicene Developments

The crisis of Nicaea was not fully resolved by the council. Arianism did not die out in the church; it went underground and surfaced at numerous points throughout the next half-century. From the time of the council in 325 till the death of Constantine in 361 and for twenty years beyond, the church still struggled mightily with its understanding and articulation of God's identity.

During the initial period of anti-Nicene reaction, 325–37, the followers of the Arian Eusebius of Caesarea were able to get pro-Nicene leaders—such as Athanasius, Patriarch of Alexandria since 328—deposed and exiled. The Arians urged that *homoousios* was unscriptural and threatened the understanding of three persons in the Trinity. After 337 various moderate formulas were promulgated at Antioch in 341, Philippopolis in 342, and Antioch in 344. These omitted the term *homoousios* but were critical of Arianism in general.

The Arians struck back at the Third Council of Sirmium in 357 and at the synods of Nice in 359 and Constantinople in 360, where they were able to get Arian creeds passed. This prompted Jerome to write, "The whole world groaned and marvelled to find itself Arian."[24] Yet because of this,

ARIANS STRUCK BACK

moderate theologians supported Basil of Ancyra's proposed use of the term *homoiousios* (of like substance). Since this term could be interpreted in several ways, there was hope that the happy ambiguity might bring a measure of unity.

The years 361–81 marked the overthrow of Arianism. During this time major theologians such as Athanasius of Alexandria and the Cappadocian fathers (Basil of Caesarea, Gregory of Nazianzus, and Gregory of Nyssa) worked to refine further the Nicene understandings. In 381 the Council of Constantinople reaffirmed and solidified the faith of Nicaea, and banned all Arian and arianizing deviations.[25]

Athanasius

The great defender of the Nicene faith was Athanasius, who was Bishop of Alexandria from 328 until he died in 373. His chief work, *Orations Against the Arians*, summarizes Arian doctrine (thus providing a major source for our knowledge of Arius's teachings) and vigorously sets forth arguments in favor of the Nicene position.[26]

Athanasius developed a rather full doctrine of the Trinity. As strongly as Arius, he affirms faith in one God: "We confess God to be one through the Triad, and . . . entertain belief of the One Godhead in a Triad . . . for there is but one form of Godhead."[27] Unlike Arius, however, Athanasisus asserts that the Word is God and not a creature: "Nor as man from man was the Son begotten so that he is later than the Father's existence, but he is God's offspring. Since he is the peculiar Son of God who always is, he exists everlastingly."[28] How the Son is generated from the Father is a mysterious process, but Athanasius holds to the strict identity of substance: the Son is "true God, *homoousios* with the true Father."[29]

Athanasius also developed a strong doctrine of the Holy Spirit. Against a group called the Tropici, who saw the Spirit as the "greatest of the angels" (citing 1 Tim. 5:21; Heb. 1:14), Athanasius argues that the Holy Spirit "is not a creature" but belongs to the indivisible "holy Triad," for "the whole Triad is one God." For Athanasius the Holy Spirit is fully divine and consubstantial (*homoousios*) with the Father and Son. Scripture teaches that "the Spirit belongs to and is one with the Godhead which is in the Triad."[30] There is thus the closest relationship between the Spirit and the Son, so that the Spirit and Son share the same essence as do the Son and the Father. The Spirit must be divine, he argues, if the Spirit is to unite individuals with the divine Son of God.

Athanasius was not a speculative theologian and thus he urged a respect for the mystery of the Trinity. His vocabulary is not always precise or fully expressive of his thought, and he leaves a number of questions unanswered. Yet he does stress the unity of the Godhead and the full participation of Father, Son, and Holy Spirit in the divine essence. "The holy and blessed Triad is indivisible and one in Itself. When mention is made of the Father, the Word is also included, as also the Spirit Who is in the Son. If the Son is named, the Father is in the Son, and the Spirit is not outside the Word. For there is a single grace which is fulfilled from the Father through the Son in the Holy Spirit."[31]

The Cappadocians Set the stage for council of Constantinople

The three Eastern theologians from the region of Cappadocia tackled the questions left unanswered by Athanasius. Basil the Great (d. 379), his brother Gregory of Nyssa (d. 394), and Gregory of Nazianzus (d. 390) were three bishops who sought to use Scripture and philosophy to refute Arian teaching. Their roots were in the *homoiousios* (of like substance) tradition, and their thought prepared the way to the Council of Constantinople in 381, which helped settle the church's response to the question Who is God?[32]

Whereas Athanasius had stressed the unity of the divine nature, the Cappadocians urged the trinity of the divine persons with an emphasis on the primacy of the Father as the one out of whom both the Son and the Holy Spirit are generated. While Athanasius also maintained the distinctions between the members of the Godhead, he had no satisfactory term with which to express these distinctions. It was a major contribution of the Cappadocians to explain how one substance can be present in three persons at the same time.

In the teachings of Athanasius and in the Council of Nicaea, there is no difference between *ousia* and *hypostasis*, but Basil insists on a distinction. He argues that the most appropriate and acceptable formula is "one substance in three persons." The distinction between the two is that between a universal and a particular. Just as each human being has his or her own individuality and yet represents universal humanity, so each person in the Godhead is set apart by that person's own characteristics but is still a part of the whole Divinity. While Origen distinguished the terms and spoke of three hypostases in the Godhead, he tended to make the Son and the Spirit lesser Gods, not as fully divine as the Father. The Cappadocians, however —like Athanasius—accepted the full divinity of the Son and the Holy Spirit. Thus Gregory of Nazianzus writes, "The Godhead is one in Three and the Three are one, in whom the Godhead is, or to speak more accurately, who are the Godhead."[33] Each of the three persons of the Godhead has certain distinguishing characteristics. Basil identifies these as paternity (Father), sonship (Son), sanctifying power (Holy Spirit).

With the stress on the one substance in three hypostases, the Cappadocians indicate God's triunity: the three are one God yet three persons.

Athanasius began with the *oneness* of God; the Cappadocians begin with the *threeness* of the persons. Whereas before Nicaea the main problem was to derive the trinity of persons from the unity of God, after Nicaea the main issue was to achieve the unity of God from the trinity of the persons.

One of the Cappadocians' contributions is to affirm the full divinity of the Holy Spirit. They also dispel any notions that the Son and Spirit are subordinate to the Father by stressing the identity of substance among the three. And they speak clearly of the divine personages and their distinctive characteristics.

Council of Constantinople 381

Fifty-six years after Nicaea, various heresies and schisms were still disrupting the church and the state. In 381 Emperor Theodosius I called a council for Constantinople to put these issues finally to rest. At this council no pope or Western bishop was represented. Of the 186 bishops present, 36 were *pneumatomachi* (literally, "spirit-fighters"), a group whom the Cappadocians wrote against and who denied the full divinity of the Holy Spirit. These 36 left when they were asked to accept the Nicene faith.

Among the documents of this council is what became known as the Niceno-Constantinopolitan Creed, commonly known today as the Nicene Creed. It became the sole baptismal confession in Eastern churches and the eucharistic creed of Christendom. An expansion on the 325 creed, this creed lengthens the statement on the Son but also includes a long section on the Holy Spirit, described as "the Lord and Giver of life, who proceeds from the Father, who together with the Father and Son is adored and glorified, who spoke through the prophets." Here the Holy Spirit is on the same level as the Father and Son, clearly affirming the Spirit's divinity and the Spirit's place in faith and worship.[34]

Augustine 354-430

With the work of the Cappadocians in the East and the teachings of Augustine (354–430) in the West, the church came to its most fully developed answer to the question Who is God? Augustine wrote a vast amount of theology, but his elaborate work *On the Trinity* (*De Trinitate*), written between 399 and 419, ranks as one of his most important. In this work he accepts the basic idea that God is triune, distinct in persons yet one in substance. Certain emphases in Augustine's work stand out.[35]

1. There is an absolute unity of the Trinity. For Augustine, all subordination of the Son and the Spirit must be eliminated: whatever is affirmed of God is affirmed equally of each of the three persons. For "not only is the Father not greater than the Son in respect of divinity, but Father and Son together are not greater than the Holy Spirit, and no single Person of the

Three is less than the Trinity itself." The corollary of this for Augustine is that the three members of the Godhead are not three separate individuals in the same way as are three human beings, but rather that the substance of each is identical with that of the others and with the divine substance itself. This Augustine maintained in order to reject the description of God as "threefold" (triplex), a term used by the theologian Victorinus, which to Augustine meant a conjunction of three individuals. Rather, as a Trinity, the divine persons indwell in each other. This also means for Augustine that whatever is said about the divine nature should be said in the singular, since there are not multiple divine natures, but only one.[36]

2. The distinction of the persons is grounded in their mutual relations within the Godhead. Although the three are identical in substance, they are distinguished by their relationships. The Father begets the Son, and the Holy Spirit is bestowed by both. By holding this, Augustine avoided the modalist idea that God simply appears in three forms or modes, saying instead that in the Trinity there are distinct persons. Augustine wished to affirm both unity and plurality in the Godhead without contradiction.

3. The Holy Spirit is the Spirit of both the Father and the Son alike. As Augustine writes in commenting on the Gospel of John, "The Holy Spirit is not the Spirit of one of Them, but of both." This view is what came to be known as the double procession. In this view the Holy Spirit is said to proceed "from the Father and the Son." The phrase "and the Son" became known as the filioque and in 1054 was one of the reasons for the split between the Eastern and Western churches. The Eastern church rejected this phrase, which was inserted into the Niceno-Constantinopolitan Creed at the Third Council of Toledo in 589. Eastern theologians argued that it was noncanonical—not grounded in the New Testament and early church tradition—and that it was dogmatically untrue and had dangerous consequences. Augustine believed that since Father and Son share all things, they also share in the procession of the Holy Spirit. To the question whether, if both the Son and the Spirit derive from the Father, there should not be two Sons, Augustine makes the distinction that the Son is "begotten" while the Spirit "proceeds." The Spirit is the mutual bond of love between Father and Son.[37]

4. The use of analogies drawn from the human soul to describe the Trinity is often seen as Augustine's most original contribution to the question of the Trinity. While he does not believe these explain the Trinity, they serve to deepen the mystery of how God can be absolutely one yet also three distinct persons. This means that Augustine finds analogies to the Trinity nearly everywhere he encounters the number three. He sees the Trinity in Genesis 1:26, where God says, "Let us [the three] make man in our image, after our likeness." Humanity bears "a kind of resemblance to

the Trinity."[38] The experience of love discloses a lover, an object loved, and the bond between them, which is the love that unites. This is analogous to the Father, Son, and Holy Spirit, the Spirit being the bond between them. There is a triad for humans of being, knowing, and willing, which for Augustine is an analogy. There are various other "trinities" of humanity: the mind, (self-)knowledge, (self-)love; memory, understanding, will; and remembrance of God, understanding of God, love of God.[39] Each of these, says Augustine, shows three elements that are coordinate and equal yet are one in their essence; and each throws light on the mutual relations among the divine persons.

Augustine's theology is embodied in the Western church in the so-called Athanasian Creed, composed sometime between 430 and 500. This creed is also called the *Quicunque vult* after the opening words in the phrase, "Whoever wishes to be saved must above all keep the Catholic faith. . . ." The creed uses the terms *substance* and *person* to speak of the divine unity and trinity: "We worship one God in Trinity and Trinity in unity; we distinguish among the persons, but we do not divide the substance." The *filioque*, or procession of the Holy Spirit from the Father and the Son, is affirmed as well. In this creed, formerly said to have originated with Athanasius but now known to have originated somewhere in the south of France, the church made a definitive expression of its faith in the Trinity and answered as well as it could the question Who is God?

2

Christological Controversy

Who Is Jesus Christ?

In the midst of the church's struggles over its doctrine of God, it also had to answer another fundamental, closely related question: Who is Jesus Christ? Descriptions and formulas of belief in the Trinity always had to include the person of the Logos, the Son, Jesus Christ. Thus, as the church's understanding of the Trinity became clearer, it also had to consider certain specific and crucial questions about the person of Jesus Christ. Every statement about who Jesus is implies a certain understanding of the Trinity. Conversely, every affirmation about the Trinity says something about Jesus Christ. Questions about Jesus revolved most importantly around the issues of his *humanity* and *divinity*. How can Jesus Christ be considered both divine and human at the same time? This issue was to occupy the church's thought for many years and lead to another crucial theological turning point. More broadly, the question Who is Jesus Christ? is the question of Christology, which the church sought to answer with its doctrine of the incarnation.

Biblical Basis

The writings of the New Testament present neither a unified picture nor an intellectually developed statement of who Jesus is. Yet there are more clear statements in the New Testament that lend themselves easily to a developing doctrine of Christ than there are for a doctrine of the Trinity. In part this must be due to the fact that the writers confronted Jesus immediately. To develop a doctrine of the Trinity, certain philosophical and theological conceptions were necessary, but as the authors wrote of Jesus, they reached for titles and ideas that were already at hand and made sense out of their relationship with him.

The varying experiences of Jesus are presented in the different perspectives of the biblical writers. Thus there are many strands of christological thought in the New Testament. As the early church sought to develop its understanding of who Jesus was, it appealed to the diverse elements in the New Testament yet also attempted to see how they all fit into a larger, more unified pattern. These writings include material describing the life and words of Jesus, interpretations of who Jesus was by his early followers, and various titles given to him, as well as theological descriptions.

To capsulize in a short space the biblical teachings about Jesus is impossible. Detailed scholarly treatments are readily available, but some of the major dimensions of the New Testament witness can be mentioned.

For the early disciples of Jesus there was no question that he was a human being just as they were. In all the Gospels Jesus walked and talked and lived among the people of Galilee like any other human person. The realities of life, such as hunger and thirst, weariness and fatigue, pain and suffering, were entirely real to him. In his crucifixion and burial he died just like anyone else (see Matt. 8:24; 21:8; John 4:6; 11:35; 19:28).

Jesus also entered into the joys and sorrows of life in his relationships with other people (Luke 10:21; Mark 10:21; Matt. 9:36; 26:37–40). He could express human emotions ranging from pity (Mark 1:41) to anger (Mark 3:5; 11:15ff.). He asked for information, showing his real human mind (Luke 8:45; John 11:34; Mark 6:35; 9:21). And he prayed (Matt. 6:9; John 17) and was tempted (Matt. 4:1–11).

Yet the early disciples were sure that Jesus was more than just another prophet sent from God. In the person of Jesus his followers encountered God in a unique and unsurpassed way, and their belief was solidified and certified by his resurrection from the dead. For Jesus' followers the Easter event produced the certainty of faith that became the central note of Christian preaching and teaching (Acts 3:15; 1 Cor. 15; Col. 1:18).

From the perspective of the resurrection, the words and actions of Jesus took on even deeper meaning for the early church. Such was the case with Jesus' baptism (Matt. 3:13—4:11), his transfiguration (Mark 9:2–8), his controversies with Satan (Mark 3:23–27), his many miracles (Mark 5:35–43; Luke 18:40–43), his relationship to the Jewish law (Matt. 5:21–48), and his views about his own suffering and death (Matt. 16:21; Mark 10:45; John

10:17, 18). The Easter event also gave new meaning to such words and sayings of Jesus as the use of *Abba* as a familiar term for God in prayer (Mark 14:36; Matt. 6:9; Luke 23:34) and his announcement of the kingdom of God as the initial proclamation of his ministry (Mark 1:15; cf. Luke 4:43; Matt. 4:23, 9:35). In John's Gospel, Jesus' "I am" sayings (6:35; 8:12; 10:7, 11; 11:25; 14:6; 15:1) and his statements of his relation to the Father who "sent" him (3:17; 9:39; 10:36) and to the Holy Spirit (14:15–17, 26; 15:26; 16:5–15) were also deepened after the resurrection.

In the New Testament the question Who is Jesus? is often answered by the ascriptions of titles to him or to his role in the plan of God as proclaimed by early Christian preachers of the *kerygma*, the gospel message. Indeed the New Testament rarely speaks of who Jesus is without at the same time referring to what Jesus does: his person and work are linked.

The New Testament uses various titles for Jesus. (1) The *Messiah*, or *Christ* (Mark 8:27–33; 14:61; 15:2), is the fulfillment of Old Testament expectations, the one in whom the coming kingdom of God is brought to earth. (2) The *Son of David* (Mark 10:47, 48; 12:35–37; Matt. 9:27; 15:22; cf. Mark 11:9–10) indicates a kingly role for the coming leader. (3) The *Son of God* (Matt. 4:3, 6; 14:33; 16:16; Mark 12:6; 15:39) signifies a special, unique relationship between Jesus and God. (4) With the *Servant of God* (Luke 22:37; Mark 10:45; John 1:29ff.) various allusions link the work of Jesus to that of the "servant of Yahweh" in the Servant Songs of Isaiah (Isa. 42:1–4; 49:1–7; 50:4–11; 52:13—53:12). (5) *Lord* (*Kyrios*: Acts 2:36; Phil. 2:9; Mark 11:3; Rom. 1:4) designates Jesus' exaltation and power with God as ruler over all creation.[1] (6) *Son of Man* (Mark 2:27; 10:45; 14:62; Luke 12:10; 17:22ff.; Matt. 24:27, 37ff.) is an image drawn from Old Testament passages (Dan. 7:13ff.; Ezek. 2:1; Ps. 8:4) and means both a human being and a coming ruler who receives eternal dominion and kingdom. (7) Jesus is the final *prophet* (Luke 7:16; Mark 6:14ff., 8:27; Acts 3:22, 7:37; John 6:14), who will fulfill all prophecy at the end of time. (8) The *Word* (*Logos*: John 1:1–14; cf. 1 Cor. 8:6; Rev. 19:13) is the supreme revelation of God, preexistent with the Father and the full expression of the mind and will of God (Heb. 1:1ff.). (9) In some texts (Heb. 1:8–9; John 1:1; 20:28; and other passages by implication) Jesus is directly identified with *God*. For the biblical writers and the early church, each of these titles conveyed an aspect of who Jesus was.[2]

Beyond the titles given to Jesus, certain passages in the New Testament stand out as christological hymns that focus direct attention on Jesus and give him direct praise. The background influences on these texts are both Jewish and hellenistic. Examples of such christological hymns are Philippians 2:6–11, Colossians 1:15–20, 1 Timothy 3:16, 1 Peter 3:18–22 (1:20),

Hebrews 1:1–4, and John 1:1–14. Taken together these passages form a concentrated expression of the early church community's perception of who Jesus is.[3]

Another major dimension of the church's scriptural understanding of Jesus comes from the writings of the Apostle Paul. Jesus' preexistence is presupposed by Paul (see Gal. 4:4; Rom. 8:3, 32; 2 Cor. 8:9; Phil. 2:6ff.; Col. 1:15). Christ is the *wisdom* of God (1 Cor. 1:18—2.16; Col. 1:15–20), hearkening back to Old Testament concepts of wisdom as existing before the world and at work in the creation of the world (Job 28:20–28; Prov. 8:22–31—cf. Bar. 3:32–38; Ecclus. 1:4, 9; 24:3–22; Wisd. of Sol. 7:25–26; 9:9–10). Paul frequently and regularly refers to Christ as the *Son of God* (Rom. 1:3, 4, 9; 5:10; 8:3, 29, 32; 1 Cor. 1:9; 2 Cor. 1:19; Gal. 1:16; 2:20; 4:4, 6; Eph. 4:13; Col. 1:13; 1 Thess. 1:10), which for him entailed consideration of both the person of Jesus and what Jesus did for the redemption of the world (Rom. 8:3; Gal. 4:4). Christ is the *image of God* (2 Cor. 4:4; Col. 1:15; cf. Phil 2:6) in whom all the fullness and glory of God dwells. Of all the Pauline designations for Jesus, the one most frequently used is Lord (*Kyrios*). With this Paul asserts—so the church believed—that Jesus is directly associated with God the Father in the exercise of supreme authority over the cosmos by virtue of his resurrection, ascension, and coming again (*parousia*: 1 Cor. 2:8; 2 Cor. 1:14; Gal. 6:17; Phil. 2:11; 1 Thess. 2:15). Paul's identification of Jesus with God also occurs in numerous passages. In their own ways the remaining New Testament books also paint similar pictures of who Jesus is.

In the biblical materials the church had much to draw upon. Jesus Christ stood in common with other humans in terms of his human characteristics, but he is also seen as one in whom God is realized and known in a special and unique way. These dual dimensions of Jesus are described with many terms and images. It remained the task of successive generations of Christians to say more fully, with more precision and in terms appropriate to their own historical and cultural contexts, how they understood the biblical data. For it is crucial that the church in every time and place say clearly who Jesus is.

Backgrounds to Chalcedon

Early Trends

In the first three centuries of the church, formulations of Jesus' identity were not explicit. As with the doctrine of the Trinity, it took decades to achieve clarity of understanding and expression. In these early times, however, certain trends arose that were judged from the perspective of later times to be outside the mainstream of church teaching. Also like the doctrine of the Trinity, Christology did not develop in a straight line. There were zigs and zags as the developing doctrine of the church moved in one direction and then another. If the task of Christology came to be a description of the person of Christ in terms of the dimensions of the human and the divine, then these early trends may be seen as "one-sided solutions" to the christological problem.

One of these movements was *Ebionism*. This group had its roots in Jewish Christianity and gradually separated itself from the main body of the church in order to move in its own direction. Ebionites (whose name means "poor ones" after the title given to the early church at Jerusalem— see Gal. 2:10; Rom. 15:26) were vigorously opposed to the Apostle Paul and John the Baptist. Christologically, they regarded Jesus as "the elect of God," "the true prophet," but they denied that he was divine. The early history of Jesus (Matt. 1–2) is deleted from their gospel, because they denied the virgin birth of Jesus, his Sonship, and his preexistence. Jesus was perceived as a man on whom the Holy Spirit descended and into whom it entered at his baptism, a view that came to be known as *adoptionism*. For the Ebionites Jesus' mission was to do away with Jewish sacrifice and bring an end to the Old Testament priesthood by fulfilling the Old Testament law. For fulfilling the law Jesus earned the title *Christ*.[4]

A second movement, *Docetism*, moved in the opposite direction from Ebionism, eliminating Jesus' humanity. The name comes from the Greek *dokein*, meaning "to seem." In this view Jesus' humanity and suffering were not real: they were only phantasms. Justin Martyr writes of the docetic view, "There are some who declare that Jesus Christ did not come in flesh but only as spirit, and exhibited an appearance (Gk. *phantasian*) of flesh."[5] Early traces of this view are found in the New Testament itself, particularly in the first letter of John (2:18, 19; 4:2, 3; 5:5, 6, 9). Ignatius referred to Docetists as "godless" people who say that Christ suffered in appearance only. The apocryphal Gospel of Peter says that Jesus, on the cross, "kept silence, as feeling no pain."[6] For Docetists Jesus' bodily makeup was an illusion. A famous docetic saying was that when Jesus walked on the beach, he left no footprints! Docetism was both a movement on its own and an attitude found in other views as well.

A third and very complicated tendency in the early church was *Gnosticism*. This was an elaborate descriptive philosophy of cosmic speculation, the details of which vary from system to system. A primary emphasis was on the way of *knowledge* (Gr. *gnōsis*). The secret knowledge that is the key to life and the universe is given to the enlightened ones, who are called the *elect*. When knowledge is mystically bestowed, the divine element within one is liberated. Christologically, Gnosticism posited a spirit world from which the divine Christ descended and united himself for a time (between baptism and death) with the person known historically as Jesus of Nazareth. Jesus' body was formed not out of flesh but out of a psychic substance, so that he was perceived as a heavenly Christ and an earthly man in "temporary juxtaposition." Thus the docetic emphasis was at the center of gnostic Christology. Gnosticism as a philosophy, or system of philosophies, completely spiritualized Christianity and was hostile to concepts of the physical body and matter. For the Gnostics spirit was good while matter was evil.[7]

Apologists and Second-Century Theologians

The theologians known as the apologists, who were concerned with building a bridge between Christianity and Greek philosophy, wanted to show the Greeks that Christianity was the true philosophy. These writers began to develop their understanding of who Jesus is by concentrating on the concept of the *Logos*. Appropriating this term from Greek philosophy (see chap. 1), they began to work on the question of the relationship of Jesus Christ to God the Father.

Justin Martyr

For Justin Martyr the Word (*Logos*) became human by being born of the Virgin Mary. "He Who was formerly Logos, and appeared now in the semblance of fire, now in incorporeal fashion, has finally by God's will become man for the human race. He preexisted as God and was made flesh of the virgin, being born as a man. The Logos made God known to people of the old covenant but now has become a human being with a body, soul, and spirit.[8] As the divine reason the Logos was the one through whom the world was formed and governed. In this sense Jesus Christ as the Logos (John 1:1–14) was a perfect expression of who God is and what God does. Yet since the Logos is begotten, or brought forth from God, the Son is inferior to the one God. The Logos is also the mediator between God and God's creatures.

For Justin the incarnation, God's becoming a human being, involved Jesus taking on real flesh and blood and enduring real, physical suffering. He did not cease to exist as Word while on earth and was at the same time "God and man." While Justin shows the reality of the two natures of Christ, he does not discuss how they can coexist in one person. The Logos who is Jesus is the same kind of logos (reason) that is in all people, but Jesus is the Logos to the fullest degree. "The Christ who has appeared for us men," wrote Justin, "represents the Logos principle in its totality, that is both body and Logos and soul."[9]

✓Melito of Sardis and Irenaeus

One of the earliest Christian historians, Eusebius, quoted a remark that Melito of Sardis was one of the "great stars of Asia" and was an important champion of the divinity and humanity of Christ. Melito saw Christ as a divine and glorious figure who became a human being to redeem humanity from the suffering and death that had come to the world through the sin of Adam. Christ is the fulfillment of the whole work of God, beginning with Moses, the divine work which was itself a "type" or preview of God's perfect work of salvation in Christ. In the death of Christ, the church has a new Passover mystery. For Melito Christ "rose from the dead as God, being by nature both God and a human being." Melito's thrust was antignostic and antidocetic. He spoke of the incarnation of Jesus as *aphantaston* (no phantasm) and thus real. He spoke of Jesus as the "perfect man."[10]

Irenaeus of Lyons was likewise antidocetic and antignostic in his christological teachings. He presented a magnificent vision of Jesus as the second Adam and thus began a new direction in christological thinking. Jesus Christ inaugurates a new, redeemed race: "A second Adam to the race and to the rescue came." In his stress on the unity of the God-man, Irenaeus rejected gnostic speculation, which separated the heavenly Christ from the earthly Jesus.

✓For Irenaeus the eternal Word became incarnate in Jesus Christ. The basic problem with gnostic thought was that it denied the true divinity of the world's Creator. Redemption could occur only if the divine Word could enter fully into human life. Against the Docetists, Irenaeus maintained that Jesus Christ was "truly God" and "truly man." If his flesh differed from humanity's in any way (except in sinlessness), the parallel is incomplete, the sin of the first Adam cannot be overcome, and reconciliation cannot occur.[11]

Irenaeus held that the ultimate God of the universe is God the Creator and that this God is actively involved with creation. In the incarnation the preexistent Logos, who was revealed in the creation of the world and in the theophanies of the Old Testament, actually became a human being. For Irenaeus, Jesus Christ "recapitulates" or "sums up" what God has done in history, particularly in the history of Israel (see Eph. 1:10). Christ also recapitulates all that humanity is and will become for God. In his famous phrase Irenaeus says of Christ, "He became what we are in order to enable us to become what He is." Jesus Christ is the climax of history, renewing and redeeming the whole human race, which was lost in sin through Adam. Whereas Justin emphasized the distinction between the Logos and the Father, Irenaeus stresses that Jesus is the form in which the Godhead is made known in human history. In Jesus Christ is the unity of the divine and the creaturely.[12]

Tertullian and Origen

Challenges to the church in the third century, in Christology as in the doctrine of the Trinity, came from Monarchianism and the dualism of spirit and matter in Gnosticism. It was Tertullian of Carthage in the West and Origen of Alexandria in the East who gave decisive direction to Christology in this period.

Tertullian faced the monarchian movement in two forms. *Dynamic Monarchianism*, also called *adoptionism*, held that Jesus was a mere man on whom the Holy Spirit descended. As he grew, he moved gradually into "deity." The second form, called simply *Monarchianism*, is also called *Modalism*, because while maintaining the oneness of God and the full deity of Christ, it erased all distinctions between Father, Son, and Holy Spirit. Both forms tried to preserve the rule and reign of God as the divine monarch of the universe and as the source from which all else flows. But in doing so, the Monarchians sacrificed essential dimensions of both the doctrines of God and the doctrine of Christ.

Tertullian was a Latin-speaking North African who was trained as a lawyer and rhetorician. While he developed the church's theology in several directions, he was eventually drawn into Montanism, a movement that laid heavy stress on the work of the Holy Spirit and remained outside the mainstream of the church. Two of his major works are *Against Praxeas*, directed against the Monarchians, and *On the Flesh of Christ*, in which he opposed the dualistic Gnostics.

The main emphasis of Tertullian's Christology asserts the two natures of Christ, using the term *substance*. For Tertullian the Word, who was preexistent with the Father, is a distinct person but of the same essence as the Father. The Word became a human for the purpose of salvation, since only a human could accomplish the work of salvation on behalf of the whole of humanity. The Word was born from a virgin as the Son of God. It is important to stress, says Tertullian, that the Word was born *from* the virgin and not *through* the virgin, as if Mary were only a channel through which Jesus passed, as the Gnostics taught. The humanity of Jesus was genuine in every respect. While he assumed a soul, the governing principle in Christ was always the Logos.[13]

Tertullian was the first theologian to deal with the issue of the two substances in relation to Christ. To the question of whether Christ was somehow changed or transformed into human flesh or whether he really did "clothe himself" in it, Tertullian answers the latter. It is inconceivable that any transformation could take place in God and the Logos, since they are by nature unchangeable, immutable. Being transformed would lead to the destruction of them both. His conclusion is that both substances, divine and human, maintained their own distinctive qualities and activities when they were united in Christ. The divinity performed the miracles, while the humanity of Jesus endured the sufferings, yet both of these belonged to the same person. The Son of God and the Son of Man were the same person (Lat. *persona*), but in Tertullian's understanding of the Trinity, Father, Son, and Spirit are three separate persons (*personae*) who each speak and act. Against the Monarchians and the Gnostics, Tertullian stresses the unity of Jesus in that Jesus Christ unites Godhead and humanity in himself without confusion or separation.

Origen of Alexandria was the church's first systematic theologian, as evidenced by his work *On First Principles (De Principiis)*, in which he deals with the teachings of Scripture in an ordered way. In this work Origen also lays out his understanding of the Logos and how it was expressed in Jesus Christ. "We believe that the very Logos of the Father, the Wisdom of God Himself, was enclosed within the limits of that man who appeared in Judaea; nay more, that God's Wisdom entered a woman's womb, was born as an infant, and wailed like crying children."[14] Origen goes on to explain how this came about, and his explanation is influenced by the Neoplatonic philosophy in which he was trained.

Origen believed in a world of preexistent spiritual beings, which includes human souls before their births. One of these souls, says Origen, was destined for Jesus. It was like all of the other souls in every way, yet from the beginning it was attached to the Logos with a kind of mystical devotion. It burned with love and the desire for justice. All other souls use their free will in wrong ways and fall away from the Logos to whom they are supposed to be attached, but one unique soul became permanently united with the Logos. This, says Origen, was a complete union—as complete as when a lump of iron is plunged into fire and becomes red-hot. Origen cited 1 Corinthians 6:17, which says that whoever is united with the Lord "becomes one spirit with him." According to Origen, this unique soul became the meeting place of the infinite Logos and finite human nature.

In the incarnation the Logos became embodied through a human birth. For Origen, Jesus was a human being (with a soul inhabiting his body) who was also divine: he had a divine and a human nature (Gr. *physis*), each keeping its own special characteristics but still forming a unity. Yet because of Origen's emphasis on the Logos as the mediator between God and the created order, his picture of Jesus is one in which the body, while real (against Docetism), could also be altered at will and was more divine than other bodies. Jesus' body had a godlike, ethereal quality, according to

Origen, since it is the reality of the Logos *in* the body that is the most important principle of mediation between God and creation.

Arius and Nicaea

From the death of Origen in 254 until the year 318, there were variations in christological thought within the churches but no major breakthroughs. It was a time of "theological twilight,"[15] but that changed with the controversy surrounding Arius from 318 to 325.

As indicated in chapter 1, Arius begins with the premise of God's absolute uniqueness and transcendence. God is eternal and the source of all reality. Whatever else exists must have come from God and been created out of nothing. Nothing of God's being, or essence (*ousia*), can be shared or communicated, for then God would have to change. If there were any other divine beings who participated in God's being, then there would be more than one God.

From these premises certain conclusions follow. First, the Logos must be a creature formed out of nothing by the command of the Father. To speak of the Father "begetting" the Son must be a symbolic way of saying that the Father "made" the Son. Thus the Son owes his existence completely to the Father's will.

Second, this Son (or Word, which Arius thought to be an inaccurate title) must have had a beginning, since he was a creature. This led to Arius's slogan: "There was when He was not." His view was summarized in his *Thaleia*, where he wrote the following verse:

> The Father is alien in being to the Son, and he has no origin. Know that the monad was, but the dyad was not, before it came into being.[16]

The thought that there could be two eternal persons implied to Arius that there were two self-existent principles and thus two Gods.

The third implication for Arius is that the Son can have no communion with or direct knowledge of God the Father. The Logos and God the Father are of different essences (*heteroousios*), according to Arius. Like all other creatures the Son is "alien from and utterly dissimilar to the Father's essence and individual being."[17]

Finally, the Son must be liable to change and even to sin. Since the Son was a creature, sin was a possibility for him. Yet, says Arius, in God's providence, God foresaw that the Son would remain obedient and thus not sin. God bestowed this grace of obedience on the Son in advance.

In Arius's view, to say that the Word is God or that Jesus is the Son of God is to confer a courtesy title. "Even if he is called God, He is not God truly, but by participation in grace. . . . He too is called God in name only."[18] For Arius the Logos became *flesh* by entering into the creature Jesus, but it did not become *human*. Since it did not take a human soul, the Logos did not truly become human like all other human beings. Jesus is a creature superior to all others, but a creature all the same.

The Council of Nicaea in 325 condemned Arianism on two christological points. (1) The Son is begotten, not made. The council condemned all who affirm that the Father existed before the Son, that the Son is a creature who is produced out of nothing, and that the Son is subject to change or development. (2) The Son is "out of the Father's substance" and is "of the same substance" (*homoousios*) as the Father. This means that the Son is fully God, sharing the same divine nature with the Father, and that the Son is coeternal with the Father—also denied by the Arians. Despite the various compromise formulas suggested, *homoousios* became the church's ongoing understanding and was reaffirmed at the Council of Constantinople in 381 and again at the Council of Chalcedon in 451.[19]

Athanasius

The Christology of Athanasius is found in his treatise *On the Incarnation of the Logos of God* and his answer to the Arians in *Against the Arians*. In the former, Athanasius tries to answer the question of why the incarnation occurred. He argues basically that the Logos became truly human so that humanity might be reconciled to God and restored to its originally intended relationship with God. Human beings are composed of both soul and body, and the true Savior must have both, just as other humans do.

Athanasius begins with John 1:14: "And the Word became flesh and dwelt among us." He writes of the Logos, "He became human. He did not enter into a human being."[20] It is only God who can save the fallen human race, and this is done by God's becoming a human being. The incarnation of Jesus did not alter the transcendent status of Christ, since "in taking flesh he does not become different, but remains the same" and "still exercises sovereignty over the universe while in a human body." But Christ did take human flesh and have a body, "appropriating" humanity to himself. He did not take another's body; he had his own. Only in this way, said Athanasius, could redemption be carried out. There was thus a true incarnation of the Logos, a true "becoming man." For Athanasius, the Logos "became flesh. He did not enter into a human being."[21] The incarnation is and must be accomplished by one who is truly and fully God and truly and fully human.

Athanasius draws careful distinctions between the Logos in his eternal being and the Logos incarnate. For him there was a perfect union of divine and human and no commingling of the two aspects. When commenting on 1 Peter 4:1, which speaks of Christ suffering in the flesh, Athanasius says,

"These things were not proper to the nature of the Word as Word, but the Word . . . was subject of the flesh which suffered them."

> For this reason the things proper to this flesh are said to belong to him because he was in it—such things as being hungry, being thirsty, suffering, getting tired and the like, to which the flesh is susceptible. But the proper works of the Logos himself, such as raising the dead and making the blind see and healing the woman with a hemorrhage, he accomplished through the instrumentality of his own body. Furthermore, the Logos bore the weaknesses of the flesh as his own, since the flesh belonged to him, while the flesh renders assistance in the works of the Godhead, since the God-head came to be within it, for it was God's body.[22]

Scriptural expressions about Jesus' emotional experiences and limitations are explained by physical factors. The "ignorance" of Jesus about certain matters as reported in the Gospels, says Athanasius, was feigned, since as the Logos Jesus must have known all things.

These questions about the relation of the divine and human in Jesus lead to an important issue concerning Athanasius's thought. Did the humanity of Jesus include a rational human soul, a conscious human selfhood? Or does Athanasius see the Logos taking the place of the human self in Jesus? Though he nowhere denies the human soul of Jesus, he does not stress it as an important dimension of what it would mean for Jesus to be truly human. When Athanasius handles the question of Jesus' ignorance by saying that the Logos restrained himself and acted "as if" he were a human being, this becomes a significant issue. Clearly Athanasius did not integrate into his thought any real place for the human soul of Jesus. Yet while he did not solve this problem, his achievement was significant in helping the church answer the Arians on the question Who is Jesus Christ?

Apollinarius

Apollinarius (or Apollinaris) of Laodicea (c. 310–90) was a friend of Athanasius who thought he had the answer to the question of whether Jesus had a human soul. His answer was no. For Apollinarius the divine Logos (reason) took the place of a human soul; Jesus was a combination of Word and flesh, just as John 1:14 says.[23]

Apollinarius affirms Jesus as both God and a human being. This is essential if Jesus Christ is to be the world's Redeemer. On the question of how humanity and divinity could be maintained within the same person, Apollinarius argues, "If a perfect God were united with a perfect man, then there would be two (sons), one by nature the Son of God, and the other by adoption."[24] In emphasizing the unity of the person of Christ, Apollinarius evolved the formula "one incarnate nature of the divine Logos."

This represents an extreme version of the Christology that starts with

the Logos and sees the Logos becoming "flesh." This Logos-flesh Christology of Apollinarius takes its understanding of humanity from 1 Thessalonians 5:23, which speaks of the spirit, soul, and body of people. In Christ the
divine Logos replaced the human mind (John 1:14; Rom. 8:3). The divine
Word was substituted for Jesus' normal human psychology or soul.
"Human" for Apollinarius means "spirit united with flesh." In Christ, who
is both divine and human, "the divine energy fulfils the role of the ani-
mating spirit and of the human mind."[25] The divine Logos can be said to
have "become human" in the sense that he shared the makeup of other
human beings, but it is the divine Logos that produces the intellectual and
physical energy for Jesus Christ.

This view made sense to Apollinarius, since there were biblical texts
that spoke of Christ being "found as a man" or "in the likeness of men." The
theological significance of the virgin birth for Apollinarius is that in this
action the divine spirit replaced human sperm and was the source of life.
Although it makes Jesus different from other humans, the elimination of
the human psychology or soul of Jesus does have the advantage, Apollinarius argues, of excluding the possibility that there were two contrary
wills or intelligences in Christ, one divine and one human. It also insured
the sinlessness of the Savior, since the human mind is enslaved to all types
of evil thoughts, but the Word is immutable and thus immune to all filthy
passions. This gives the Word the power to conquer sin and death and to
convey the "life-giving spirit" to all who are united with the Word.

Thus Apollinarius insists that Jesus Christ is one, an organic, vital
unity, just as other humans are a unity of body, soul, and spirit. Jesus is
"one composite nature" in which the divine intellect (Logos) and human
flesh share the same life. This unity means the body may be termed divine
and the Logos may be properly called human. The later phrase used to
describe this exchange of characteristics is *communicatio idiomata*, the
sharing of the properties of one nature of Christ with the other. For
Apollinarius, Christ is the divine Logos enfleshed. In this he follows
Athanasius, but he goes on to draw out explicitly the implications of the
Logos-flesh model of the person of Christ. The human center of life and
consciousness is not forgotten by Apollinarius as it was by Athanasius: it is
simply denied. For this reason the followers of Apollinarius were called
Monophysites, meaning "one nature," since they saw Christ as having only a
single nature. These teachings of Apollinarius were condemned by church
bodies at Rome (377), Antioch (378), Constantinople (381), Rome (382), and
Chalcedon (451).

Cappadocian Reaction

To the Cappadocian theologians, the formulation by Apollinarius was
docetic: it made Jesus Christ only "seem" to be a true human person. In

reaction the Cappadocians began to stress the real humanity of Christ. As Gregory of Nazianzus writes, the Logos "comes to His own image, and bears flesh for the sake of my flesh, and conjoins Himself with an intelligent soul for my soul's sake, cleansing like by like, and in all points, sin excepted, becomes man."[26]

The Cappadocians stressed the two natures of Christ, which led to their slogan, "two natures concurring in unity" in the God-man. Jesus Christ is twofold," they said, "not two, but one from two." He is not "two sons." As Gregory indicates, the two natures are distinguishable in thought and can be referred to as "the one" and "the other." There are not two persons but rather a unity formed by their "commingling, God having become man and man God." The two natures are "substantially conjoined and knit together," says Gregory: it is not just a union of grace, as when God is said to be united with the prophets or the saints. Like Origen, Gregory explains this by saying that the rational soul of the Logos provided a meeting place for the joining together.[27]

Since Gregory so strongly stresses the unity of the person of Christ, he can fully use the "communication of the properties" concept; that is, what is true for one nature can be used in speaking about the other nature. Thus he describes God as "born from a virgin" or "God crucified" and Mary as "God-bearer" or "mother of God" (theotokos). Yet while the Cappadocians recognized the true humanity of the mind of Christ, they did not fully use it to explain his growth in knowledge, his ignorance of the end of the world, his agony in Gethsemane, and his cry of dereliction from the cross. Thus, while the Cappadocians advanced beyond Apollinarius, they did not satisfactorily resolve the issue of the relationship of Christ's divinity to his humanity.

Antiochene Christology: Theodore of Mopsuestia

The greatest need at this stage in the church's understanding of Jesus' identity was for an honest acknowledgement of his real life and experiences and of the importance of his human soul. The Antiochene school of the fourth and fifth centuries helped meet this need.

Thus far, the controlling framework for Christology had been the Logos-flesh model, which began with the Logos and went on to speak of his incarnation or becoming flesh. This led to a variety of questions relating Jesus' mind, body, and soul to each other. In the midst of this, a fundamental shift occurred. A new framework was developed which was more indebted to Aristotle than to the Platonism of the prevailing pattern. The Word-flesh model with its roots in Origen radiated from Alexandria; the new school was centered in Antioch. Its framework was Word-human. Each of the two schools came to represent one side of the church's view of who Jesus Christ is, but as each moved further in its own direction, errors

crept into the church's teachings. This led at some points either to con-
fusing the two natures of Christ or to separating them completely. While
the church rejected both errors, at the same time it confessed the truth that
was rooted in each.[28]

Two major figures of the Antiochene school who wrote on Christology
were Diodore of Tarsus (d. c. 394) and his student Theodore of Mopsuestia
(d. 428). Both were significant Scripture scholars as well as bishops. The
Word-human framework that Theodore helped develop presupposes a
complete and independent human nature for Jesus. This means that Jesus
underwent real growth in knowledge, including the knowledge of good
and evil, as well as in physical development. Jesus had to struggle with real
temptations. Theodore speaks of the humanity as "the man assumed": "Let
us apply our minds to the distinction of natures; He Who assumed is God
and only-begotten Son, but the form of a slave, he who was assumed, is
Man."[29] Thus in Christ there were "two persons" and "two natures," against
the teaching of Apollinarius, which proclaimed one person and one nature.

This sharp distinction between the divine and the human does not lead
Theodore to say there were two Sons, as if there were two separate,
objective realities in Jesus. He argues that "the distinction of natures does
not prevent their being one."[30] To explain this *hypostatic union,* or union of
the person, Theodore uses the metaphor of *indwelling*. The incarnation
shows a special kind of indwelling in which Jesus is a human being who
shares the nature of the Logos in a unique way, different from any prophet,
apostle, or saint. The human nature is a "garment" in which Christ's body is
wrapped. It is a shrine or temple in which the Godhead dwells. There is
thus an ethical union between the two natures of Christ. From the moment
of Jesus' conception, the Logos was united with him. As Jesus grew,
matured, and struggled against evil, the reality of this union with God
became ever more real. It grew to its greatest expression in the resurrection,
where the human being and the Logos are seen in their ever-present reality
as one being or person.

There is thus a unity of divine and human in the man Jesus. For
Theodore, what is said of one nature may be said of the other, but "the Son
is unique, because of the perfect conjunction of natures operated by the
divine will." "The two natures are, through their connection, apprehended
to be one reality."[31]

Thus there is a unity of will rather than substance in Antiochene
Christology. God has graciously taken the initiative and become completely identified with humanity by becoming a real human being. A single
person results from this coming together of the Logos and humanity. As
Theodore puts it, "The natures have in virtue of the union brought about
one *prosopon* (person)."[32]

The Antiochene school, as represented by Theodore, sought to do justice to the full humanity of Jesus Christ, but it too had difficulty in defining the nature of the union of divine and human in the person of Jesus. Its tendencies were toward adoptionism and thus toward something less than a full incarnation. Theodore's teachings were condemned at the Fifth General Council at Constantinople in 553, where his views about the union of the divine and the human were rejected as heretical.

Turning Point: The Chalcedonian Crisis

An important period for the development of Christology occurred between the Nestorian controversy of 428 and the Council of Chalcedon in 451. This was a time of crisis: the formulations of earlier periods were tested and probed for their weaknesses while other, more satisfactory understandings were sought. At this point there were two major types of Christology: (1) the Word-flesh framework, which concentrated on the Logos and spoke of the Word being united with a human body but had less interest in the human soul or the personality of the Logos, and (2) the Word-human framework with its emphasis on the humanity of Jesus but less clarity on the nature of the Logos as the divine dimension of Jesus. Each of the views had its positive and negative aspects, but there was a great need for a formulation that did justice to both the divine Logos and the human Jesus. The church's christological understanding was formalized at the Council of Chalcedon in 451, but the route to Chalcedon ran through periods of crisis and clashes of politics and personality.

Nestorius

Nestorius was an Antiochene monk and follower of Theodore of Mopsuestia who became Bishop of Constantinople in 428. When asked to comment on whether it was appropriate to use the term *theotokos* (God-bearing) as a description of Mary, Nestorius got into trouble with Cyril, bishop of Alexandria. This question actually posed a hidden test. To affirm *theotokos* would be to affirm the unity of divinity and humanity in Jesus. To deny it would imply that at some point Jesus must have become divine (as in adoptionism). In what sense, then, can one say that divinity and humanity were united in him?

Nestorius said it was doubtful that this term was valid unless combined with *anthropotokos* (human-bearing). Better, said Nestorius, would be the term *Christotokos* (Christ-bearing), and Mary should properly be called *theodochos*, the "recipient of God."[33] The sermon in which Nestorius made these statements did not sit well with Cyril, who was of the Alexandrian school, which sanctioned the use of *God-bearer* for Mary. The Alexandrians believed in the "communication of the properties": what was said of one nature of Christ could also be said of his other nature. For Cyril the issue was christological.

Nevertheless, Nestorius rashly fanned the flames of controversy with his writings against *theotokos*; he argued that God cannot have a mother and no human could bear the divine. Mary bore a man, the vehicle of divinity, but not God. No Godhead, claimed Nestorius, could be carried for nine months in a womb, be wrapped in baby clothes, suffer, die, and be buried. Behind this, said Nestorius, was the Arian belief that the Son was only a creature or the Appolinarian view that the true humanity of Jesus was incomplete.

In a flurry of letters, Cyril denounced Nestorius to Pope Celestine and urged Nestorius to change his views. In his correspondence Cyril adopted a phrase he believed had been coined by Athanasius but which in fact had been used by Apollinarius: Jesus Christ is "one incarnate nature of the divine Logos." Cyril said Nestorius had turned Jesus into "two sons" linked together by only a moral union. Others said Nestorius's views showed tendencies toward adoptionism, but the picture drawn by Nestorius's opponents was that he split the God-man into two distinct persons.

Nestorius rejected this picture of his Christology and argued that the two natures of the incarnate Christ must be maintained as unaltered and distinct. "I divide the natures, but I unite the worship." He wished to hold to the two natures without mixture or confusion.[34] Nestorius wanted to avoid saying that in the incarnation the Word underwent any pain or suffering; thus he rejected the Alexandrian descriptions of Jesus as "God born and dying" or of "Mary bearing the divine Word." These, said Nestorius, were opposed to Scripture and creed. He also wanted to safeguard the understanding that Christ's life was genuinely human in every way, including growth, temptation, and suffering. For the "Second Adam" must be a real human if the redemption of the race is to occur. There can be no fusing of divinity with humanity. The divine and human must exist side by side in such a way that each maintains its own properties and operations. Each is a *nature (physis)*, and each nature has its own form as an individual (*prosopon*) and its own concrete subsistence (*hypostasis*). In this he wanted to stress the reality of each nature.

This language led to the impression that Nestorius believed Jesus Christ was two persons artificially linked or glued together. Yet Nestorius wanted to say that Christ was a single, unitary person (*prosopon*). "Christ is indivisible in His being Christ but He is twofold in His being God and man."[35] There was one person who combined in himself two elements, God and humanity, with all the characteristics proper to each. To the question of what is the nature of this unity, Nestorius preferred not to speak of a "hypostatic union," as did Cyril, who meant a union of the persons.

Nestorius preferred the term *conjunction* and spoke of the "perfect," "exact,"
or "continuous" conjunction of the natures, meaning their interpenetration
of each other.

1 Person
2 Natures

Thus Nestorius taught that Christ is one person (as seen outwardly),
but that this one person is the result of a coming together, or union, of two
distinct natures. Neither was the Godhead transformed into human nature,
nor was the human nature of Christ deified (against the Cappadocians).
Each took the form of the other, so that the Christ was one person while
remaining twofold in nature. This strong stress on the two natures meant
Nestorius wished to keep the natures apart and to see the human dimensions of Christ, his actions and experiences, assigned to his human nature,
while the divine traits of Christ are attributed to his divine nature.

Not only Bishop Cyril but also the church as a whole rejected Nestorius's teachings. They felt his accounts of the two natures of Christ and
their union did not give an adequate account of how divinity and humanity
existed in Jesus Christ. His Christology did not appear to give a strong
enough account of the substantial unity of the person of Christ. It appeared
to speak of the union as only moral or ethical.

Cyril of Alexandria

Bishop Cyril maintained that Nestorius's views turned the incarnation
into an illusion and his Christology denied that the divine Logos became
truly human. What was needed, Cyril argued, was a much stronger statement of the intimate union of the eternal Word with the human in the
person of Jesus Christ. Thus as a good Alexandrian and follower of
Athanasius, Cyril upheld the Word-flesh christological schema.

This meant that Cyril believed in two stages, or phases, of the Logos,
one before and one after the incarnation. At the incarnation the Logos
continued to exist in the form of God but now also added earthly existence
as a servant (John 1:14; Phil. 2:5–11). For Cyril this did not mean the divine
Son underwent a change (though Nestorius argued it must mean this), but
that prior to the incarnation the Son existed "outside flesh" and at the
incarnation was "embodied." The nature of the Word became "enfleshed."
Thus the Word became incarnate, and Cyril's formula is "one nature, and
that incarnate, of the divine Word." There was a complete fusion of the
divine and human in the incarnation.[36]

There was no division in the incarnate One for Cyril. The human
nature of Christ included a real, rational soul (against Apollinarius); the
humanity of Christ was true and genuine. While there were two aspects of
Christ's being, or two "natures," Christ was completely one, "the single,
unique Christ out of two different natures."[37] The union of divine and
human in Christ was absolute and complete. Cyril describes it as "natural"

or a "hypostatic union," a total union of the person of Christ. The human nature of Christ never existed on its own (as in the Antiochene position): from conception on, this nature belonged to the Word. Jesus was not bipersonal, and Cyril maintains there was no mixture or confusion of the two natures that coalesced in him. There was no intermingling of the Word and the humanity of Christ, since they are utterly different in essence; each kept its own properties. Cyril's illustration is the union of body and soul in a person. Each can be described separately, yet they are indivisibly joined together in a human person. Thus the union of the person is absolute for Cyril. While a distinction between the natures is always perceived, they are not separate. This means Cyril can use the "communication of the proper-ties" fully and say things such as, "The Word of God suffered in flesh, and became first-begotten from the dead."[38] With this strong passion for the union of Christ's person, Cyril was horrified at Nestorius's language about the two natures of Christ, because for Cyril this endangers the whole process of redemption and salvation.

From Ephesus to Eutyches

The struggle between Nestorius and Cyril came to a sharp focus at the Council of Ephesus in 431, which was called at the request of Nestorius to the Emperor Theodosius. While both sides were represented, the feelings were so strong that separate meetings were held, in which each party excommunicated the other. When authorities eventually recognized the meeting over which Cyril presided as the proper council, Nestorius was condemned and sent into exile. He was never rehabilitated and died in 451. On the positive side, this council canonized the Nicene Creed as Christian orthodoxy (right teaching) and cited Cyril's second letter to Nestorius as the authoritative interpretation of the creed.[39]

In the years following Ephesus there were vigorous efforts to reconcile the Antiochene and Alexandrian understandings of Christology. A Symbol of Union was constructed in 433. This document induced the Antiochenes to recognize the propriety of the term *theotokos* for Mary (with safeguards) and led the followers of Cyril to speak of "two natures" with descriptions distinguishing the attributes proper to Christ's humanity and divinity.

For the next fifteen years, however, neither party was completely happy, and in 448 another crisis developed. The symbol for all who disliked the union was a man named Eutyches, who came to be regarded as the founder of Monophysitism, which held that the humanity of Jesus was completely absorbed by his divinity, leaving Jesus only one nature (Gr. *monophysis*). After the incarnation the body of Christ was not of the same substance as that of other humans. Eutyches declared, "After the birth of our Lord Jesus Christ I worship one nature, viz. that of God made flesh and became man."[40] Christ was of two natures only before the union with humanity. For "after the union I confess one nature." In this, Eutyches saw himself as continuing the Alexandrian tradition.

At the Synod of Constantinople in 448, Eutyches was declared a heretic, but political issues arose. Dioscorus, nephew of Cyril and his successor as bishop of Alexandria, would not recognize Eutyches' excommunication. At the Council of Ephesus in 449, Eutyches was restored, and Flavian, bishop of Constantinople and presider of the synod that had condemned Eutyches, was deposed. The Symbol of Union was said to have exceeded the bounds of the Ephesus council of 431, and the subsequent confession of two natures was condemned. For these actions the council came to be known as the Robber Synod of Ephesus.

Leo I

The pope of the Roman church at this time was Leo I. He wrote to the emperor condemning Eutyches and accepting the action of the Constantinople synod. This document, known as Leo's *Tome*, sets out what had become the picture of Jesus in the Western church. Although his work is not original, it draws together the best of Western Christology. Several points stand out.[41] Leo's Tome

1. The person of Jesus Christ as the God-man is identical with the person of the divine Word or Logos: "He who made humanity while remaining in the form of God is the same one who in the form of a slave became human." The Word was not diminished by the incarnation. Instead, "while continuing to be beyond time, he begins to exist from a point in time."

2. The divine and human coexist in this one person and are not mixed (against the Cappadocians) or confused (against Cyril). Each maintains its own properties "without defect, and just as the 'form of God' does not remove the 'form of a slave,' so the 'form of a slave' does not diminish the 'form of God.'"

3. Although the natures act separately, they always act in concert with each other. Leo argued that "each 'form' carries on its proper activities in communion with each other. The Word does what belongs to it, and the flesh carries out what belongs to it." This prevents Jesus from being viewed as a split personality.

4. The oneness of the person of Christ means it is legitimate to use the "communication of the properties" in speaking about Jesus Christ. Thus, said Leo,

> we read that the Son of man came down from heaven (since the Son of God took on flesh from the Virgin of whom he was born), and conversely we say that the Son of God was crucified and buried (even though he endured

these things not in that divine nature in virtue of which, as Only Begotten, he is coeternal and consubstantial with the Father, but in the weakness of his human nature).

Leo's *Tome* picks up concerns of both the Antiochenes and the Alexandrians. For the Antiochenes there is the affirmation of the duality in Christ, the reality and independence of two natures. For the Alexandrians there is the identity of the person of Christ with the incarnate, eternal Word. As Leo put it in a Christmas sermon, "It is one and the same Son of God Who exists in both natures, taking what is ours to Himself without losing what is His own."[42]

The Chalcedonian Formula

In 450 the Emperor Theodosius, who maintained the views of the Robber Synod of Ephesus, fell from his horse and died. His successor was Marcian, a man who favored the two-natures doctrine. Under pressure from Leo and others, Marcian called a new church council to deal with christological problems. It met at Chalcedon in 451, with more than five hundred bishops taking part.

The goal of the council was to establish a unified faith throughout the empire for the benefit of both church and state. Needed was a christological formula that all sides could sign as a truthful expression of their view of who Jesus Christ is. The crucial question was how the confession of one Christ could be understood along with the belief in Christ as "truly God and truly human," "perfect in Godhead, perfect in manhood."[43]

The documents of the Council of Chalcedon include a preamble, a reaffirmation of the Nicene Creed of 325 as the standard of Christian orthodoxy, and the recognition of the Niceno-Constantinopolitan Creed of 381 as the refutation of heresies that had arisen since Nicaea. The council also canonized the two letters of Cyril against Nestorius as a sound interpretation of the creed and Leo's *Tome* as the answer to Eutyches and a confirmation of the true Christian faith. The council's formal confession of faith said this:

> Following, therefore, the holy fathers, we confess one and the same Son, who is our Lord Jesus Christ, and we all agree in teaching that this very same Son is complete in his deity and complete—the very same—in his humanity, truly God and truly a human being, this very same one being composed of a rational soul and a body, coessential [*homoousios*] with the Father as to his deity and coessential [*homoousios*] with us—the very same one—as to his humanity, being like us in every respect apart from sin. As to his deity, he was born from the Father before the ages, but as to his humanity, the very same one was born in the last days from the Virgin Mary, the Mother of God [*Theotokos*], for our sake and the sake of our salvation: one and the same Christ, Son, Lord, Only Begotten, acknowl-

edged to be unconfusedly, unalterably, undividedly, inseparably in two natures, since the difference of the natures is not destroyed because of the union, but on the contrary, the character of each nature is preserved and comes together in one person [*prosopon*] and one hypostasis, not divided or torn into two persons [*prosopa*] but one and the same Son and only-begotten God, Logos, Lord Jesus Christ—just as in earlier times the prophets and also the Lord Jesus Christ himself taught us about him, and the symbol of our Fathers transmitted to us.[44]

This Chalcedonian formula gave equal recognition to both the unity and the duality in Jesus Christ. It spoke of "one person and one hypostasis" who is "not divided or torn into two persons." Yet in spite of his "two natures," Christ remains without division and without separation. The divine Word is a unity existing in two natures, each of which is complete and retains its own distinctive properties and operation.[45] Thus, the incarnate Christ is the one Son of God, who is truly and perfectly divine and human. Chalcedon affirmed both the distinction and the completeness of Jesus Christ as being God and a human being at the same time.

Aftermath of Chalcedon

The Chalcedonian settlement gave the church a definitive answer to the christological issues surrounding its question Who is Jesus Christ? It was a crucial turning point in that it adopted a description of Christ that has stood through the centuries as an authoritative expression of the church's faith, but it did not answer all christological questions or bring ultimate peace. It evoked a hostile reaction in Eastern churches, where those with monophysite leanings fought against it. In the sixth century the Second Council of Constantinople (553) interpreted the formula in line with Cyril. Since Christ was one person with two natures, the question arose as to whether he had one will or two. The Third Council of Constantinople (680–81) settled the *monothelite* (one-will) controversy by saying, "In our Lord, Jesus Christ, there are two natural wills, and two natural operations, indivisibly, inconvertibly, inseparably, without any fusion, as the holy fathers have taught, and that these two natural wills are not contrary, as wicked heretics have said." In taking this position, the church sought to restore the Chalcedonian balance and express the full reality of the incarnation of Jesus Christ as understood from Holy Scripture.[46]

3

Ecclesiological Controversy

What Is the Church?

The overwhelmingly important questions Who is God? and Who is Jesus Christ? occupied the major theological interest of the church in the earliest centuries. As the church began to answer these questions, attention turned to other issues and doctrines. While these doctrines were also emerging in the early periods, they did not develop as rapidly or with as much urgency as the doctrine of the Trinity and Christology.

At some point the church needed to reflect seriously on what the church is and what God intends its nature to be. For a doctrine of the church to develop, sustained theological effort was crucial. As the early church was finding its way through the Near Eastern world, it faced a number of challenges and threats to its own existence. In many areas the most immediate questions were ones of survival. It is not surprising then that the early church was identified first and foremost with emerging structures based on its primary sources of authority: its leadership (councils), its rules of faith (creeds), and its holy writings (canon). Sustained theological reflection on the nature of the community of faith was not a pressing need.

In a broad sense the early church did not have enough experience to gain a perspective on what it truly was. It struggled to understand what God was calling it to be, but in the formative years understanding came slowly. It was not conveyed full-blown into the church's reservoir of knowledge. While the church always sought to know itself, it did not have all the needed resources at its command. In many ways, too, the day-to-day reality of living in communion with Jesus Christ surrounded by fellow believers helped postpone detailed theological interpretations. Yet doctrinal controversies, persecutions, and the continuing interactions of Christians among themselves and with the sources of their faith all helped prepare the way for serious wrestling with the question What is the church?

Biblical Basis

In the New Testament the Greek term *ekklēsia* is usually translated "church." The word is found in many New Testament writings, but the idea is also present in books that do not explicitly use the term.[1] Behind the New Testament usage is a history is both the Greek language and the Old Testament.

The word *ekklēsia* comes from the verb *kalein* (to call) and its compound form *ekkalein* (to call out). In classical Greek literature the citizens of a city are called out by a herald, who summons them to come together. The terms has an official connotation, since the people were to assemble for officially sanctioned purposes.

Of greater significance for the New Testament usage of *ekklēsia* is the use of the term in the Septuagint (the translation of the Hebrew Old Testament into Greek, made in Alexandria, which was complete by the end of the second century B.C.). In this translation the term *ekklēsia* occurs about one hundred times, most often to translate common Hebrew terms for the gathering of people ('*ēdhāh* and *qāhāl*: see Deut. 9:10; Josh. 8:35; Jer. 26:17).[2] More important, the Old Testament often stresses who is assembled or who called the assembly by indicating that it is an "assembly of the Lord" (see Deut. 23:2ff.; 1 Chron. 28:8; Neh. 13:1; Mic. 2:5). In this sense the term took on a technical theological meaning to refer to the people of Israel, especially as they gathered before God. Such important events as the receiving of the law (Deut. 5:22), the dedication of Solomon's temple (1 Kings 8:14ff.), and the reading of the book of the law by Ezra (Neh. 8:2) took place with the assembly gathered together.

In the New Testament *ekklēsia* describes congregations of Christians who by their relationship are united with Jesus Christ. The term is used by Paul for Christians gathered in a particular place, such as in a house (Philem. 2; Col. 4:15) for the purposes of worship (1 Cor. 11:18; 14:19), prayer, instruction, or deliberation (see Acts 11:26; 12:5; 1 Cor. 14:4–5, 28, 34–35), but also for all Christians in a wider area, such as a city. Thus Paul spoke of "the church of the Thessalonians" (1 Thess. 1:1; 2 Thess. 1:1).

Christians in a province (Galatia: Gal. 1:2; Judea: Gal. 1:22) or wide area (Asia: 1 Cor. 16:19; cf. Rev. 1:4, 11) are designated when the term is used in the plural. In the broadest sense Paul can speak of "all the churches of Christ" (Rom. 16:16).

The character of the *ekklēsia* is indicated primarily when the church is referred to as the *church of God*. The designation *of God* is sometimes added to the singular form (see 1 Cor. 1:2; 10:32; 11:22; 15:9; Gal. 1:13; 1 Tim. 3:5, 15) and to the plural (1 Cor. 11:16; 1 Thess. 2:14; 2 Thess. 1:4). Even when the phrase *of God* is not added, it is implied in the context of the passages. Theologically this indicates that the church gains its identity and purpose from the fact that it is a people "called by God": God is the one who summons and gathers the church. It is God who is at work in and with the church (see 1 Cor. 12:28). Also, the church is sometimes referred to as the *churches of Christ* (Rom. 16:16; Gal. 1:22) or *the churches of God in Christ Jesus* (1 Thess. 2:14; cf. 1:1; 2 Thess. 1:1). The interchangeability of these phrases indicates the closest possible connection between the church as the people of God (cf. Heb. 4:9; 1 Peter 2:9–10) and as the body of Christ (1 Cor. 12:12–27).

Although the church is formally identified by the term *ekklēsia* in the New Testament, there is much more to the concept of the church. There are nearly one hundred different images or descriptions of the church in the New Testament.[3] These extend through minor images such as the salt of the earth, ark, one loaf, branches of the vine, God's building, citizens, and exiles to major images—the people of God, the new creation, the fellowship in faith, and the body of Christ—around which a cluster of other images can be seen. These include the themes of the saints and sanctified, believers and faithful, slaves and servants, the people of God, kingdom and temple, household and family, the new exodus, vineyard and flock, one body in Christ, and the new humanity.

As the church developed its ecclesiology, or doctrine of the church, this variety of images was employed in numerous ways. The full biblical picture of the church was allowed to emerge instead of playing the images off against each other and thus emphasizing only a limited aspect of the New Testament teachings. Despite the church's struggles and failures through the centuries, it has maintained that Jesus Christ is the head of the church (Col. 2:10; Eph. 1:22ff.; 5:25) and that the realities to which the images point find their true expression in Christ. Thus the church may be seen as the true Israel of God in Jesus Christ, who himself is the true Israelite. The church is the family of God in Christ, who is the true Son of God. The church is the planting of God in Christ, who is himself the true vine or grain of wheat. Just as the fullness of Christ himself can never be exhausted by any one description, so the church also needed the full variety of biblical imagery.

Yet it also recognized that it is in Christ and not in itself that the true reality of the church must be seen.

Early Ecclesiology

It was about 250 years after the birth of Christ before the Christian church had its first theological treatise devoted directly to discussing the nature of the church; this was *On the Unity of the Church*, written by Cyprian, bishop of Carthage (248–58). Yet while there was no extensive theological formulation of the nature of the church in the early centuries, foundations were laid that were later built upon and further developed. As the church struggled with questions about the Trinity and the person of Christ, it realized that these articles of belief also had implications for the church's understanding of itself. Thus in a sense theologians did describe what they believed about the church even though they did not deal with it fully as a theologian problem.

There are many dimensions to the doctrine of the church, including the church's order, government, structure, discipline, authority, mission, and relation to the state. In the early church period all these issues were encountered, even if not thoroughly addressed.

Apostolic Fathers

As with the doctrine of the Trinity and Christology, the early Apostolic Fathers for the most part adapted New Testament themes and imagery in discussing the church. Empirically, early Christians were most aware of being members of local congregations spread throughout the Mediterranean world. Each congregation had its own structure, officers, and life. Yet at the same time there was a deep awareness of a bond of unity that linked all who confessed Jesus Christ as Lord. Ignatius of Antioch was the first to give expression to the universality of the church by using the term *katholikos*, "catholic" meaning "universal": "Wherever Jesus Christ is, there is the catholic church."[4] This church stands in contrast to the local church, which is located only in the area presided over by a bishop. As the aged martyr Polycarp faced death, he prayed for "the whole Catholic Church throughout the world."[5] In the *Shepherd of Hermas* the church gathers its members from the whole world, forming them into one body, which is united in understanding, mind, faith, and love.[6] Justin Martyr spoke of all who believe in Christ as united "in one soul, one synagogue, one Church, which is brought into being through His name and shares in His name; for we are all called Christians."[7] Other biblical images of the church in the early theologians are the new Israel, the body of Christ, the bride of Christ, God's building, and the temple of the Holy Spirit.

An important ecclesiological theme running through this early period is that of the church as a "new people" called to be God's agents and servants in the world. This picks up a theme already found in the New Testament: Jesus Christ is the "last Adam," who reverses the sin and death of the "first Adam" and brings new life to a new humanity whose members are united with him by faith (see Rom. 5; 1 Cor. 15:45; cf. James 1:18; Rev. 14:4). The *Epistle of Barnabas* refers to "the new people" called by God, and Aristides notes three sorts of people: pagans, Jews, and Christians, who are called "a third race" in *The Preaching of Peter*.[8]

The writer of the second-century *Epistle to Diognetus* elaborated on this theme. He developed Paul's idea that the true citizenship of the Christian is in heaven (Phil. 3:20) and also defined how the church is universal. The writer describes the Christians he calls "this new race":

> The distinction between Christians and other men, is neither in country nor language nor customs. . . . While living in Greek and barbarian cities, according as each obtained his lot, and following the local customs, both in clothing and food and in the rest of life, they show forth the wonderful and confessedly strange character of the constitution of their own citizenship. They dwell in their own fatherlands, but as if sojourners in them; they share all things as citizens, and suffer all things as strangers. Every foreign country is their fatherland, and every fatherland is a foreign country. . . . They pass their time upon the earth, but they have their citizenship in heaven. They obey the appointed laws, and they surpass the laws in their own lives. They love all men and are persecuted by all men.[9]

Though the author was heavily influenced by Platonic notions of the body as the prison of the soul and thus the idea that Christians are imprisoned by the world, he does indicate the uniqueness of the Christian life and thus the life of the church. This distinctiveness comes in its being "in the world, but not of the world," a characteristic of the church found in every land where Christians dwell.

Irenaeus

Irenaeus's views of the church developed in the context of the threats posed by Gnosticism. The Gnostics claimed to possess a secret tradition of truth passed down from the Apostles. To counter them Irenaeus argued that the church possesses the true apostolic tradition, which is not secret but available to all in the Scriptures. This tradition is found in the canon of truth taught openly to all who will follow Christ through the church.[10] By proclaiming this canon or rule of truth throughout the world, the church, though scattered, is actually "one." It is the "new Israel," "Christ's glorious body," "the mother of Christians." The Spirit of God is openly at work in the church: "Where the Church is, there is the Spirit of God; and where the Spirit of God is, there is the Church and all grace; and the Spirit is the truth."[11]

For Irenaeus the guarantee of the church's continuity of apostolic teaching is the unbroken succession of official guardians (*episkopoi*, "bishops") of the canon of truth in local congregations. "It is within the power of all . . . who may wish to see the truth, to contemplate clearly the tradition of the apostles manifested throughout the whole world; and we are in a position to reckon up those who were by the apostles instituted bishops in the churches, and (to demonstrate) the successions of these men to our own times."[12] Irenaeus lists all the bishops of Rome as proof of this apostolic succession. He counts those who held the "see" or "teaching chair" (Gr. *kathedra*) of the local church—not those who laid on hands during consecration—for they were responsible for faithfully conveying apostolic teaching and doctrine. Thus the recognized and ordered office of the bishop is integrally related to the true nature of the church; he is the church's conveyer and preserver of the purity of the Christian gospel.

Tertullian

In the West the teachings of Tertullian are very similar to those of Irenaeus at a number of points. He too sees the Christian church as the unique place where the Spirit of God works and the only location of the apostolic teachings that are passed on through the unbroken succession of bishops. "We are a body knit together by the bond of piety, by unity of discipline and by the contract of hope."[13]

In the year 207, however, Tertullian joined the Montanists. Named after its founder, Montanism arose in Phrygia about the middle of the second century. Along with two women, Prisca and Maximilla, Montanus claimed to be inspired by the Holy Spirit and to have received divine revelations through ecstatic trances. These revelations were passed on through epigrammatic oracles, which his followers began to consider more authoritative than the Scriptures.[14] In addition the Montanists took a rigorous stand on discipline: there can be no forgiveness for sins committed after baptism, asceticism must be practiced, people should refrain from marriage, and martyrdom is welcomed as the type of death most truly glorifying Christ.

Tertullian's connection with Montanism also affected his perception of the church. In this later stage of his life, he saw the church primarily in terms of the Spirit: the work of inspired prophets is of more importance than that of bishops; and if the church is primarily spiritual, it must be composed of pure, undefiled people. In his work *Modesty* Tertullian argues that since the church is "the bride of Christ" and is to have "neither spot nor wrinkle," it cannot permit impure, adulterous, and other demon-inspired sinners in its fellowship nor, particularly, in its leadership. In later controversies about the nature of the church, Tertullian's arguments were to be used again. For in addition to questions about the truth or apostolicity of the church's teachings, there was another major question in emerging ecclesiological doctrine: What constitutes the purity or holiness of the church?

Origen

Origen of Alexandria became head of the catechetical school in Alexandria in the year 203. This school, which had a wide influence in training in the Christian faith, had previously been led by Clement of Alexandria (c. 150–215), a man who sought to combine his knowledge of Greek philosophy with his understanding of Scripture. Like Clement, Origen was greatly influenced by the philosophy of Plato—especially when it came to his understanding of the church.

Also like Clement, Origen distinguishes between the church on earth and "the church on high," that is, the historical, empirical, observable church and the mystical, spiritual body of Christ, which exists in heaven. Origen speaks of "the true church" in contrast to the church seen in history. The observable church is organized for ministry, which is carried out on the basis of the apostolic teachings safeguarded by the church through apostolic succession.[15] The church is the "congregation of Christian people," the "assembly of believers," the body of Christ.[16] But, says Origen, this church on earth does not exist without spot or wrinkle: "I can confidently say that the treasury of the Lord is his Church, and in that treasury . . . there often lurk men who are vessels of wrath . . . chaff with the grain, and fish which have to be thrown out and destroyed together with good fish which have all come into the net."[17] The true church, according to Origen, existed before the creation of the world and consists of all who attain perfection on earth and become united with the Logos. The church on earth prepares one to become, through Christ, part of the church on high, which is "the assembly of all the saints" and "all those souls which have attained perfection."[18]

Both Clement and Origen were universalists: they believed all creatures will ultimately be saved. The biblical images of "everlasting fires" in hell are not to be taken literally, for humanity is being educated and prepared for the salvation that is its final destiny. Some souls endure punishments along the way, but the final word is the salvation of all. Thus the church in history and the church "on high" are not contrasting realities; they are in continuity with one another.

Turning Point: The Question of the Lapsed

The Christian church faced various periods of persecution during the early centuries. The last years of the second century meant mostly peace for the church, since the Roman Empire was involved in civil wars and efforts to preserve its borders against roving barbarians, but the third century was a period of more intense persecution by Roman officials. In 202 the Emperor Septimius Severus issued an edict aimed especially at new converts and those who taught them. Two famous martyrs of that period were Perpetua and Felicitas, whose martyrdom was chronicled by Tertullian.[19] Irenaeus also may have been killed in this period.

During the next half-century, persecutions subsided while the Christian church continued to grow, but in 249 Decius became emperor. His desire to return Rome to the glories of its ancient past included restoring Rome's ancient religion. Decius wanted to do more than his predecessors, who simply punished those who would not worship the emperor: he wished to reestablish the ancient religion by systematically stamping out all opponents. For him the survival of the empire itself was at stake.

Earlier Tertullian had stated that "the blood of the martyrs is the seed of the church." The persecution initiated by Decius, however, was designed not to create martyrs but apostates. Decius made worship of the Roman gods mandatory throughout the realm. Everyone had to offer a sacrifice to the gods, burn incense before the emperor's statue, and taste sacrificial meat. The penalty for noncompliance was death.

Many Christians rushed to comply with the emperor's decree. A most graphic description of the situation in Alexandria comes from Dionysius.

> And what is more, the edict arrived, and it was almost like that which was predicted by our Lord, wellnigh the most terrible of all, so as, if possible, to cause to stumble even the elect. Howsoever that be, all cowered with fear. And of many of the more eminent persons, some came forward immediately through fear, others in public positions were compelled to do so by their business, and others were dragged by those around them. Called by name they approached the impure and unholy sacrifices, some pale and trembling, as if they were not for sacrificing but rather to be themselves the sacrifices and victims to the idols, so that the large crowd that stood around heaped mockery upon them, and it was evident that they were by nature cowards in everything, cowards both to die and to sacrifice. But others ran eagerly towards the altars, affirming by their forwardness that they had not been Christians even formerly; concerning whom the Lord very truly predicted that they shall hardly be saved. Of the rest, some followed one or other of these, others fled; some were captured, and of those some went as far as bonds and imprisonment, and certain, when they had been shut up for many days, then forswore themselves even before coming into court, while others, who remained firm for a certain time under tortures, subsequently gave in.[20]

As a result, the Christian church nearly collapsed.

The actual number of deaths under Decius's persecution was not large. Instead of being martyred, prisoners were promised, threatened, and tortured in order to produce apostates. Christians who maintained their faith even in the midst of severe torture were called "confessors" and were greatly honored by other Christians. When Decius died in battle in June 251, his persecution ended, but the church was left with the question of what to do with the "lapsed," those who had capitulated to the authorities during the persecution. This led the church to reflect on its very nature as the people of God and to face the crucial question What is the church?

LASPED

Cyprian and Novatian

The important question of the lapsed was also a difficult one, since not all had compromised their faith in the same way or to the same degree. Some had immediately sacrificed to the emperor, others purchased fraudulent certificates saying that they had, and still others gave in but then found strength to confess their faith again and seek readmittance to the church while persecution was still occurring. Some members argued that the confessors should decide who would be readmitted. Many bishops, however, claimed the church hierarchy alone had the authority to restore the lapsed. Others went further: they demanded that great rigor and no leniency be shown in the whole question.

In the ensuing debate Cyprian, bishop of Carthage (248–58), and Novatian, leader of the "rigorist" party, played key roles. Cyprian had become bishop not long before the persecutions began. He was a follower of Tertullian and, like his master, trained in rhetoric; when danger arose, he believed it his duty to flee to safety and continue to act as bishop through letters. Some interpreted this as cowardice, and when the persecution ended, many believed the confessors in Carthage should have more authority than the bishop, especially on the question of the lapsed.

When Cyprian returned to Carthage, he found the church in disarray. Many in that city and in others were willing to make sacrifices in the temple and then participate in the Eucharist the following week. Soon after Cyprian's return, however, the church began to recover rapidly. Within the church there were those who urged that the lapsed be reaccepted with very little discipline or punishment. There were others, though, who wished to apply the church's ancient rule that apostates are to be permanently excommunicated. Cyprian believed a council of North African bishops should make a ruling. Soon after Easter in 251, he convened a council, which decided that no one should be wholly or permanently barred from penance. Each case of the lapsed was to be determined on its own merits by the clergy. Lapsed clergy were not to be readmitted to their orders, but others could be received after suitable discipline.

In Rome similar questions were posed. On June 4, 251, Cornelius was elected to succeed Pope Fabian. On this issue Cornelius favored a policy similar to Cyprian's, but Cornelius was opposed by the presbyter Novatian, who split the Roman church over this issue. The Novatianists argued that a church containing lapsed members could no longer be considered a church. To readmit the lapsed was to lose its holiness; to embrace the apostate was to forfeit its existence. The Novatianists themselves were doctrinally orthodox; they accepted the canon of faith and apostolic teachings. Thus the church could no longer claim that the basis of its unity was apostolic teaching alone. A new way had to be found for the church's unity to be expressed and guaranteed in history.

Bishop Cyprian rose to this challenge in his book *On the Unity of the Church*, written around 251. In this work he argues vigorously that the unity of the church is found in its episcopate. The Novatianists claimed to have their own episcopate, since their bishops had been consecrated by other validly consecrated bishops. Cyprian claims that these were not really bishops, for to be a true bishop one must succeed to a vacant see. The schismatic Novatianist bishops had done so neither in the case of Maximus, who had been set up in Carthage as a rival to Cyprian, nor in the case of Novatian himself in Rome. The important point is the bishop's office, not who consecrated him.

This led to Cyprian's basic principle, "No bishop, no church." It is church leadership that forms the bond by which the church's unity is assured. "You ought to know that the bishop is in the Church, and the Church in the bishop; and if any one be not with the bishop, that he is not in the Church. . . . The Church, which is catholic and one, is not cut or divided but is indeed connected and bound together by the cement of priests [*sacerdotes*, i.e., bishops] who cohere with one another."[21] Each bishop is entitled to his own views and to administer his own diocese, and mutual respect is to be given among bishops. The church is governed by the bishops, the successors of the Apostles, and therefore obedience to the bishops is an absolute necessity.

For Cyprian, since God is one, the church must be one. Each community is to be led by one leader who, as bishop, maintains the peace and unity of the churches. Because the church is found in the bishops and the bishops are in the church, the Novatianists had no standing whatsoever in Cyprian's view. Since their so-called bishops were not proper bishops, they had no power to ordain, baptize, absolve sins, or celebrate the Eucharist. When Novatianists asked to be readmitted to the catholic church, Cyprian ordered them to be baptized. For him the genuine sacraments and means of salvation could come only through the true church. "There is no salvation outside the church," and "he can no longer have God for his Father who has not the church for his Mother."[22]

Cyprian's strong stand for the unity of the church is rooted in Scriptures such as Matthew 16:18–19, John 20:20–23, and Ephesians 4:4–6. First granted by Jesus to Peter and the other Apostles, that unity is now found in the college of bishops, who constitute the ruling authority of the church, which is the ark of salvation.[23] It was not enough for Cyprian to seek the unity of the church in common agreements on doctrine; he looked instead to the episcopacy. He answered the Novatianists—who said the holiness of the church depended on the purity of its members in having no dealings with the lapsed—by arguing that the catholic church is united through its bishops, in whom the church's theology, organization, and sacraments are one.

Turning Point: The Mystical Body

Bishop Cyprian became the first bishop-martyr of Africa on the evening of September 14, 258, during a persecution by the Emperor Valerian. In the following decades the Christian church grew in numbers and strength among all classes and social groups, but while church discipline was still officially strict in practice it was often lax in the churches of North Africa.

Within fifty years another severe persecution had broken out. Begun by the Emperor Diocletian and later known as the "Great Persecution" (303–12), it sought to recall Christians to their duty in recognizing Roman gods. Diocletian insisted that no blood be shed, so that the church would not gain further strength from its martyrs. Instead, he ordered Christian churches throughout the empire to be destroyed, sacred books to be handed over to be burned, and all Christians in public office to be removed. Upper-class citizens who were Christians in private life were to lose all their privileges, particularly the right to bring suit in court. In addition, Christian slaves were not to be freed. In the next several years, subsequent edicts ordered the imprisonment of clergy; forced sacrifices by clergy and general sacrifice by all Christians were ordered by Diocletian's successor, Galerius, in 304. For nearly a decade there were further periods of violence and calm, as well as political wranglings that divided the empire. The church had experienced its most violent fury of persecution, before the end came with Constantine becoming emperor and issuing the Edict of Milan in 313, which gave Christianity full freedom and legality.

As in the time of Cyprian, this period of persecution forced the church to examine itself and ask What is the church? Cyprian had grounded the church in its structure and hierarchy, through which the sacraments were administered; his view was highly influential for many years. After the Great Persecution, however, other issues arose that also shaped the church's view of itself. Specifically, the church had to deal with the problems raised by the Donatist schism.

Donatism

As with Novatian, the Donatist controversy concerned those who had lapsed during persecution, which in North Africa had been particularly intense. Bishops and other Christians in charge of Scriptures were threatened with death if they did not hand their books over to the Roman authorities. Those who did were called *traditores* (traitors). As with the earlier persecutions, not all capitulated in the same way. Some bishops handed over heretical books and led the Romans to believe they were sacred Scriptures. Others surrendered the true books and claimed they were avoiding bloodshed, which was their pastoral duty. But many in the churches, both leaders and others, worshiped the pagan gods, and some reported that pagan temples were filled to overflowing.[24]

As in earlier persecutions, there were also Christians who remained firm in their faith and thus faced imprisonment, torture, and death. The confessors who survived tended this time to be very rigorous about re-admitting the lapsed. They insisted that not only those who worshiped pagan gods but also the *traditores* should be barred from the church. These traitors were unholy, and even those who had dealt with them lost holiness and ceased to be church members. Sacraments and all other ecclesiastical actions performed by such people were seen as invalid.

A specific controversy arose over the consecration of Caecilian as bishop of Carthage. The rigorist party claimed one of his consecrators, Felix of Aptunga, was a *traditor*, and thus his consecration was invalid. In opposition they elected Majorinus, but he died soon after becoming the rival bishop. In 313 Donatus of Casae Nigrae was elected in his place and gave leadership to this party for the next fifty years. Thus the Donatist controversy meant a division of the African church. Caecilian and his followers called themselves "catholic," since they were in communion with churches throughout the whole world. Donatus saw himself as heading the "church of the martyrs" and upholding righteousness in the midst of the fallen world.

The bishop of Rome and leaders in other important cities declared Caecilian the true bishop of Carthage, and Majorinus and the Donatists were declared usurpers. After an investigation into whether Felix was actually a *traditor* and an appeal to the emperor, the Council of Arles (314) ruled in favor of Caecilian. Constantine, determined to have a unified church as a key ingredient in his unified empire, fell in line with the council's ruling and ordered his officers in North Africa to deal only with Caecilian and his associates. Since tax exemption for the clergy was one of Constantine's offerings to the church, this decision was an important and most practical one. After a brief period of repression and persecution against the Donatists (317–21), Constantine realized that this policy would not restore religious unity to Africa, since martyrdom was no detriment to the Donatists. On May 5, 321, he granted toleration to the Donatists, and until his death in 337, the issues of the Council of Nicaea (325) claimed most of his attention.

Throughout the fourth century the schism continued, at many points fueled by nationalistic feelings among the native Berbers, who opposed any institution that was backed by imperial Rome. Many North African churches became Donatist and, claiming to be the true church, set up their own bishops and systems of church administration. In many cases, the Donatist bishops even ascended to vacant sees through the help of sympathizers. They could thus claim the authority of Cyprian as a support for their position as successors to the Apostles.

Augustine

The theological issues raised by the Donatist schism were crucial for the church. Donatus and his followers argued that the validity of any sacrament depends on the personal worthiness and holiness of the administrator. Related to this is the question of whether an ordination or consecration performed by an unworthy bishop is valid. Donatus believed that the church is one, just as God is one, but the supreme mark of the church is purity. Christians aspire to a martyr's death, since they must witness to their faith in a sinful world. They are sealed by their baptism with the power and joy of the Spirit, who enables them to triumph and conquer as martyrs and confessors. To the question Where is the church? the answer was in Africa—in the community of Donatus. It was proper for these followers to separate from the followers of Caecilian, since their true holiness should have no contact with an apostate. If a member of Caecilian's party should ever wish to become a Donatist, that person would have to be rebaptized, since the Donatists would not recognize the validity of any other baptism. As one Donatist bishop put it, "There is one baptism, which belongs to the church; and where there is no church, there cannot be any baptism either."[25] For the Donatists the unity and the catholicity of the church depended on its prior holiness. The Donatist Petilian writes, "By doing violence to that which is holy you cut asunder the bond of unity."[26] The "communion of the saints" means the communion of the "perfected" saints.

The Donatists were challenged theologically by Optatus, bishop of Milevis in North Africa, and much more fully by Augustine (354–430), bishop of Hippo Regius, a region about one hundred miles west of Carthage. Optatus's chief arguments in his *Schism of the Donatists* are that the validity of the Christian sacraments depends on the work of God and not on the worthiness of the one who administers them, just as the holiness of the church is rooted in God's work and not in the holy piety of the church's members. "The church is one, and its holiness is produced by the sacraments. It is not to be considered on the basis of the pride of individuals."[27] Catholicity, according to Optatus, means the church is worldwide in scope and united in its communion with the see of Rome, whose first bishop was Peter. Donatism, however, was confined to North Africa and had no relationship with the Roman see. Thus the Donatists were severed from the true church.

Optatus's thought was developed much further by Augustine, a theological giant in the Western church for centuries to come. When he became bishop in 396, the Donatist schism had been part of the church's life for many years, and he devoted several writings to the issues it raised.

At the Synod of Arles (314), the church had recognized Donatist sacraments and doctrinal orthodoxy. Catholics had argued, as Optatus and Augustine did later, that the validity of the sacraments did not depend on the moral condition of their administrator. Augustine, however, denied that the Donatists really represented the church. He regarded them as a "false" church, "heretics" who had led the catholic church into schism. Indeed, Augustine believed that he himself would be personally liable at the last judgment if the Donatists were not returned to the church catholic.[28]

Augustine answered the question What is the church? by saying it is the mystical body of Christ, the bride of Christ, the mother of Christians. Echoing Cyprian, Augustine affirmed that there is no salvation outside the church.[29] While the Donatists could have an orthodox faith and even the sacraments (contrary to Cyprian's view), they are "of no avail for the forgiveness of sins" and thus unprofitable, since the Holy Spirit is given only in the true church.[30] Augustine clearly claims that the catholic church has the true faith of the Apostles, the sacraments, and the ministry. This church, with its hierarchy centered in Rome, is catholic in that it teaches the whole truth (and not fragments of it) and is universal, in distinction to sects that appear only in limited localities.[31]

Yet Augustine also recognized that the church is a "mixed company": there are true Christians in the church as well as those who do not truly believe. Biblical passages referring to the purity of the church (e.g., Eph. 5:25–27) refer to the church's future state. The church here and now, for Augustine, is more properly characterized by biblical stories such as Noah's ark, where the clean and unclean animals existed together, or the parable of the Tares (Matt. 13:24–30), where wheat and chaff exist side by side until the final judgment. Thus for Augustine there had to be a theological distinction between the outward organization of the church and the church as the communion of the saints.[32]

The head of the church is Jesus Christ, and the church exists in organic union with Christ. The bond between Christ and Christians is love, which is personified in the Holy Spirit.[33] Love is the essence of the church, where faith and hope also reside. The church is a fellowship of love, a fellowship of the Spirit. The unity of the church is its unity of belief in the gospel of Jesus Christ, but also its unity of love, which binds members together around the deepest loyalty they know in life, God's love in Jesus Christ. One cannot belong to the church if one does not love God and others.[34] Such disregard for love put the Donatists outside the church, according to Augustine. For, as he wrote of the schismatics, "All things [i.e. the sacraments] were indeed theirs before, but profited them nothing, because they had no charity. For what truth is there in the profession of Christian charity by him who does not embrace Christian unity?"[35] The antithesis of love is schism, and schism is sacrilege.

Augustine's distinction between the outward or *visible* church and the heavenly or *invisible* church rests on Scripture and also on the observation that some in the church seem to have no part in "the invisible union of love," which is the true nature of the relationship of Christians to Christ and to others. The "elect" are those predestined to share this relationship; in the strictest sense they constitute the true or essential church, "the congregation and society of saints."[36] Yet Augustine also believed that those who outwardly seem to be within the bosom of the church and to enjoy this "invisible fellowship of love" may not actually be truly Christian. Thus Augustine could say of the church, "Many sheep are without, and many wolves are within."[37]

For Augustine the church is the true people of God, the mystical body of those united with Christ by faith and love. The church is catholic in that it is worldwide and includes churches in communion with the see of Rome as well as other Christian churches.[38] It is also universal in respect to time, since it embraces all those in true communion with God (the elect) from the beginning to the end of history.

The church is "holy" not by virtue of the personal virtues of its members but in the holy grace of God communicated through the church, particularly through the sacraments. This means, against the Donatist view, that baptism "belongs to Christ, regardless of who may give it."[39] For "the genuineness and holiness of the sacrament [does not depend upon] what the recipient of the sacrament believes and with what faith he is imbued."[40] The holiness of the church is rooted in the grace of God and not in human members.

The church is also "one" and "apostolic" for Augustine because it stands in the tradition of the Apostles' teachings; it is united in this faith and in the bond of love between Christ and Christians. The church has its unity when it receives the grace of God. In the catholic church, says Augustine, one obtains "the root of charity in the bond of peace and in the fellowship of unity."[41]

After Augustine

Augustine's ecclesiology formed the basis for understandings of the church developed in the Middle Ages and later. His view that unity is expressed by communion with the see of Rome gave impetus to the growth of power and supremacy in Rome and to the development of the papacy. His arguments against the Donatists shaped understandings of the "holiness" of the church that pointed beyond the ability of humans to be virtuous by their own power and toward the objective grace of God as the source of the church's life. Augustine's teachings on the visible and invisible church as grounded in the election of God were recaptured by Calvin and served as the basis of his ecclesiology as well.

Thus the church was forced to reflect on its nature through the first four centuries chiefly because it faced the problem of persecution and the question of what to do with those who had lapsed from their faith. The church's self-understanding arose out of practical, pastoral situations. Crucial theological turning points were faced and theological proposals made on how to understand the nature and purpose of the *ekklēsia* in history and beyond. The formative concepts laid down in these early periods set fundamental directions for centuries to come. They did not, of course, solve all the problems or answer all the questions, but they did provide a framework and a basis for further reflections, which continued through the following centuries and into the present day. As contemporary churches in vastly different cultures and settings struggle to understand their own lives and ministries, they are still informed by these earlier conflicts. They are guided as well by the insights that developed as Christians wrestled with the question of who they were as followers of Jesus Christ. In one sense that question is never fully answered, for each new context and situation is the place where ecclesiological controversy and reflection take place. In that sense Christians will always have to ask the question What is the church?

4

Anthropological Controversy

What Is Humanity?

During the fifth century the church not only faced the question of its own nature but also questions about the nature of those who make up the church. The Trinity, Christology, and ecclesiology continued to claim attention, but the church also began to examine its understanding of human nature and destiny. Who are church members without and within the church? If the church is composed of those united to Jesus Christ in his "mystical body," in "the ark of salvation," why is this important and even crucial? What is the nature of humanity—both apart from Christ and in union with Christ? This question led ultimately to the doctrines of sin and grace (see chap. 5) as the church looked inward at its own body and its many members (1 Cor. 12:12).

Although there were extensive controversies over the Trinity and Christology in the early centuries, there was no protracted discussion of the nature of humanity prior to the fifth century. The only creedal reference to humanity's nature or condition involves "the forgiveness of sins." Though notions of humanity were certainly formed in the early years, no consensus on the issue was needed. The church contained a variety of opinions on the question, at times appearing to be contradictory. In the longer view, the church has never pronounced any one view of humanity orthodox over against all others. Occasionally definitions were laid down and some views

condemned, but in comparison to Christology and the Trinity, anthropology has never received an exact and definitive treatment. Thus the question
remains: What is humanity?

Biblical Basis

There are a number of questions that cluster around the issue of
humanity. These are all important and each has undergone its own historical development.

Old Testament Perspectives

There are several Old Testament Hebrew terms that refer generically to
humanity, as well as terms that refer to a male. The opening chapters of
Genesis provide two accounts of the creation of humanity. In the first (Gen.
1:26–30), humanity is portrayed as the last of the living things created, the
climax of creation. Genesis 1:27 states that God created both male and
female. They are said to be in the "image" and "likeness" of God (1:26) and
are given "dominion" over the world with its living creatures (1:26, 28). In
the book of Psalms this position of honor and dignity for humanity is also
highlighted (Ps. 8).

The second account (Gen. 2:7–8; 18–23) pictures humanity at the center
of creation. Here humanity is "formed" as a potter would form a vessel (cf.
Job 10:8–11; Ps. 139:13–16). Humans gain life when God breathes into them
so that they become living beings (Gen. 2:7). The first humans are given
names in the biblical account; the man is named *Adam* (Heb. ʾādhām),
meaning "human being" or "humankind," and the woman is named *Eve*
(Heb. ḥawwāh), meaning "life" (Gen. 3:20; cf. 4:1).

Theologically these two creation accounts show the dependence of
humanity on God. Humans are created by God and rely on God for their
continuing life and existence. They are also seen as distinct from God: God
is the Creator; they are the creatures. The creation of humans in the image
and likeness of God, whatever it might fully signify, at least means that
there is a relationship between creatures and their Creator. It is, however, a
relationship in which the distinctiveness of each party is recognized.
Throughout the Old Testament the contrast between God and humankind
is clearly drawn (Hos. 11:9; Num. 23:19). Humans are seen in a creaturely
relationship with God, on whom they depend, and yet they are distant
from God in terms of their lives (see Isa. 45:11; Job 10:8–12).

The nature of the special relationship between God and humanity is
bound up with the description of humans as created in the *image* and
likeness of God. Through the centuries there have been many interpretations of these terms. Among the most important are the image of God
understood as corporeal form, spirit, physico-spiritual being, dominion,

male and female, rational and moral personality, and "sonship." Such
interpretations say something about the perceived nature of humanity but
also about the perceived nature of God. Theologically, views of the nature
of the image of God (*imago Dei*) are also related to views of the nature of sin
and salvation.

A number of other dimensions are related to the nature of humanity as
portrayed in the Old Testament. While individual terms are used to
describe the constitutive parts of a human being—such as liver, kidney,
heart—the Old Testament view of humanity is not one that divides human
nature into numerous parts. There is a basic wholeness of the person rather
than a duality or plurality of parts.

Humanity is also portrayed in the Old Testament as social and corporate in nature. Humans cannot live by themselves: there is always a
dependence on God and on other human beings, as well as obligations to
God and to others. In that sense there is solidarity throughout humanity as
humans are bound to each other and to God. In the story of Israel throughout the Old Testament, the connection of the individual with the larger
social unit is particularly strong. The individual in Hebrew thought is
summed up in the community, while the larger community is also reflected
in the individual. This concept has been captured in the term *corporate
personality*.[1] In the case of the sin of Achan, for example, the guilt of the one
man is carried through the whole community (Josh. 7:24–26; cf. 2 Sam. 14:7;
21:1–14; 2 Kings 9:26). Conversely, David and Solomon do not act purely
for themselves as individuals but also as representatives of the whole
nation.[2]

The Old Testament is also quite clear that the relationship between
God and humanity is severely restricted by sin (see chap. 5), which affects
all people (1 Kings 8:46; Ps. 143:2; Prov. 20:9; Eccl. 7:20) and is introduced in
Genesis 3 through the transgression of Adam and Eve. While the Old
Testament is not explicit on how sin spread through the race, the biblical
pictures of human solidarity and corporate personality suggest that the
continuity of human generations one after another is the context in which
the sinfulness of humanity spreads. The presence and power of sin are so
real that one writer traces it to the origins of the individual (Ps. 51:5). This
sin is ultimately against God (Ps. 51:4) and constitutes the rupture of the
relationship that God intended humanity to have and enjoy.

New Testament Perspectives

New Testament views of the nature of humanity are part of the
inherited legacy from the Old Testament. In the sense that humans are
seen as intimately related to and dependent on God, the study of humanity
is always theological anthropology. Humanity is never portrayed as ulti-

mately separable from its Creator and thus is not viewed alone or on its own. Since humans are always seen in their relationship to God, statements about humanity always have the closest possible relation to views about the nature of God.

Such dimensions as human intelligence, freedom, and responsibility are assumed especially in the teachings of Jesus (Luke 16:19–31; Matt. 25:1–13, 31–46). The parables of Jesus show humans freely making decisions on the basis of their own judgments and then facing the consequences of their decisions and responsibilities. At the same time, Jesus shows that humans are of great concern to God and deeply loved by God. The individual person, Jesus declared, is of more value than all the birds of the air and beasts of the field (Luke 14:5; Matt. 10:31). The parable of the Prodigal Son (Luke 15:11–32) and the other parables about "lostness" (Luke 15:3–7; 8–10) reveal the depth of love God has for humans (cf. John 3:16), and they show the plan and purpose of God to reestablish relationships that are broken by sin. Jesus' own attitudes and life-style highlight this through his acceptance and love for social outcasts such as the tax collector Matthew (Matt. 9:9), Zacchaeus (Luke 19:1–10), the woman of Samaria (John 4:7–26), and the woman taken in adultery (John 8:2–11). Even the humblest and most helpless of humans, a child, is not to be despised (Matt. 18:10) but honored as the model citizen in the kingdom of God (Matt. 18:4; cf. Mark 10:15; Luke 18:17). Jesus' healing miracles also indicate how he values and loves humans as precious in the sight of God.

The nature of humanity and the human relationship with God is explored more fully in the writings of the Apostle Paul. Paul employs numerous terms to express his views on the nature of humanity, including *flesh*, *body*, *spirit*, *heart*, *mind*, *remorse* or *conscience*, *soul*, and the *inner person*.[3] While each of these has its own meaning and usage in Paul (and they overlap at points as well), in a broader sense he shares the Old Testament perspective that unites the constituent parts of a person. There is a certain interchangeability of terms in Paul, for example, when he writes, "Present your bodies as a living sacrifice, holy and acceptable to God . . ." (Rom. 12:1), and "Let every person [*psychē*: lit., 'soul'] be subject to the governing authorities" (Rom. 13:1). In these instances *body* and *soul* do not indicate individual and exclusive entities but are rather terms applied to the whole personality.

Most striking and most developed in the Pauline literature on humanity are his descriptions of humans under the power of sin, as well as humans redeemed by Jesus Christ and living the Christian life in the community of the church. For Paul, as for the Old Testament, sin is a pervasive fact of life that is rooted in the origins of the race in Adam (Rom. 5:12–14) and dramatically affects the lives of all humans (Rom. 3:23). Sin brings death (Rom. 6:23), and its curse is relieved only by the death and resurrection of Jesus Christ (Rom. 3:21–26), which is received and accepted by faith (Rom. 5:1–2). One's relationship with God is restored, and reconciliation becomes a reality (2 Cor. 5:16–21), a new life that produces peace (Eph. 2:15ff.; Col. 1:20), hope (Rom. 15:13), and love (1 Cor. 13:13).

For Paul human nature finds its model and fulfillment in Jesus Christ. Paul draws parallels between the "first man" who was "from the earth, a man of dust" and the "second man," Jesus Christ, who is "from heaven" (1 Cor. 15:47). The "first Adam" brought sin and death; the "second Adam" brings life and salvation (Rom. 5:12–19; 1 Cor. 15:21–22, 44–49). In two passages Paul refers to Jesus Christ as the "image" (RSV "likeness") of God (2 Cor. 4:4) and the "image of the invisible God" (Col. 1:15; cf. Phil. 2:6— Christ "in the form of God"). These two accounts are in many ways reminiscent of the creation story (Gen. 1:3 is cited in 2 Cor. 4:6). Both deal also with the visibility and the illumination of the glory of God in and through the glory of Jesus Christ. This light now shines on the world in Jesus Christ, as did the light at creation when God said, "Let there be light." Now "the light of the knowledge of the glory of God" is seen "in the face of Christ" (2 Cor. 4:6).

Paul asserts that believers in Christ have undergone a radical transformation in which they pass out of death and slavery into life and freedom by the command of God. Paul speaks of this "new life" in the category of creation (Gal. 6:15; 2 Cor. 5:17; Eph. 2:10, 15; 3:9; 4:24; Col. 3:10; Titus 3:5). The "old nature," "old person," or old life in "the flesh" (see Rom. 6; 7; Gal. 5:16ff.; Eph. 2:3ff.; 4:22) has now become new (Eph. 4:24; Col. 3:10). This newness is "created after the likeness of God in true righteousness and holiness" found in Jesus Christ (Eph. 4:24; cf. 2 Cor. 3:18). Believers are "to be conformed to the image of [God's] Son" (Rom. 8:29; cf. 1 Cor. 15:49). Christ is "formed" in believers (Gal. 4:19), just as they have been created in him (Eph. 2:10). This renewal in the image of God comes through baptism (Gal. 3:27; Rom. 6:4), in which one "puts on Christ" and thus becomes a new person, part of the "new humanity" in Christ Jesus.

Anthropology East and West

In discussing the development of theological anthropology, or the relationship of humans to God, a number of other doctrines are involved. In particular, the doctrines of sin and God's grace must be considered. As anthropological understandings developed in the church, answers to questions about the nature of sin, the work of Christ, and the grace of God all affected or were affected by views of the nature of humanity. In what follows, primary attention will be given to views of how humans are able or unable to respond to the grace of God. This issue took its sharpest form in the fifth century in the controversy between Augustine and Pelagius. The question is directly related to the nature of humanity and more especially to the question of sin and human will. It is only one part of the larger picture of theological anthropology, but it is an important part. The Augustinian-Pelagian controversy marked another significant theological turning point, which was focused on the question What is humanity?

Early Anthropology

The writings of the Apostolic Fathers do not present a systematic doctrine of humanity. These primarily practical works do not spell out formal descriptions of the concepts they use, but, like writers already mentioned, the Fathers make extensive use of scriptural language.

With the apologists, however, the beginnings of a view of humanity begin to emerge. In these writings, humans are perceived as dichotomous, composed of *body* and *soul*. Consistently, the apologists hold that humans have the free will either to accept or to reject the offer of grace from God. Justin Martyr argues that while we have no choice in being born, we do have a choice in living our lives in ways pleasing to God. This power of choice is decisive for Justin. "Those who choose what is pleasing to [God] will, because of that choice, be counted worthy of incorruption and of fellowship" with God, for they choose "by the rational powers which he has given us." Consequently, humans are fully responsible for their choices and are without excuse before God when they do wrong or sin. Justin's views are also echoed by Athenagoras, Theophilus, and Tatian.[4]

Justin's position stands over against prevailing notions of human helplessness. One of these contemporary views was the Stoic belief in fate. An ancient philosophy, Stoicism taught that the universe is subject to a universal reason, or *logos*, which is implanted in the structures of the world. From this follows the notion that everything has a universal natural order, and therefore so does life. This order is *natural law*. To be virtuous, humans have to submit themselves in obedience to this power or fate, which has already decreed and predetermined each person's actions. Popular astrology, on the other hand, taught that everything was controlled by the heavenly bodies.[5] Gnosticism, another prevalent system, taught that humans are by nature unable to avoid evil or choose good. From birth they are doomed to sin. To counter these systems, Justin developed his views on human responsibility. He answered objections that Christian belief in prophecy means there can be no free will; God does not predetermine human actions, says Justin, but only foresees how humans, through their freedom, will choose to act. This is then announced to the prophets.[6]

Justin and the other apologists believed that origin of evil in humanity
was with evil demons who infected the race and put it under a curse. He
did not draw a link between the sin of Adam and that of later persons, but
they, "becoming like Adam and Eve work out death for themselves," and
"so shall each be by himself judged and condemned like Adam and Eve."[7]
In the more fully developed explanation of Tatian and Theophilus, the sin
of Adam is seen as the point of entrance for sin into the world but as
nothing more than a prototype or model of the sin that all humanity
chooses.[8]

Irenaeus

An alternative stream of thought regarding sin can be seen in the views
of Irenaeus. Like Theophilus he taught that Adam and Eve did not possess
complete perfection at creation but had the potential to grow into it. God
could have given this perfection, Irenaeus believed: "A mother, for example, can provide perfect food for a child, but at that point he cannot digest
food which is suitable for someone older. . . . Humanity, however, was
immature and unable to lay hold of it."[9] God gave the gifts of immortality
and incorruptibility to humans along with the knowledge of good and evil,
"so that they might choose the better things intelligently." This freedom can
make humans good. Knowing the difference between good and sin,
humans can appreciate and choose the good, but Adam disobeyed God
and thus lost the "image and likeness" with which he was endowed. Each
individual, following Adam, likewise sins by willful disobedience.
"Through the disobedience of that one man who was first formed out of the
untilled earth, the many were made sinners and lost life."[10] Irenaeus's
doctrine of *recapitulation*, in which Jesus Christ recapitulates, or sums up,
the history of the race, explains how the human situation of sin and death
is redeemed. As the second Adam, Christ reverses the sentence of the first
Adam.[11]

Tertullian

The themes of human nature and sin often recur in the writings of
Tertullian. "The entire [person] consists of the union of two substances,"
that is, of body and soul,[12] but in this union the soul predominates.
"Without the soul we are nothing; there is not even the name of a human
being, only that of a carcass."[13] Yet in the union of body and soul they are
so closely commingled that it is "deemed uncertain whether the flesh bears
the soul or the soul the flesh."[14]

Tertullian believed Adam was the source of all souls,[15] but after Adam
and Eve sinful parents have passed on sinful souls to their children.
Though it was Satan who enticed Adam to transgress the command of

God, human beings, "having been consequently given over to death, made the whole race from that time onward, infected from his seed, the bearer also of his condemnation." This led Tertullian to speak of the "birthmark of sin" and how sin has spread through the human race. All humans share in Adam's sin, for "we have borne the image of the earthly through our participation in transgression, our fellowship in death, our expulsion from Paradise."[16] This sin of humanity is the "fault of our origin" (Lat. *ex originis vitio*), and thus Tertullian coins the term *original sin*.[17] The soul still possesses "a portion of the good" of its original and created nature. Human free will, the ability to choose good or evil, is not snuffed out. Human nature is shaped by the "power of choice, which is called 'self-determination.' This faculty belongs to our nature and is capable of change; and thus whithersoever it inclines, our nature inclines the same way."[18] In his opposition to infant baptism Tertullian shows he does not believe that humans inherit the guilt of Adam, just the inclination to choose evil because of inherited sinful souls.

Clement and Origen

The theologians of the East do not follow Tertullian in positing a view of original sin in which the transgression of the first parents is passed on to posterity. Clement of Alexandria sees disobedience as the first sin in the Garden of Eden but denies that it is passed on to offspring. For "involuntary action is not judged, whether due to ignorance or compulsion," and "actions which are not the result of free-will are not imputed."[19] Although Clement stresses the ability of humans to make free choices, all are sinful and may be called sick or blind or ignorant. Their condition may even be termed "death." Yet this does not mean that all are involved in Adam's guilt. Against the Gnostics, Clement is vehement on the point that only personal misdeeds can be considered sin. Sin leaves humans disoriented and vulnerable to the irrational elements of their nature. Victory over sin is the conquest of rationality over instinct and sinful passion. Those who conquer attain likeness to God.

Origen's doctrine of creation affects his view of humanity. Heavily influenced by Neo-Platonism, Origen holds that a set number of rational essences were created by God and were all equal and alike. These pre-existent souls are endowed with free will (against the Gnostics). Each soul can advance by imitating God or fall away by neglecting God. All souls (except for Christ's) choose to be disloyal to God and thus fall into sin. When souls sin, they take on flesh as human beings.

Origen often allegorizes the story of Adam and Eve; their coat of skin, for example, can be understood as the surroundings of a body for a fallen soul.[20] Injustice in the present world can be understood as the judgment some receive for the sins of their preexistent souls. Adam and Eve represent every human being: the fall into sin in Genesis 3 is the story of all of humanity. The practice of infant baptism, which Origen advocates, is needed for purification, not from Adam's sin, but simply from the stain of the soul's contact with the flesh.[21]

The idea of human freedom is of crucial importance for Origen. The church believes that "every rational soul is possessed of free-will and volition." One can follow either the sinful ways of one's parents or the righteous ways of God. Souls who consistently follow God may become God's angels, while those who consistently sin may be numbered among the devil's angels. Sin and evil may be impossible to avoid completely, but the Christian is called upon to struggle against them. While the human will according to Origen is not sufficient to attain salvation by itself, it receives God's graceful assistance. "Our perfection does not come about by our remaining inactive, yet it is not accomplished by our own activity; God plays the greater part in effecting it."[22]

Fourth and Fifth Centuries

In the fourth and fifth centuries the doctrine of humanity began to take an important place in the church's theological discussions. Beside the views developing in the theological writings of both East and West, another dimension of human life is found in the ascetic tradition.

From the beginning local Christian communities had promoted fasting, almsgiving, continence, and even virginity. In the third century the drive toward these practices grew stronger. Christians faced chaotic social conditions, an unstable imperial government, added taxes, and outbreaks of persecution. These evils of the social environment drove some Christians into a life of solitude and isolation. Many of these ascetics looked forward to the life to come and their ultimate reward for keeping themselves pure by retreating from the world.

Ascetics often stressed the capacity for good that resides within the human person. God wished Adam to do the good but also allowed him the freedom to do evil. This would have made his preference for the good virtuous and worthy of reward. Like Adam, humans now can turn their backs on God and do evil. When this occurs, a pattern is established, and it becomes increasingly hard to turn in a new direction. A societal group that makes such choices can orient a whole culture toward sin. The sin of Adam commenced a process in which the environment is more likely to lead to sin than to obedience to God. While humans still have free choice, it is very difficult to reverse the pattern and follow God. Thus the Christian life is a struggle to be obedient to God in the midst of a threatening environment. Only a Christian community with godly people can provide a model of obedience to reverse the tendency to sin. God's grace is available to those who choose it, but it is the freedom to choose that constitutes God's divine image in humanity. These ascetic views, presented by such figures as Anthony of Egypt and Martin of Tours, come to full expression in the writings of the British monk Pelagius (fl. 383–410).[23]

Athanasius and the East

Though mainly concerned with establishing who Jesus Christ was, Athanasius also touched on the nature of humanity. Humans are God's special creations, impressed with the image of God. They receive thereby the gifts of immortality and incorruption. Yet God knew, according to Athanasius, that the will of humans "could incline either way." By free choice humans chose to sin and thus "despised and rejected the contemplation of God, and devised and planned wickedness for themselves . . . and received the threatened condemnation of death." But the loss of immortality for the body does not mean for Athanasius that the image of God is completely lost or that humans no longer have free choice.[24]

These same emphases are also found in Eastern theologians such as Basil of Caesarea, his brother Gregory of Nyssa, and Gregory of Nazianzus (the Cappadocians). Humanity was created in a primal state of happiness and blessedness. While sin derives from the misuse of freedom by Adam and Eve, the Eastern theologians do not go on to say that this guilt is passed on to later generations of humanity. Both Gregorys, along with John Chrysostom (c. 345–407), teach that newborn children are exempt from sin. Chrysostom interprets Romans 5:19, which says that "by one man's disobedience many were made sinners," to mean only that later generations were made liable to punishment and death. "For unless a man becomes a sinner on his own responsibility, he will not be found to deserve punishment. . . . That one man should be punished on another's account seems to most people unreasonable."[25] Thus, while in some way all humanity shares in Adam's fall and must live with the resulting weakness, these theologians do not say that humanity as a whole shares in Adam's guilt. Crucial for them is the view that the human will remains free and capable of making decisions pleasing to God. As Chrysostom writes, "Since God has placed good and evil in our power, he has granted free decision of choice, and does not restrain the unwilling, but embraces the willing." For "the Lord has made our nature free to choose."[26]

Ambrose and the West

In the fourth century the West focused more attention than the East on the effects of Adam's fall into sin. Following Tertullian, Western theologians like Ambrose of Milan (c. 339–97) stress that the fall of Adam plunged humanity into a sin that is all-encompassing in its effect. "We all sinned in the first man, and by natural inheritance an inheritance of guilt [Lat. *culpae*] has been transferred from one man into all. . . . Adam was in each of us: For in him human nature sinned, because through one man sin passed over into all." "In Adam I feel, in Adam I was cast out of Paradise, in Adam I died."[27] Ambrose bases his views on Psalm 51:5 "In sin did my mother conceive me." The fall was a cosmic catastrophe that affected all humans. The original sin is passed on through the sexual act of procreation. Baptism removes personal sins, and foot washing can cleanse hereditary sin.[28] Yet Ambrose also retains the concept of freedom of choice: "By free will we are either disposed toward virtue or inclined toward vice."[29]

Turning Point: Pelagius and Augustine

The issues surrounding the question What is humanity? came into sharp focus in the debates between Pelagius and Augustine. Pelagius was born in Britain in the middle of the fourth century and came to Rome to study law around 380. There he was baptized a Christian. Pelagius took the Christian life seriously and wanted to live strictly by God's law as the duty of all Christians. Pelagius interpreted this to mean he should give up his legal practice and become an ascetic in order to achieve perfection. He began to proclaim his views and soon gained the conversion of an important lawyer named Celestius. Pelagius also sought to persuade others of his views through a series of formal letters of exhortation.[30]

When Alaric conquered Rome in 410 Pelagius and Celestius fled. In Hippo, in northern Africa, they sought a meeting with Bishop Augustine, but since he was out of the city dealing with the Donatist controversy, Pelagius and Augustine never met. Pelagius then went to Palestine, where his ideas were well received. Celestius, however, went to Carthage, where he sought ordination in the church but was soon declared a heretic because of his views on sin, the fall of Adam, and baptism. A local synod condemned his teachings (which followed Pelagius's thought), and in 412 a council of the North African church, held in Carthage with Augustine presiding, declared Celestius's views unacceptable. In that year Augustine wrote *On the Reward and Remission of Sins* and *On the Spirit and the Letter*, in which he dealt with the same issues.

Pelagius's views drew fire two years later because of his letter to the nun Demetria. The vehement response to this letter came from two important Western theologians, Jerome and Orosius; they were opposed to Pelagius's emphasis on the freedom of the human will, which had been strong in the Eastern church. Eventually, 214 Western bishops condemned Pelagianism at a general council in Carthage in 418, a judgment reaffirmed by the ecumenical Council of Ephesus in 431. Pelagius's views, in a modified form known as *semi-Pelagianism*, continued to cause controversy in the church through the next century, until the Synod of Orange in 529 put an end to the struggles.[31]

Pelagius believed in the complete freedom of the individual, who is thus responsible for every action taken. Every sin is a result of individual choice and therefore a deliberate act of contempt against God. "We have within us a free will which is so strong and steadfast to resist sin, a free will which the Creator implanted in human nature universally," for "there is no congenital evil in us, and we are begotten without fault; and before the exercise of a man's own will there is nothing in him except what God has created."[32] Pelagius reacted to Augustine's prayer in his *Confessions*, "Give what Thou commandest, and command what Thou wilt," because it seemed to turn humans into puppets with no freedom for themselves.[33]

For Pelagius humans can "be without sin, and can keep the commandment of God" if they wish. Pelagius did not argue that in actual practice anyone ever remains sinless throughout life, but that one can turn from sin through one's own effort and the grace of God. A person "does not become incapable of conversion" because of sin.[34] It was important for Pelagius that individuals have the power to choose the good if good and evil are to have any meaning. Thus humans can choose to work toward perfection or toward evil: either choice is a real possibility.

Pelagius believed also that this freedom is an act of God's grace. "I mean by grace that state in which we were created by God with free will."[35] The sin of Adam did not affect posterity; it concerned Adam alone. Although it introduced sin into the created order, bringing with it both physical and spiritual death and setting before humanity the habit of disobedience, Adam's sin is passed on to later generations only by "custom" or "example." "Doing good has become difficult for us only because of the long custom of sinning, which begins to infect us even in our childhood. Over the years it gradually corrupts us, building an addiction and then holding us bound with what seems like the force of nature itself."[36] God assists humans to resist sin by giving them guides in the form of the law and the promise of reward to those who do good. The freedom to obey the law comes to humanity through God's grace, which is given "to make the fulfillment of God's commands easier." This leads to Pelagius's conclusion that people can—if they so desire—"observe God's commandments without sinning."[37]

In a series of anti-Pelagian writings, Augustine rejects these positions. Whereas Pelagius believed that the human will was free by nature, Augustine argues that it is only free by God's grace. For Pelagius the freedom of the will lies in humanity's power to choose. Augustine holds that true freedom rests only in the power of the will to achieve, and this can be accomplished only by the direct aid and grace of God. For Pelagius the answer to the question What is humanity? is that humans are emancipated from God as children from a parent: "This is the strongest exhortation possible, for Scripture to call us the children of God."[38] But to Augustine the relation between humans and God, though also like that of children to parents, is more aptly conceived as the relation between a baby and a mother. The baby is utterly dependent upon and intimately involved with all good and evil that springs from the parent as the only source of life.[39]

Augustine believed Adam was created perfect, holy, and "able not to die" if he ate from the tree of life. This first man had "the ability not to sin, not to die, not to desert the good," and also the power to persevere in this state of perfect freedom.[40] Humans are created in the image of God, which is found in "the rational or intellectual soul"; thus they can "employ reason and intellect to apprehend God and to behold him."[41] Yet Adam's condition, described by Augustine as "able not to sin" (Lat. *posse non peccare*), was permanently affected when he sinned. Adam's freedom was lost, for with the fall into sin, he became "not able not to sin" (*non posse non peccare*) and thus subject to death. Adam sinned out of pride, which led to his disobedience.[42]

This is original sin, and Augustine believed that the guilt of Adam's sin is transmitted forever after to all who are born.[43] The fall stemmed from Adam's misuse of freedom, and his transgression contaminated all humankind, since all humanity is "in the loins" of Adam.[44] The guilt of sin, according to Augustine, is transmitted by the physical act of generation. Since Adam was the first parent of the human race and since the Scriptures say "all sinned in him," argued Augustine, then all are involved in Adam's sin. "In the misdirected choice of that one man all sinned in him, since all were that one man, from whom on that account they all severally derive original sin."[45]

One result of this original sin passed on through the generations is that true freedom has been lost. For Augustine the power of free choice remains in all sinners. People can choose what they wish among various courses of action—for example, to make a trip or to stay at home—but freedom from sin and freedom for righteousness and a right relationship with God have been lost for all who come after Adam. The liberty to avoid sin and do good has been replaced by bondage to the power of sin. Thus humans who act according to their nature now act as sinners. Humans now sin by "necessity" because although "we always enjoy a free will," this will "is not always good."[46] Given choices, humans always choose the sinful alternative. Humans have "freedom to sin" (*posse peccare*) but not "freedom not to sin" (*posse non peccare*). Humanity as a whole is infected with what Augustine called "concupiscence," or self-centered desire, which directs one toward the self as the center of attraction instead of toward God.[47] For Augustine humankind is a "lump of sin," a "mass of perdition" (*massa perditionis*), and can be saved from sin and death only by the grace and predestination of God.[48] True freedom of the will can be achieved only when God acts by bringing one to new life in Jesus Christ, in order to restore the image of God, which sin has deformed and defaced.

What Is Humanity?

The controversy between Pelagius and Augustine brought to a head two different conceptions of the nature of humanity. For both theologians humans are created by God in the image of God. For both, humans are distinct from God and yet are in relationship with God. For both, this relationship has been broken by sin.

Pelagius and Augustine did not agree, however, on humanity's ongoing nature. For Pelagius humans tend to imitate Adam, the first person, by sinning. Yet sin is essentially "superficial," a matter of one's free choice. Choices can be reversed: wrong choices toward sin can be overcome by subsequent right choices toward the good that is found in God's law. Obedience for Pelagius is the hallmark of the Christian life, and the assurance of one's salvation is found in one's obedience to the law and the other aids provided by God.

For Augustine the question What is humanity? has to be answered differently. The first person, Adam, plunged humankind into sin, and all humans are now born with the guilt of sin from the common ancestor of the race. In Augustine's view the original freedom of humanity to choose obedience to God has been profoundly and permanently damaged. Humans now sin habitually in that they act according to their sinful nature, inherited from their origins as human beings. Only God can restore humanity to a right relationship and heal it of the deep cause of its sin. Through grace God has done this by creating a "new humanity" in Christ Jesus.

5

Soteriological Controversy

How Are We Saved?

One's views on the nature of humanity and especially the effect and power of sin have many theological consequences. Basically, sin indicates a rupture in the relationship between humanity and God. If it is to be repaired and harmony between creature and Creator reestablished, something must happen. That something is what the church has understood as *salvation*, and the study of salvation is called *soteriology*. How salvation occurs and how it is described involve a number of related theological issues, including the grace of God, the work of Christ, and human ability or inability to respond by faith. Further, the doctrine of salvation or redemption encompasses the atonement (what was accomplished by Christ's death) and justification (how one becomes righteous before God), as well as sanctification (the growth and development of the Christian life).

To keep our focus on major turning points in the history of Christian theology, we will look at the doctrine of salvation as it is expressed in various understandings of justification. As the controversy between Pelagius and Augustine shows, the church of the fifth century faced two major views of humanity and the power of sin. When these opinions about humanity and sin were clarified, there was a need to know their implications for the doctrine of salvation. The Pelagian and Augustinian positions, as well as the variation known as semi-Pelagianism, include a doctrine of salvation that describes how sin can be overcome and a right relationship with God established.

The doctrine of salvation is intertwined with the doctrines of the atonement and justification. Before Anselm of Canterbury (1033?–1109) wrote *Cur Deus homo* (1097–98), there was no systematic account of the atonement. In the early church period there were prominent themes describing the work of Christ, but none of these were fully developed. Anselm's view was challenged by Peter Abelard (1079–1142), and numerous theological descriptions of the death of Christ appeared subsequently.[1]

After the time of Augustine, the major turning point for the doctrine of salvation came in the sixteenth century when Martin Luther (1483–1546) challenged the doctrines of the Roman Catholic church. Luther and other Protestant Reformers rejected the views of salvation taught by the Roman Catholic theologians of the medieval church. Luther focused attention on the doctrine of justification by grace through faith as the way in which the biblical teachings on salvation can best be understood. At the Council of Trent (1545–63) the Roman church set forth its own teachings, which continued to be its official view. Today Protestant and Roman Catholic theologians often try to find as much common agreement and convergence as possible. For this to occur, however, it is important to understand the historical turning points on the important question How are we saved?

Biblical Basis

It is impossible to survey the issue of salvation in a short space, because the concept pervades both the Old and New Testaments. There is a wide variety of biblical terms and images used to describe aspects of salvation in the broadest sense. Many of the images developed in the New Testament have their roots in the Old Testament, but the focus is a bit different. New Testament writers give their attention to explaining how God has provided salvation in Jesus Christ. In the following discussion the primary emphasis is on the New Testament views, but connections are also made to their Old Testament roots.[2]

1. *Salvation and Redemption.* The New Testament represents salvation with the Greek term *sōtēria* (Luke 1:69, 71, 77; Acts 4:12; Rom. 1:16; 2 Cor. 7:10; Eph. 1:13) or its verbal form *sōzein* (Matt. 1:21; John 3:17; Acts 2:21; Rom. 5:9; 1 Cor. 1:21; Eph. 2:5). The Hebrew equivalents of these terms (*yāshī; pālat*) mean simply "help," often with legal support implied. This call for help in the midst of distress is seen particularly in the Psalms (18:27; 72:4; 109:31); God is the one who is "help" (40:17; 79:9; 85:4). In texts written after the exile in Babylon, God's help comes in the future (Isa. 25:9; 60:16; Zech. 8:7, 13).

In the New Testament, *sōzein* has the meanings "save" and "heal." Jesus sees as his mission "to seek and to save the lost" (Luke 19:10). This salvation is linked with the forgiveness of sins (Mark 5:34; Luke 17:19) and with faith (Luke 7:50; 15:11–32; 19:9). Jesus as the one who brings salvation and help is the "Savior" (Luke 2:11; John 4:42; Acts 5:31; Eph. 5:23; Phil. 3:20; 2 Peter 1:1; 1 John 4:14).

In the writings of Paul, the whole life, death, and resurrection of Jesus Christ is seen as the saving act of God (Rom. 4:25; 5:10; 2 Cor. 4:10–11): through the work of Christ on earth and particularly through his death on the cross (Rom. 3:25; 5:9; Eph. 1:7; Col. 1:20; cf. Heb. 9:12; 13:12; Rev. 1:5) forgiveness of sins is received by humanity. Through Christ, according to the New Testament, God has acted to redeem and help a people held captive by the evil effects of sin. Through faith (Acts 16:30–31; Rom. 5:6–11; 10:9; 1 Cor. 1:23–24) those who trust in Jesus Christ as their Lord and Savior receive a new relationship of communion with God through Jesus Christ and the Holy Spirit (Eph. 1:19ff.; Rom. 1:16; 1 Cor. 1:18; Phil. 3:10; 2 Thess. 1:11; 2 Tim. 1:7–8). This salvation is both a present reality (2 Cor. 6:2) and a future hope (Rom. 8:24; Gal. 5:5). The Christian life in the present and in the future is marked by faith, hope, and love (1 Cor. 13:13; Col. 1:4ff.; Rom. 15:13; 1 Tim. 1:3; Eph. 4:4).

2. *Freedom from Slavery.* In the Old Testament God is portrayed as rescuing people from danger by leading them out (see Pss. 68:6; 107:14; 142:7). The supreme example of this is God freeing the people of Israel from slavery in Egypt; thus the terms also mean "liberation from the house of slavery" (see Exod. 13:3; 20:2; Deut. 5:6; 8:14; Jer. 34:13).

The New Testament also presents salvation in terms of rescue. It is "Jesus who delivers us from the wrath to come" (1 Thess. 1:10), and in the Lord's Prayer Jesus instructs his disciples to pray for deliverance from evil (Matt. 6:13). God in Jesus Christ delivers from deadly peril (2 Cor. 1:10), from the present evil age, and redeems from the "curse of the law" (Gal. 3:13). God has "delivered us from the dominion of darkness and transferred us to the kingdom of his beloved Son" (Col. 1:13). Thus Jesus means freedom from the constraints of slavery in all its various forms.

3. *Liberation through Ransom.* Related to freedom from slavery is the New Testament picture of redemption through a ransom (see Luke 1:68; Rom. 3:24; 8:23; Eph. 1:7; Heb. 9:12; 1 Peter 1:18). The Hebrew background is the redemption of a slave by paying a ransom (Exod. 21:7–11) or freeing a poor person who is unable to pay a debt (Job 6:23). In Deuteronomy the liberation from Egypt is also such a redemption (Deut. 13:5; 15:15; 24:18). It is God who is the "redeemer" (Job 19:25; Pss. 72:13–14; 119:154; Lam. 3:58), who protects weaker ones (Jer. 50:34), and who in the Exodus reclaims the lost nation of Israel (Exod. 6:6; Ps. 74:2; Isa. 63:9).

In the New Testament the distinction between purchase by ransom and repurchase of a lost possession is practically nonexistent (see Luke 24:21; Rom. 3:24; 1 Cor. 1:30; Heb. 11:35), but the image continues to be linked with the death of Jesus as the means by which liberation is accomplished (Mark 10:45; 1 Peter 1:18–19; Eph. 1:7).

4. *Reconciliation.* One of the major images of salvation used by Paul is reconciliation after a dispute. In this image, as former enemies are turned into friends, so humanity is said to be reconciled with God through Jesus Christ (Rom. 5:10; Eph. 2:14; Col. 1:21–22). It is not God who is reconciled to humanity, but humanity—formerly estranged from God because of sin— which now is reconciled to God (2 Cor. 5:20). God "reconciled us to himself" (2 Cor. 5:18–21; cf. Col. 1:22; Eph. 2:16) and also to other humans. It is Jesus Christ who brings about this reconciliation (Col. 1:22; Eph. 2:16). This leads to changed relationships between God and humanity and among human beings. Humans need no longer be enemies and godless, helpless sinners (Rom. 5:6–8); they are now a "new creation" (2 Cor. 5:17) since sin is forgiven and the love of God is now in their hearts (Rom. 5:5). Reconciliation through Jesus Christ makes us sinless before God's judgment (Col. 1:22); we are friends again with God and people of peace (Eph. 2:15).[3]

5. *Peace with God.* Closely related to reconciliation with God as establishing a bond of peace is salvation as peace (Heb. *shālōm*, Gr. *eirēnē*). Jesus Christ is "our peace" (Eph. 2:14) and is himself the content of the "gospel of peace" (Eph. 6:15). Numerous New Testament letters begin with the salutation, "Grace to you and peace from God our Father and the Lord Jesus Christ" (Rom. 1:7; 1 Cor. 1:3; 2 Cor. 1:2; Gal. 1:3; Eph. 1:2; Phil. 1:2; Col. 1:2). Through Jesus Christ, we have "peace with God" (Rom. 5:1), which was promised in the annunciation by the angels at the birth of Jesus (Luke 2:14). This "good news of peace by Jesus Christ" is preached as the gospel message by the early church (Acts 10:36) and by Jesus himself to both Jews and Gentiles (Eph. 2:17).[4]

6. *Forgiveness of Sin.* The New Testament often links the forgiveness of sin with the death and resurrection of Jesus Christ (Luke 1:77; Acts 5:31; Rom. 4:5; 5:6; Gal. 3:22; Eph. 1:7; 2:5; Col. 1:14). In the Old Testament the Hebrew word *sālaḥ* means to "bestow forgiveness," an act that only Yahweh can do (Pss. 86:5; 130:4; Dan. 9:9; Neh. 9:17), though it is often carried out through the work of a priest (Lev. 4:5; Num. 15:25–26, 28). The term means more precisely covering sin (atonement), leaving sins behind (Isa. 38:17), or casting them into the depths of the sea (Mic. 7:19). God is a God of forgiveness (Neh. 9:17), who is always ready to forgive (Lev. 26:40– 41). At times this forgiveness is described as wiping away the record of guilt (Isa. 43:25; Ps. 51:3), removing a burden (Mic. 7:18; Pss. 32:1; 85:3), passing over guilt (Amos 7:8; 8:2), and passing over sin as an act of forbearance

(Amos 7:2, Jer. 5:1; Deut. 29:19; Ps. 103:3). Sometimes sin is expiated through a sin offering made by a priest (Lev. 4:26, 31; 5:6, 18; 14:18). In the New Testament Jesus Christ is the one who "takes away the sin of the world" in the sense of bearing the consequences for sin (John 1:29; 1 John 3:5). Jesus is portrayed as the atoning sacrifice, the perfect offering who as both priest and victim secures salvation (see Heb. 2:17; 9:11ff.; 10:10ff.).

7. *Salvation as Justification*. The imagery of salvation as justification is developed most fully in the writings of the Apostle Paul, who also employs other imagery as noted above. As with the other New Testament images, the Old Testament background provides the overall context for interpreting the concept. In this case the New Testament Greek term for *justify* is *dikaioō* (and related words), which stems from the Hebrew root ṣdq.[5] English translations have rendered words with the *dikaio-* stem as "justice" and "righteousness," adjectives as "just" and "righteous," and verbs primarily as "justify."

The contexts in which justification language is used are forensic, or related to law courts. At certain places, however, Paul was apparently repeating primitive confessions of faith. Examples of these are, "You were justified in the name of the Lord Jesus Christ" (1 Cor. 6:11) and "Jesus our Lord, who was put to death for our trespasses and raised for our justification" (Rom. 4:24–25), as well as Romans 3:24–26a (cf. 1 Cor. 1:30; 1 Peter 3:18; 1 Tim. 3:16; and perhaps 2 Cor. 5:21).

More clearly than anyone else, however, Paul described what God did for humanity in Jesus Christ by relating it to grace and faith. For Paul a person "is not justified by works of the law but through faith in Jesus Christ" (Gal. 2:16). This justification is by "the grace of God" through faith and not through the law (Gal. 2:21; Rom. 3:22, 24). Faith in Christ is a gift of God (Eph. 2:8–9); it arises from hearing the gospel proclaimed (Gal. 3:2; Rom. 10:17) and leads to a new life of obedience (Rom. 1:5; cf. 16:26). Faith expresses itself through love (Gal. 5:6). Paul speaks also of God's judgment of human works (2 Cor. 5:10; cf. Rom. 2:6–8). Justification, however, is accomplished through Christ "once for all" and involves not only a past but also a present and future tense. It is based on what Christ has done in the past (Rom. 5:6ff.), which brings a new relationship with God through Christ in the present (Rom. 5:1), while being also a "hope of righteousness" for the future (Gal. 5:5). The action of God in salvation leads to a personal responsibility to live obediently in the new life. Thus Paul urges Christians to "work out your own salvation with fear and trembling," while also recognizing that "God is at work in you, both to will and to work for his good pleasure" (Phil. 2:12–13). Any good works done by believers and presented to God in the future (1 Thess. 1:3; cf. Rom. 2:7) are done by the power of God in the Christian's life.

Salvation in the Early Church

The various biblical ways of speaking about salvation provide many theological strands for theologians to draw upon in describing the nature of salvation and how it is accomplished. The development of a structured doctrine of salvation took several centuries, since the concept includes many other theological ideas. Even when some views of salvation solidified—as in Pelagius and Augustine—they went through further refinements and still continue to develop today. Expressing what humans receive by virtue of the life, death, and resurrection of Jesus Christ and how they receive it is an ongoing challenge. Several major, overlapping themes began their development in the early church and are presented here in the views of the major representatives of the period.

Salvation as Illumination: Apostolic Fathers and Apologists

The early Apostolic Fathers spoke of numerous benefits that come from Jesus Christ, but their major emphasis was on what Jesus imparted to humanity: new knowledge, new life, faith, immortality. Thus Jesus is seen primarily as a teacher, and salvation flows from the knowledge (gnōsis) of God that brings eternal life.[6] As Clement of Rome says of Christ, "It was through him that he [God] called us 'from darkness to light' [Acts 26:18], from ignorance to the recognition of his glorious name"; "Through him the Master has willed that we should taste immortal knowledge." For Clement we are "justified by our deeds, not by words": "Happy are we, dear friends, if we keep God's commandments in the harmony of love, so that by love our sins may be forgiven us."[7] Thus for salvation faith is joined with the keeping of the law and piety before God, who gives grace to those who perform the commandments and are worthy.[8] Since Jesus is the Christian's example and source of illumination, Clement exhorts his readers to follow that example and "unhesitatingly give ourselves to his will, and put all our effort into acting uprightly."[9]

The apologists also stressed the illumination Christ brought from ignorance, error, and bondage to demons. As the Logos of God Christ is the fulfillment of the longings of all nations and the answer to the speculations of the Greek philosophers. In the incarnation God's reason (logos) was fully revealed in Jesus Christ, the teacher of the race, the "new law-giver," who imparts a saving knowledge to humanity. In opposition to Gnosticism, which stressed the impartation of saving knowledge to only a few (the "elect"), Justin maintains that the knowledge of Christ is free and open to all, for Christ is "the Word [Gr. logos] of whom all mankind have a share."[10]

For Justin, however, Christ not only imparted divine knowledge; he also conquered the powers of evil that lead humans away from God. The

purpose of the incarnation was the conquest of the serpent, and throughout his whole life and ministry Jesus showed his power over all evil spirits
and was hailed as "Lord of the powers."[11]

In stressing salvation as illumination early Christian theologians
looked to Christ as the source of enlightenment and the example by which
a new life, free from ignorance, unbelief, and death, might come to the
world. Jesus is the greatest example of human freedom, and salvation is
secured by following his example, which humans are free to do or not to
do. The gospel message includes the chance to shake the powers of evil and
ignorance and to live a morally responsible life illumined by the life and
teachings of Jesus Christ.[12]

Salvation as Restoration: Irenaeus

The notion of the imitation of Christ has its most profound expression
in the third century in the work of Irenaeus. For him the Christian's
imitation of Christ had its origins as part of God's plan of salvation, which
began with Christ's imitation of Adam. Irenaeus's theory of *recapitulation*
(Eph. 1:10; Rom. 13:9) means "our Lord summing up universal humanity in
himself even to the end, summing up also his death."[13] This was the
purpose of the incarnation: for Christ to repair the damage done to
humanity by Adam's disobedience. For Christ passed through all stages of
human growth and redeemed each by being made for all—infants, children, men, and women—"an example of piety, righteousness, and sub-
mission."[14] He thus identified himself completely with humanity. At the
same time, Christ restored humanity to the image of God, which it lost
through Adam's fall, by incorporating them into his own obedience. Jesus
Christ, "when he was enfleshed and became a human being . . . summed up
in himself the long history of the human race and so furnished us with
salvation in a short and summary way, to the end that what we had lost in
Adam (namely, to be after the image and likeness of God) we might
recover in Christ Jesus."[15]

In his understanding Irenaeus follows the parallelism between the first
and second Adam (Adam and Christ) drawn by the Apostle Paul (see Rom.
5:14–17; 1 Cor. 15:20–22, 45–49). In restoring humanity by becoming "what
we are, in order that he might make us what he himself is," God acted in a
way that is "fitting" to God's nature, that is, in gentleness rather than by
force.[16] Christ restores humanity by reversing the sentence of death
incurred by Adam. In this Irenaeus appealed to a number of types and
parallels between the "old Adam" and the "new Adam." For example,
whereas our bondage to sin is caused by the fruit of a tree, in Christ we are
redeemed by the fruit of another tree, the cross. Whereas Adam was
tempted to disobedience by the virgin Eve, in Christ we are saved through

the obedience of the Virgin Mary. Whereas the fall of humanity was caused by the disobedience of the first Adam, the restoration and salvation of humanity come through the obedience of the second Adam.[17] By his complete identification with the human race at every point in its existence, Jesus Christ restores fellowship with God by "perfecting humanity according to God's image and likeness." This union of humanity and God occurs through the Spirit of God: "The Lord . . . pours out the Spirit of the Father to unite God and humanity and bring them into communion, bringing God down to human beings through the Spirit and, conversely, bringing humanity up to God by his own incarnation."[18]

Like earlier theologians, Irenaeus shows Christ as a teacher and example. He goes beyond them, however, by also indicating that Christ's obedience was offered to God in place of the disobedience of humanity spread through Adam's fall. It is the whole life of Christ, the incarnation itself, that brings salvation as the restoration of what humanity was originally intended to be.

Salvation as Satisfaction: Tertullian

The great Western theologian Tertullian introduced a concept into the meaning of salvation that developed in many significant ways in later centuries. He uses the legal term *satisfaction* to describe the need of the sinner to be reconciled to God: good deeds acquire merit with God, but bad deeds require satisfaction. After baptism, a penitent sinner wishing to be freed of the sinful offense committed against God must not only be contrite and confess the sin, but also offer satisfaction. This satisfaction is the discharging of an obligation in a way that is agreeable to the one who was wronged. In the "second repentance" of the Christian, God observes the person's sorrow and takes that as the basis for annulling the penalty of the sin.[19]

Tertullian speaks of God as "one to whom you may make satisfaction." A person who repents has "begun to make satisfaction to the Lord"; to lapse after repentance "will give satisfaction to the devil." For it is necessary "to satisfy the offended Lord" in order that "I may reconcile to myself God, whom by sinning I have offended." Through tears, fasting, prayers, alms-giving, and sin offerings the sinner renders satisfaction to God; and through the punishment of one's self, eternal punishment is avoided, and sin forgiven.[20]

Unlike later theologians Tertullian does not directly relate his view of satisfaction to the work of Christ.[21] More than Irenaeus, he puts great stress on Christ's death and asks, "Who has ever redeemed the death of another by his own, except the Son of God alone? . . . Indeed, it was for this purpose that he came—to die for sinners." For "it was necessary for him to be made a sacrifice for all nations, and he delivered himself up for our sins."[22]

Tertullian's view of satisfaction made by the sinner also gave rise to a doctrine of merits and the doctrine of penance. Here the process of salvation is made a legal and ethical one in which God is an injured party, because of sin, and humans must "appease" their angry God. This is done by acts of self-humiliation to win God's favor. If one does more than is needed, one gains merits and puts God in debt to oneself. Tertullian's principle was, "A good deed has God as its debtor." If a Christian refrains from sin and does more than God commands through obeying the law, "like deed involves like merit." In this way salvation may be achieved, and in eternity God will reward differently "for the variety of merits."[23]

Tertullian's introduction of satisfaction and his views on Christ's sacrifice for sins were developed by later theologians into various judicial views of the atonement in which Christ substituted himself for the sinner and paid the price of reconciliation by satisfying God's divine honor (Anselm), God's justice (Luther), or God's wrath (seventeenth-century Lutherans and Calvinists). Tertullian's views also began a movement toward a doctrine of merit and a whole theology of penitence, which became prominent in medieval theology.

Salvation as Victory: Origen

While Tertullian and other theologians of the Western church began to emphasize the death of Jesus as the focus of God's work of salvation, some Eastern theologians looked to the resurrection of Christ as God's crowning work of salvation. In Irenaeus, along with his view of salvation as restoration, and also in Origen, the dominant view was that salvation was the great triumph of Jesus Christ over Satan and the forces of evil. This *Christus Victor* view of salvation graphically displays God's cosmic victory over the devil and all evil powers: they are defeated in the work of Christ and subjected to God's power and will. The crucifixion and resurrection are closely related in this struggle, representing the last battle against evil and the final victory.[24]

For Origen, Christ is the great physician, teacher, lawgiver, and example. Yet as the divine Logos Christ was also engaged in a life-long battle with the hostile evil forces that encircle the earth. In his incarnation he broke through the band of demons surrounding earth and at every turn in life struggled with Satan. Origen looks to Colossians 2:15 to see in the death of Christ both the supreme divine example and the trophy of Christ's victory over the devil, who was effectively nailed to the cross along with the evil principalities and powers. "Through his Resurrection He destroyed the Kingdom of Death, whence it is written that He freed captivity."[25]

One of the major images Origen uses to express this theme is the image of *ransom*. Origen speaks of Jesus handing over his soul to Satan in exchange for the souls of humanity, which the devil claimed to own because humans are sinful. When Satan accepted this exchange, he found that the soul of Jesus could not be held because Jesus was sinless, and the sinless soul of Christ caused Satan agonizing torture. Thus the devil miscalculated the transaction and deceived himself because Christ proved too good for him; Satan could not hold such a one in his kingdom. Origen concludes by exclaiming: "So also Death thought that it had him in its power, but it had no power over him who became 'free among the dead' [Ps. 88:5] and stronger than the authority of death, and so much stronger, that all who wish to follow him can do so, though overcome by death, since death has now no strength against them: for no one who is with Jesus can be seized by death."[26]

Origen's view that Christ's victory over evil provided for the salvation of the world is closely tied to his ultimate view of the restoration of all things (Acts 3:21). Origen was heavily influenced by 1 Corinthians 15:24–28 with its prophecy of the eventual victory of God over all enemies, including death, and the handing over of the kingdom by Christ to God the Father. "The goodness of God, through his Christ, may recall all his creatures to one end, even his enemies being conquered and subdued." These enemies include death (the "last enemy") and also Satan, who holds the sinful world under evil power. God will be "all in all" only when "the end has been restored to the beginning, and the termination of things compared with their commencement. . . . And when death shall no longer exist anywhere, nor the sting of death, nor any evil at all, then truly God will be all in all."[27]

Origen's grand vision and the *Christus Victor* view in general certainly finds support in many statements of Scripture, but he tends not to consider fully other biblical statements about sin and guilt. While the image of Christ the victor provides a framework and context for understanding the meaning of salvation, later theologians also felt the need to develop descriptions of how the work of salvation is accomplished by God in individual lives.

Salvation as Deification: Athanasius and the Eastern Theologians

Another important theme in the early church was salvation as *deification*. This was seen as the final result of the saving knowledge of God, the forgiveness of sins, and the rescue from death, which Christ accomplished in his death and resurrection. Deification became a primary description for salvation among theologians of the Eastern church. As Western theologians developed the theme of salvation as justification, Eastern writers stressed the union of believers with Christ's divine nature and thus with

God.[28] While images in theologians of this period tend to overlap, it is possible to see the strand of salvation as deification in many different writers.

For the Eastern fathers divinization and deification are synonymous. The terms indicate how the blessings of salvation—immortality or incorruption—are experienced gradually by believers in this life. Deification describes a believer's personal encounter with God and the work of God's grace, whereby through the Spirit of God believers experience a communion with God and are regarded as children of God. In the words of Clement of Alexandria, "The Logos of God had become man so that you might learn from a man how a man may become God."[29] The completion of divinization occurs only at the final consummation.

Biblical support for salvation as deification comes from passages such as Psalm 82:6: "I say, 'You are gods, sons of the Most High, all of you" and 2 Peter 1:4: ". . . and become partakers of the divine nature," as well as passages from Paul (such as 1 Cor. 15:49; 2 Cor. 8:9; Rom. 8:11) and John 10:34, where Jesus quotes Psalm 82:6. Eastern theologians taught that believers will be recreated in the likeness of Jesus Christ, the Son of God. This involves both transformation and renewal.[30]

Early theologians such as Ignatius of Antioch speak of immortality and being part of an imperishable life.[31] Irenaeus also speaks of the restored humanity in Jesus Christ as united with the divine nature of the Logos.[32] For Clement of Alexandria deification comes by illumination and the teaching of the Logos. In baptism a believer is illuminated and made a child of God, is perfected and made immortal as in Psalm 82:6. The knowledge of God brings incorruptibility, which is divinization. Origen too uses the Greek terms for divinization to describe knowing God, being re-formed in God's likeness, and eventually being perfected so that we become like God.[33]

Athanasius provides a full description of salvation as deification. For him the goal of Christ's work is to restore the divine image in humanity. "The Word was made man in order that we might be made divine." Against the Arians Athanasius wrote that "by becoming man He made us sons to the Father, and He deified men by Himself becoming man."[34] Athanasius's analogy is that of a damaged portrait. To restore it to its original condition, the original model had to sit for it once again. Thus it is crucial for Athanasius that Christ be truly God. God himself must be the model, and Christ as the agent of salvation must be truly God. The ultimate result of the incarnation and of salvation is divinization by the grace of God. For Athanasius the human soul (or human being) becomes deified as the person is restored to God's image. God has "assumed the created and human body in order that having as creator renewed it, he might deify it in himself and bring us into the kingdom of heaven according to God's likeness."[35]

Salvation as deification was continued in the Eastern tradition by the Cappadocians, Cyril of Alexandria, John of Damascus, and others.[36] The ascetic tradition, with its emphasis on contemplation and Christian mysticism, finds the soul's union with God a possibility even in this life. Instead of emphasizing the fall of humanity into sin, this theme stresses the human potential of being united with God. In baptism this process begins, in the present life of obedience and responsibility it is carried out, and in the future, deification will be complete.

Turning Point: Augustine and Pelagius

Salvation as Justification

The basic pattern for describing salvation in the Western church arose out of the controversy between Augustine and Pelagius in the fifth century. Augustine emphasizes the Pauline model of salvation as justification more strongly than Eastern theologians with their emphasis on salvation as deification. At points Augustine links deification with justification by stating that justification implies deification since through justification humans are adopted into the household of God as children.[37] Augustine's primary emphasis, however, is on the point that justification effects a transformation of the individual, thus making a person righteous.[38] This transformation takes place through God's grace. At stake in Augustine's debate with Pelagius and the Pelagians is the extent to which God's grace is necessary and sovereign in the process of salvation.

For Augustine the process of salvation centers on the work of Jesus Christ. In his theology, however, Augustine used and developed several motifs from the early church. For him the incarnation is connected with sin and its remedy: "If man had not sinned, the Son of God would not have come." For the human race to be redeemed, it was essential for God to become a human being.[39]

In the course of his writings, Augustine used a number of images to describe what Jesus Christ had accomplished. Many of these strands are woven together in one passage in his *Enchiridion*.

> For we would not be liberated even by means of "the one mediator between God and man, the man Jesus Christ" [1 Tim. 2:5], were he not also God. When Adam was created, he was certainly righteous, and there was no need of a mediator. However, when sins had made a wide rift between mankind and God, it was necessary that we should be reconciled to God, and even brought to the resurrection to eternal life by means of a mediator who alone was without sin in his birth, life, and execution: so that man's pride should be shown up and cured by the humility of God, and man

should be shown how far he had departed from God, since it was through the incarnation of God that he was recalled, and through the God-man that an example of obedience was offered to the insolence of man. And so a fountain of grace was opened, not for any antecedent merit, by the taking of "the form of a servant" [Phil. 2:7] by the Only-begotten; and a proof of the bodily resurrection promised to the redeemed was given by anticipation in the person of the Redeemer himself. The devil was overcome by means of that very nature which, he rejoiced to think he had entrapped.[40]

Here Augustine clearly describes Christ as the mediator between God and humanity,[41] as the example of obedience,[42] and as the conqueror of Satan and evil.[43] In other places he makes it plain that Christ is our Savior from death[44] and the High Priest who is also the sacrifice to God on behalf of humanity.[45] All in all, Jesus Christ has reconciled human beings to God and rescued them from the power and guilt of sin, so that humans are freed to follow the example of Christ and share his victory over the powers of evil. Thus humans are reconciled, restored, and also, as noted above, in some sense ultimately partakers of the divine nature in deification.

How salvation is personally appropriated and how the grace of God is applied to one's life are the crux of the issue in the debates between Pelagius and Augustine, which focus on the issue of justification and how a person is "made righteous." They also involve, of course, the doctrine of grace and, for Augustine, the issue of predestination.

Pelagius taught that humans possess a genuinely free will that is capable of either sinning or not sinning (see chap. 4). Grace is not a special work of God but rather a "natural grace" or "grace of creation." Pelagius also believed in a "grace of revelation" or "grace of teaching," through which God shows humans how to live and enlightens their reason so that they can see God's will, which is expressed particularly through the law of God. There is also, according to Pelagius, a "grace of pardon" or "grace of redemption," which is freely given by God in conversion and baptism when humans freely choose to repent of evil and to act as God desires. For Pelagius predestination is God's foreknowledge of those who will choose to follow God; it is not a sovereign decree or choice on God's part. Pelagius said simply, "To predestine is the same as to foreknow."[46]

For Pelagius grace is God's help or assistance, which is focused most clearly in God's teaching and in the revelation of God's will and the rewards promised to those who act uprightly. Grace enlightens one's understanding and motivates the will toward obeying God. Grace is supremely shown in Jesus Christ who, by his example and teachings, has given the grace, or help, necessary for humans to resist the temptation to sin and do wrong. Faith, for Pelagius, is entirely a matter of one's own free choice. Justification is by faith followed by works of righteousness. Pelagius constantly reminds his readers to act in such a way that they will merit heavenly rewards. Justification is by faith at the point of a person's (adult) baptism. Righteousness follows after baptism and at the judgment of God is accompanied by the "works of righteousness" done in life. Throughout life the believer appropriates the grace of the teaching and example of Christ, using freedom of choice to obey the gospel and to merit the final rewards of the kingdom of heaven. In sum, "Faith in the first instance is reckoned as righteousness for this reason, that [a person] is absolved as to the past, justified as to the present, and prepared for the future works of faith."[47]

For Augustine, however, the picture is much different. His view of original sin (see chap. 4), whereby in Adam the whole of humanity became enslaved to the power of sin, radically shapes his understanding of God's grace in salvation. In the state of sin the human will is incapable of choosing to do the will of God and humans are incapable of not sinning (*non posse non peccare*). In this captivity of the will, "no one, therefore, either has been freed, or is being freed, or will be freed from this state except by the grace of the Redeemer."[48] All freedom for righteousness has been lost, and it is only by the grace of God that the true freedom of the children of God can be restored.

For Augustine, in contrast to Pelagius, God's grace is not the condition God provides for the good life. Grace is rather the internal operation of the Holy Spirit that makes possible the free use of the will for the righteous purposes God intended. God's grace does not simply teach us what to do; it enables us to do the good that God desires: to do justice, live well, and observe God's commandments.

Augustine's concern is to show that the grace of God is absolutely prior to all human endeavor and that the full work of salvation, expressed as the justification of the sinner, rests with God. The grace of God is sovereign because God is sovereign. To express this, Augustine distinguishes four different aspects of the grace of God.

(1) Prevenient grace is Augustine's way of saying that God comes first: it is always God who begins the action of salvation without being at all dependent on human endeavors. Augustine derived this from Psalm 59:10 translated from Latin as, "His mercy will go before (*praevenient*) me." God initiates whatever good a person may think or will. God roots out and forgives sin and gives the Holy Spirit as a gift. With the Spirit God gives the faith needed to receive God's grace and the new will needed to fight the power of sin. Yet it is God who gives it all as a sheer gift of gratuitous love. For Augustine grace "predisposes a man before he wills, to prompt his willing. It follows the act of willing, lest one's will be frustrated." God does

not override human will but moves it from within and makes it an instrument of God's will.[49]

The term *justification* for Augustine refers to the process by which one becomes righteous, as the Holy Spirit sheds the spirit of love in one's heart. The person receives a new will that wills what God wills and expresses itself in deeds of love. Justification occurs at baptism and continues through life as an internal growth of righteousness in the believer.[50]

Augustine also spoke of (2) cooperating or accompanying grace, which is the continuing work of God in the lives of believers. Sin is never completely overcome in this life, but through ongoing grace God does good works in the lives of believers. God "provides the will, and by co-operation brings to fufilment what he begins by his operation. . . . We have no power to perform the good works of godliness without his operation to make us will, and his co-operation when we will."[51]

Augustine's term (3) sufficient grace is the grace Adam possessed in paradise that enabled him to be able not to sin (*posse non peccare*) and to persevere in this condition if he so willed. (4) Efficient grace is given to God's elect, the Christian believers, to enable them to do what God expects.[52] Augustine's emphasis throughout is on grace as the free gift of God that cannot be earned by human deeds, since humans are totally captive to the power of sin and thus capable of no good acts in the sight of God.

Augustine's views on sin and grace led him to the conclusion that God's grace is irresistible and that God predestines those who come to faith. Since all humans are gripped by the power of sin, all are incapable of anything but sin. Their wills always choose evil, and God's grace is the only power that can change this situation. When God's grace enters a person's heart, the will is changed; a person who is justified begins spontaneously to will what is good. "The grace of God is always good; and through this grace it comes about that a man is 'a man of good will' [Luke 2:14], whereas he was formerly a man of bad will. Through this grace it also comes about that good will, which has just come into being, is increased and becomes strong enough to be able to fulfil the divine commands which it has willed, when it has willed them strongly and entirely. . . . Grace makes the will healthy, so that by that will righteousness may be freely loved."[53] The gift of perseverance maintains the believer till the end, and thus salvation is fully a work of God's grace.

For Augustine this also means that since salvation comes only through grace and grace does not depend on any human effort, it must be God and God alone who freely gives grace to those whom God chooses. This is God's eternal election, or predestination, in which God chooses the "elect" out of the "mass of perdition," that is, the rest of humanity. Those who do not receive God's grace are left in their sin. Augustine, who believed his views were biblically based, sought above all else to uphold the absolute primacy of God in the work of salvation.[54]

Continuing Controversies and the Synod of Orange

Augustine's doctrine of predestination evoked much reaction in the Western church. In Egypt a monk named Vitalis argued that all good a human does is due to the grace of God, but the beginning of faith is a human work, in which God does not intervene. Augustine responded in 427 with his *On Grace and Free Will* and *On Rebuke and Grace*, which stress the unmerited nature of grace.

In southern Gaul strenuous opposition came from a monastery at Massilia presided over by Chrysostom's disciple and friend John Cassianus (Cassian). He and his colleagues rejected Augustine's views on predestination, although they followed him in other teachings. Cassian condemned Pelagius, as did the Synod of Carthage in 412 and 418 and the Third Ecumenical Council of Ephesus in 431. Wanting to avoid the extremes of Augustine, however, Cassian wrote, "As soon as he [God] sees in us the beginning of a good will, he illumines, stimulates, and urges it towards salvation, giving growth to that which he himself planted, or to that which he has seen spring *out of our own efforts*."[55] Cassian, along with Vincent of Lérins, Faustus of Riez, and others, are called "semi-Pelagians," though they may also be considered semi-Augustinians. For several decades the controversies continued.[56]

In 529 a synod gathered at Orange adopted a position that may be described as a moderate form of Augustinianism. Among other things the synod affirmed the following tenets: the fall of Adam corrupted all human-kind; grace precedes every part of justification (including the beginning of faith); because of sin, free will in itself cannot lead one to baptism; grace is not based on merit; and grace is fully necessary for avoiding evil and doing anything good.[57]

While the Synod of Orange rejected major elements of the semi-Pelagian position, it was silent on some major elements of Augustinianism, such as predestination, the irresistibility of grace, and election. Instead, emphasis was placed on the grace given in baptism and on the believer's cooperation with God to "fulfil the things which please" God after baptism.[58]

Turning Point: Luther and Trent

The debate between Augustine and Pelagius remained alive in the centuries following their deaths. Pelagius represented a concern that a Christian's faith is validated in works of perfection, love of God and neighbor, and a life-style that approximates the high standards set by the Sermon on the Mount. Augustine's concern was to show why humans, who are fatally damaged by the fall into sin, must acknowledge their weakness and look solely to the call and grace of God for salvation. The underlying theological questions of the two traditions come down to the effects of the fall on humanity (original sin) and the way humans experience the saving grace of God initially and in their Christian lives.

In the Middle Ages virtually all theologians saw themselves as anti-Pelagian, but throughout the period charges of Pelagianism were frequently hurled. The growth of medieval theology can be considered as a series of Augustinian syntheses, as certain elements in his thought became emphasized and combined with other views to produce a plurality of medieval viewpoints within the Roman Catholic church.[59]

In the sixteenth century the debate over justification became a central feature of the Protestant Reformation. In the writings of Martin Luther (1483–1546) and other Protestants the focus in justification was not only on the grace of God but also on the nature of faith and righteousness. Their views had far-reaching implications for every dimension of Christian faith and practice.

Luther and Salvation

Martin Luther was an Augustinian monk whose emerging theology began to take shape in the midst of his teaching at the University of Wittenberg. There he taught biblical studies and gave lectures on Psalms (1513–15), Romans (1515–16), Galatians (1516–17), and Hebrews (1517–18). At some point prior to 1518, Luther experienced a conversion that, in conjunction with his biblical studies, led him to initiate what came to be known as the Protestant Reformation.[60]

In his personal quest for salvation, Luther was plagued by anxieties and doubts, which he labeled *Anfechtungen* (Ger., "temptations") and *tentationes* (Lat., "trials"); he expressed them in the question, "How do I find a gracious God?"[61] His study of the Bible led him to seek the proper meaning of *righteousness*. He wondered whether righteousness belongs to God and thus any righteousness for a creature would be an "alien righteousness," or if righteousness is something a creature can attain through good works. Can a person live in such a way as to merit or earn salvation?[62]

Luther's struggles focused particularly on the "righteousness of God" in Romans 1:17. In 1545, when he was sixty-two years old, he wrote about his discovery of the meaning of righteousness:

> I hated the word "righteousness of God," which, according to the use and custom of all teachers, I had been taught to understand philosophically

regarding the formal or active righteousness, as they called it, with which God is righteous and punishes the unrighteous sinner. . . .

At last, by the mercy of God, meditating day and night, I gave heed to the context of the words, namely, "In it the righteousness of God is revealed, as it is written, 'He who through faith is righteous shall live' [Heb. 2:4]." There I began to understand that the righteousness of God is that by which the righteous lives by a gift of God, namely by faith. And this is the meaning: the righteousness of God is revealed by the gospel, namely, the passive righteousness with which merciful God justifies us by faith. . . . Here I felt that I was altogether born again and had entered paradise itself through open gates.[63]

Thus whereas Luther had earlier viewed God's righteousness as punitive, chastising sinners who fell short of the law, he came to view it as God's acceptance of sinners while they are still in their sin. The righteousness "of God" (Lat. genitive: *Dei*) means righteousness belongs to God alone. Thus no human righteousness can earn God's righteousness through "good works." Salvation as righteousness before God, or justification, comes as a gift of God's grace received by faith.[64]

This, for Luther, is the good news of the gospel. God pronounces the sinner righteous, not on the basis of the sinner's works, but through the righteousness of Jesus Christ. God considers and declares a person righteous (Lat. *justum reputare* or *computare*) because the judgment and death that sin deserve have been taken on by Jesus Christ. The righteousness of Jesus, who was himself fully righteous as the Son of God, is credited, or imputed (*imputare*), to the sinner by God.[65] God sees the sinner as one with Christ, forgives the sinner, and considers the sinner righteous because of Jesus Christ. Thus, says Luther, "we are considered righteous on account of Christ";[66] righteousness is not a human quality but a free gift of God given in Christ. For "all become righteous by Another's righteousness." The sinner is passive in this act of God, only receiving what God has done.[67]

The sinner receives this justification by faith, by believing and trusting in Jesus Christ. To believe is to recognize and grasp that the love of God has been extended in Christ. Faith is intensely personal, since one must recognize that Jesus Christ has died "for me." "Accordingly, that 'for me' or 'for us' if it is believed, creates that true faith and distinguishes it from all other faith, which merely hears the things done. This is the faith which alone justifies us." Faith is the work and gift of God to overcome the will, which is enslaved to sin.[68] Faith is the means by which justification comes, and "faith justifies because it takes hold of and possesses this treasure, the present Christ."[69] It is the Holy Spirit who gives the gift of faith which is a "living, audacious reliance upon God's grace [that] makes one happy, bold and cheerful toward God."[70]

For Luther justification by faith has two results: first, the forgiveness of sin and imputation of the righteousness of Christ to the sinner (justification) and, second, the establishment of the person as a new being who is righteous in himself or herself because of the righteousness of Christ (sanctification). For Luther these two always go together. The righteousness within us is the work of God that begins new but will be completed only in the future. Thus Luther says of the Christian, "Our justification is not yet complete. . . . It is still under construction. It shall, however, be completed in the resurrection of the dead."[71] In that sense justification is both an event and a process.

This also means that the Christian is, in the words of Luther's famous formula, "*simul justus et peccator*" (at the same time righteous and a sinner).[72] The Christian's sins are forgiven completely in justification, so that the believer has a new standing and relationship with God. In that sense the Christian is righteous but in this life is still a sinner who must constantly battle against temptation and the lure of evil. The Christian is always both saint and sinner and will remain so throughout life. For "both sin and righteousness are present in us. . . . Faith fights against sin. . . . Sin fights against faith." To put it simply, "We are [God's] children, and yet we are sinners."[73]

Salvation, for Luther, is by God's grace alone (*sola gratia*) through faith alone (*sola fide*) in Christ alone (*sola Christi*). Yet Luther is also clear that although good works can neither cause nor preserve salvation, good works follow from salvation. "Faith is a divine work in us, which changes us and makes us new from God . . . faith is a lively, diligent, active powerful thing, which makes it impossible that it shall not unceasingly do good works." The gospel transforms the righteousness of faith into a righteousness of love as a consequence—not as a condition—of justification. Love is the new motivating power in the Christian's life to move the sinner from being "turned in upon the self" (*curvatus in se*) to having unselfish love for others. The good works done are done because of faith. As Luther puts it, good works do not make a person good, but a good person will do good works.[74] "We must therefore most certainly maintain that where there is no faith there also can be no good works; and conversely, that there is no faith where there are no good works. Therefore faith and good works should be so closely joined together that the essence of the entire Christian life consists in both."[75] For Luther one is justified by faith alone but not by a faith that is alone. Good works are "a certain sign, like a seal on a letter, which make me certain that my faith is genuine. As a result if I examine my heart and find that my works are done in love, then I am certain that my faith is genuine." Through good works the Holy Spirit bears witness that one is saved.[76]

Luther frequently cites the centrality of justification by faith as "the sum of Christian doctrine" and the "principal teaching of Christianity" that produces and maintains the church. "If this article stands, the church stands; if it falls, the church falls."[77] Luther's presupposition in his doctrine of salvation is an Augustinian anthropology that stresses the corruption of humanity in sin, the helplessness of humanity, and the priority of God's grace for those God would save.[78] Luther frequently called the medieval theologians of the Roman Catholic church Pelagians because he believed they denied the unmerited nature of grace and salvation through God-given faith. Luther reacted to the doctrine of penance and the doctrine of merits in late-medieval Catholicism, particularly as expressed in the sale of indulgences. Luther wished instead to stress the divine work (*monergism*) in justification and reject any notion of merit on the sinner's behalf: "How do endeavor and merit accord with a righteousness freely bestowed?"[79]

Trent and Salvation

During the sixteenth and early seventeenth centuries the Roman Catholic church experienced an extensive movement for inner reformation and church reform. With its roots in Spain and in the work of Erasmus of Rotterdam, this reform movement was more than just a reaction to the emerging Protestant teachings of Luther. Yet the spread of Lutheran influence throughout Europe did stir in many Roman Catholics a desire for church reform that included administration, morality, and doctrine. Eventually the demand for a general church council was heard. In 1542, after a number of attempts and postponements, Pope Paul III called for a council to meet at Trent, south of the Alps. The council met first on December 13, 1545, but without the Lutherans, since they had demanded the council be "free, general, and not a papal council." During the next eighteen years the Council of Trent held twenty-five sessions in three main periods under three popes: 1545–47, 1551–52, and 1562–63. It dealt with several major theological issues, including original sin, justification, grace, and merit.

An earlier attempt to find common ground between Protestants and Roman Catholics on the issue of salvation and justification had been made at the Diet of Regensburg, arranged by Emperor Charles V in the spring of 1541.[80] The formula worked out there speaks of a "double justification," including an "inherent righteousness," by which the sinner's will is healed, and an "imputed righteousness," which is given to believers on the basis of Christ's merits. Both Rome and Luther rejected the results of the Regensburg colloquy.

The debate on justification began at the Council of Trent on June 22, 1546; the decree on justification was issued on January 13, 1547. This decree builds on Trent's teaching that original sin affects "the whole human race." Through the grace of baptism both this sin and the resulting punishment are remitted. The sin of concupiscence, however, still remains among the baptized.[81] The sixteen chapters of the justification decree make positive affirmations in explaining Catholic doctrine, while the thirty-three canons, or anathemas, draw conclusions from formulations that the council rejected.

In the major chapters on justification, a number of key points are made.

1. *Nature*. Justification is defined as a "translation" from the natural state of the first Adam to the state of grace in the second Adam, Jesus Christ. Christ died for all and granted grace, "through the merit of his passion," to those reborn in him. Without rebirth these is no justification (chaps. 3, 4).

2. *Preparation*. Justification begins for adults with the "predisposing grace of God through Jesus Christ." Through God's "quickening and helping grace" they may "convert themselves to their own justification by freely assenting to and cooperating with that grace; so that, while God touches the heart of man through the illumination of the Holy Ghost, man himself neither does absolutely nothing while receiving that inspiration since he can also reject it, nor is he able by his own free will and without the grace of God to move himself to justice in His sight" (chap. 5).

3. *Process*. The process of justification is defined as follows: "Aroused and aided by divine grace, receiving *faith by hearing* [Rom. 10:17], they [adults] are moved freely toward God, believing to be true what has been divinely revealed and promised" (chap. 6). In this, Trent affirmed that faith originates with God rather than humans; it comes through the gospel preached, is free (in that it can be rejected and leads to freedom), aims toward God, and accepts revealed truths and promises. In canon 1, the council rejects the view that human works done by one's "own natural powers or through the teaching of the law, without divine grace through Jesus Christ" can begin the process of justification.[82]

4. *Causes*. Trent described the nature of justification, using scholastic categories of causality: final cause: glory of God, Christ, and eternal life; efficient cause: the merciful God, who washes and sanctifies gratuitously; meritorious cause: Jesus Christ, who has merited our justification by his passion; instrumental cause: sacrament of baptism; formal cause: justice of God, "not that by which He Himself is just, but that by which He makes us just." The sinner who is justified is not only "reputed but we are truly called and are just, receiving justice within us" (chap. 7). For in justification comes not only the remission of sins but "all these infused at the same time, namely, faith, hope and charity." These inspired gifts come to everyone (cf. 1 Cor. 12:4–11) "according to each one's disposition and cooperation."

5. *Increase*. Justification is preserved by obeying the commandments

and by "faith cooperating with good works," an "increase in that justice received through the grace of Christ" is received, and humans are "further justified" (chaps. 10, 11: cf. Ecclus. 18:22; James 2:24). Although justification can be lost through mortal sin, it can be regained through the sacrament of penance (chaps. 14, 15).

6. *Fruits.* Trent speaks also of eternal life given "as a grace mercifully promised" to believers in Christ Jesus and "as a reward promised by God himself, to be faithfully given to their good works and merits (Rom. 6:22)." Because Christ "continually infuses strength into those justified," the works of the justified can be considered to have "fully satisfied the divine law according to the state of this life and to have truly merited eternal life, to be obtained in its [due] time, provided they depart [this life] in grace (Rev. 14:13)" (chap. 16). Christians should not trust or glory in themselves, but rather in the Lord, whose "bounty" to all is "so great that He wishes the things that are His gifts to be their merits."

Divergences and Convergences

Since the Council of Trent and the further theological writings of Protestants, the Roman Catholic church and Protestantism have remained divided on the issues surrounding salvation. Many Catholic theologians have seen Trent as condemning Luther, though his name does not appear in the decrees;[83] and Protestants have remained uneasy about such matters as the definition of grace, the place of merit and good works, the nature of faith, and human response and cooperation.[84]

Although the Second Vatican Council did not give explicit attention to justification, there have been numerous attempts by both Catholics and Protestants—particularly Lutherans—to come to a more common understanding and to emphasize, not the divergences between Catholics and Protestants, but rather points of convergence. Many of the past difficulties have stemmed from different concerns and different patterns of thought in the various traditions. The aim today is to seek new theological modes that may be able to find patterns of complementarity where before there were points of difference. Even at points where divergence still exists, one hopes that these can be points of creative tension rather than division.[85]

6

Authority Controversy

Where Is Authority?

The controversy over salvation focused on the very center and heart of the Christian faith. But underlying the theological turning points involved in that controversy, as well as those related to other doctrines, was the basic issue of authority. In all the controversies theologians turned to sources to substantiate their positions. They appealed to the various resources at hand to anchor their arguments and bolster their positions. Frequently Scripture was the primary point of theological reference, but as the church developed, other sources of authority began to find their places as well. In the early church these included confessions of faith and the church itself in terms of church tradition. By the Middle Ages the Roman Catholic church was the established church in the West and was governed through its ecclesiastical hierarchy, with the pope, the bishop of Rome, at its head. At the time of the Protestant Reformation, the question of authority was examined by the Reformers Martin Luther and John Calvin. They argued that Scripture should be the sole source of authority for the church (*sola Scriptura*) and that the office and powers of the pope were not legitimately based in Scripture. As Protestantism developed further, other theologians and church denominations appealed in various ways to different channels of authority, using various implicit principles of interpretation (hermeneutics).

The question of authority is thus many-faceted and at times quite complex. Highlighted below are the major movements and directions prominent in various historical periods. As our turning point we will concentrate on the sixteenth-century controversy between Roman Catholics and Protestants on the issue of the locus of authority for the church.

Biblical Basis

In biblical usage authority is connected with the concept of power (Gr. *exousia*). Its meanings include the use of power, the right to exercise power by legal or moral means, the dominion that power exercises, and the person or source used to legitimate what is done. In both the Old and New Testaments, the ultimate authority is God, the Creator of all and the One to whom all life owes its origin and support (Gen. 1). The New Testament witnesses to the same power of God as expressed in the life, words, and work of Jesus Christ. The earliest churches acknowledged this authority as they acknowledged Jesus as Lord (1 Cor. 1:2; Acts 9:14, 21; 22:16; 2 Tim. 2:22).

In the Old Testament there is no one Hebrew word directly translated as "authority." In the Septuagint, the Greek translation of the Old Testament, a number of Hebrew terms are rendered by *exousia*. In particular, the term is used for the power of God, whose authority is absolute (Dan. 4:34–35). The structure of Israelite society reflects channels of authority. God is the supreme Lord, but human structures and agents assist in exercising God's authority. Thus the king, prophets, judges, and priests are those who carry out the divine authority and the divine will. Kings are to rule with righteousness, judges to judge justly, priests to offer sacrifice for sins, and prophets—ultimately responsible only to God—are to speak God's word.

In the New Testament the term *exousia* is used most significantly in relation to God, who is completely free to act and is the only true source of all other authority and power (Luke 12:5; Jude 25). God is both creator and ruler of the universe. God controls the forces of both nature and history in order to carry out the divine plan and purpose (Luke 1:35; Rom. 9:21; Rev. 19:1).

The New Testament also recognizes subservient powers and authorities (1 Cor. 15:24; 1 Peter 3:22; Eph. 1:21). Civil authority may be exercised through kings, magistrates, priests, and stewards (Luke 7:8; Mark 13:34; Acts 9:14; Rom. 13:1–3; Titus 3:1). Yet all secondary powers—including evil "principalities and powers" (Rom. 8:38; cf. John 19:10–11)—have only the power permitted them by God (cf. Rev. 2:10; 1 John 4:1–6). Ultimate authority always belongs to God (Rom. 13:1).

In Jesus Christ, however, the disclosure of God's authority becomes clear. Jesus taught as one with authority (Mark 1:22). His authority came from himself (Matt. 5) and extended to forgiving sins (Mark 2:10), casting out demons (Mark 3:15), teaching (Matt. 7:29), and judging (John 5:27). This authority was granted by God (John 5:30) to be used by Jesus (John 10:18; Rev. 12:10ff.). In the defeat of Satan, Christ's power and authority is acknowledged (Luke 4:1–13, esp. vs. 6; 1 John 5:19). Christ's kingdom is universal and eternal (2 Peter 1:11; cf. Matt. 28:18).

In some respects Jesus transferred his authority to his disciples, including the authority to forgive sins (Matt. 16:19; 18:18; John 20:23), to heal diseases (Luke 9:1), and to cast out demons (Mark 6:7). They are also authorized to proclaim the kingdom of God that is to come (Matt. 10:7–8; Mark 3:15; 6:7). Those who hear his disciples hear Jesus (Luke 10:16; cf. Matt. 10:40; John 17:18; 20:21). Later the Apostles believe their own authority to preach the gospel of Jesus Christ as "witnesses" (Acts 1:8) comes from Jesus himself (2 Cor. 10:8; cf. Matt. 10:1; Mark 3:15; 2 Thess. 3:9). This apostolic authority is a derivative authority that is not absolute or inherent; it has its origin in Christ rather than in the Apostles themselves. Apostolic authority, including the right to preach and teach, is based on God's revelation in Jesus Christ (see Gal. 1:11–16). The Apostle Paul recognizes the function of teaching and the teacher as one of the gifts given to the church (Rom. 12:7; 1 Cor. 12:28) and thus one of the ways in which, through the work of the Holy Spirit (1 Cor. 12:3; John 15:26–27), the continuing presence and authority of Jesus Christ is experienced in the Christian churches.[1]

Sources of Authority in the Early Church

The passing of the generation of the Apostles left the early church with a fundamental problem. How would God's authority through the Apostles be continued? The emergence of various sources of authority in the early church provided different answers to that question, as well as a foundation for further theological understanding and doctrinal development. Each of these sources underwent intricate growth through the centuries and at various times and places have been weighted differently as to their authority for settling disputes, enlarging knowledge, and fostering theological growth. None of the sources can be viewed in total isolation from the others, for each provides a component in the total authority of the church, while pointing beyond itself to the ultimate source of authority, God in Jesus Christ, who is the "head of the church" (Eph. 5:23).

Canon: Old and New Testaments

One major source of authority for the early church was the canon of Scripture. The term canon (Gr. kanōn; Heb. qāneh) literally meant a measuring rod. It later became a rule or norm of faith and eventually a catalogue or list. In both Judaism and Christianity a canon of authoritative writings arose and provided a way to pass on theological understanding.[2]

From the beginning the Christian church appropriated the sacred Scriptures of Judaism as part of its holy writings. Israel had conceived of itself as part of a divine-human discourse: it believed God spoke to the nation. The main method God used was to speak through human beings and especially through the office of the prophet, who was a spokesperson for God, a message-bearer from God to the king, to the nation at large, or to other nations.

The words of God's messengers, remembered and recorded, became a major part of the divine-human discourse with Israel. Eventually there was a large body of such texts, consisting of various types. (1) The Torah, or law, was the central text that set forth the way in which people were to guide their lives. The commandments given through Moses became the standard by which faithfulness to God was judged (see Josh. 1:2–9; 1 Kings 2:2–9; 2 Kings 10:31; 2 Chron. 31:3–4). (2) Historical works covered the period from the end of Moses' life through the events in the books of Joshua, Judges, 1 and 2 Samuel, and 1 and 2 Kings. (3) Prophetic writings recorded the words of Amos, Hosea, Micah, Isaiah, Jeremiah, Ezekiel, and others. (4) Psalms and songs played key roles in Israel's cultic celebrations and worship. (5) Wisdom writings indicated the way of life to be followed.[3]

According to Jewish tradition the Old Testament was canonized in three stages. The *Torah*, or Pentateuch (Genesis–Deuteronomy), was declared sacred around 400 B.C., and the *Prophets* (including historical works) around 200 B.C.. Finally, a council of rabbis met at Jamnia in A.D. 90 and ratified a collection called the *Writings*. The early Christian church appropriated these Jewish Scriptures and interpreted them in light of its faith in Jesus Christ as God's Messiah, using the hermeneutical methods of allegory and typology.[4]

The New Testament canon was formed through a long process that began with oral traditions about Jesus, which eventually formed the Gospels. As time went on, the word *tradition* became a technical term to describe what is handed on and came to refer to the Christian truth that the early church received through its writings (see 1 Cor. 11:2; 2 Thess. 2:15; 3:6; cf. 1 Cor. 11:23; 15:3). The written word served as a check on oral traditions, as well as preserving them.[5]

Not till the time of Irenaeus (c. 180) did a Christian Bible begin to take shape. This growing library of sacred books included as its "Old Testament" the Greek translation of the Hebrew Bible known as the Septuagint (translated between 285 and 132 B.C. in Alexandria for Greek-speaking Jews) and as its "New Testament" the four Gospels and a collection of Paul's letters. Irenaeus also cited Acts, Revelation, 1 Peter, and 1 and 2 John.[6]

The earliest list of New Testament books is in the Muratorian Fragment, which is said to represent the tradition of the Roman church at the end of the second century. It lists as Scripture the four Gospels; Acts; the letters of Paul, Jude, and John; "John's Apocalypse and Peter's"; and the Wisdom of Solomon. It also denounced the writings of the Gnostics, Marcionites, and Montanists as having no Christian standing. Since many works claimed authority, it was crucial to establish criteria for judging them. In this light the church decided that the major test should be "apostolicity": only those books that preserved the Apostle's witness to Christ could claim authority. An internal test was also applied as the church asked itself whether it experienced spiritual power in the book; thus the book's authority arose ultimately from its content.[7]

In the third and fourth centuries the components of the New Testament canon became more precise. The first official church document listing the twenty-seven books of the New Testament accepted by both Eastern and Western churches was the Easter letter of Bishop Athanasius in 367. In the Western church the complete canon was approved by councils in Hippo in 393 and Carthage in 397.[8]

Once the full canon was established, various theological statements began to appear on the "authority" of the Bible. The church presupposed a basic unity between the Old and New Testaments. In the life, death, and resurrection of Jesus, the church saw the Old Testament fulfilled. The church also regarded the Scriptures as inspired by God on the basis of New Testament texts such as 2 Timothy 3:16 and 2 Peter 1:21. The early church extended the meaning of these texts to include the whole canon of Scripture itself, both Old Testament and New.

The growth of the canon as a source of authority in the early church also raised the question of the relation of Scripture to tradition. Irenaeus and Tertullian refer at times to the Christian tradition as that which transmits Christ's teachings, which come to the church through the Scriptures; neither theologian contrasts tradition with Scripture.[9] In opposition to the Gnostics, Irenaeus insisted that the church's tradition is open rather than secret.[10] Tertullian extended the concept to include what the church had practiced for generations as custom, such as the triple immersion at baptism, receiving the Eucharist in the early morning, and making the sign of the cross. All of this raised continuing questions about the relationship between Scripture and tradition.

By the fourth and fifth centuries the Bible was clearly the church's primary doctrinal norm and authority. Athanasius wrote against the Arians that "the holy and inspired Scriptures are fully sufficient for the proclamation of the truth."[11] Cyril of Jerusalem said, "With regard to the divine and saving mysteries of the faith no doctrine, however trivial, may be taught without the backing of the divine Scriptures. . . . For our saving faith derives its force, not from capricious reasonings, but from what may be proved out of the Bible."[12] Yet there were also bodies of tradition outside Scripture that were considered apostolic and in line with Scripture. The practices of the liturgy and of spiritual devotion played important roles as authorities, for they were regarded as providing the necessary keys to scriptural understanding. As time passed, the writings of the church fathers also came to have substantial theological authority.

It became apparent by the mid-fifth century that not all authorities were equal in weight and not all that claimed to stand in line with the Apostles were in a true apostolic succession. This led Vincent of Lérins (d. 450) to try to clarify the concept of authority in his 434 *Commonitory*. What constitutes the orthodox tradition, he says, is that which has been believed "everywhere, always, by all," and the criteria for orthodoxy are "universality, antiquity, and consensus."[13] By this point it was important for the church to recognize which forms of witness and teaching could be considered truly apostolic.

Creeds and Councils

From the start the Christian faith concerned a body of teachings. In the New Testament, summary formulas of apostolic teaching and Christian faith can be found. Early church theologians such as Ignatius of Antioch and Justin Martyr also supply christological formulas that indicate emerging conceptions of what it is important to confess about Jesus Christ.[14]

With the growth of the church and the arrival of new converts to the faith, the church needed statements that could educate candidates for baptism. In their earliest forms these statements are difficult to describe with precision. They are not fully developed creeds but rather summary statements to prepare new Christians for the sacrament. Normally they are in the form of questions posed to the candidate. In Justin Martyr's formula the questions read: "Dost thou believe in the Father and Lord God of the universe? Dost thou believe in Jesus Christ our Saviour, Who was crucified under Pontius Pilate? Dost thou believe in the Holy Spirit, Who spake by the prophets?"[15] Later formulas expanded the question about Jesus Christ.

One of the oldest creeds (c. 150), and the one that formed the nucleus of the Apostles' Creed, was the Old Roman Creed. It too had three parts, which were later expanded. In the fifth century Rufinus wrote a commentary on the Apostles' Creed, which contains the earliest known version of the creed. Probably originating in southern Gaul in the late sixth or seventh century, the Apostles' Creed became the sole baptismal formula of the Western church.[16]

Along with baptismal and declaratory creeds, rules of faith (*regula fidei*) were also used to convey Christian teaching. These were similar in content to creeds but were more open-ended and less stereotypical in form. There is reference to such a rule in Irenaeus, who spoke of the "rule of truth," and in Tertullian, who often associated the *regula fidei* with the term *disciplina*, referring to Christian ethical actions.[17] Origen spoke of the "rule prevalent among the majority of the Church" as "canon."[18] He linked this closely with the Scriptures in conveying "church instruction and teaching" and in providing "the foundation-doctrines of the Church."[19] Other writers such as Cyprian, Novatian, and Dionysius of Alexandria provide further examples of such rules of faith. While they differ from each other, they are broadly similar. They provided material for catechetical teaching prior to baptism and also served as standards by which deviations from scriptural teaching could be measured. For theologians such as Irenaeus, Tertullian, and Origen, the content of the *regula fidei* was derived directly from Scripture.[20]

Because they were perceived to be scripturally based, the various rules of faith served as standards by which orthodoxy could be maintained against heretics. This was particularly true in the period prior to the Council of Nicaea in 325. After Nicaea, when the church spoke with a united voice against the errors of Arianism, the statements of church councils began to serve as standards in place of the rules of faith from local communities.[21] As later history shows, church councils appealed to Scripture as the basis for their pronouncements. Yet history also shows that not all Christians agreed with conciliar decisions.

Church Leadership

The early church also found a source of authority in its own ongoing, orderly ministry. In the life and teaching of the church, its leaders possessed various degrees of authority in setting the church's course. The role of the Apostles was so significant for the church's government that canon, creed, councils, and tradition all pointed back to their "apostolicity." The Apostle Paul appealed to his apostolic position when his authority was challenged (1 Cor. 9:1). Other forms of church leadership also emerged: prophets, teachers, bishops (Gr. *episkopoi*), deacons, presbyters, and evangelists (1 Cor. 12:28; Phil. 1:1; Titus 1:5). The crucial notion of a succession to the Apostles became interpreted to mean a succession in doctrine, in office, or in both.

The evolution of church offices took many turns. Of particular significance for church authority, however, was the emerging office of *bishop*. In the New Testament *episkopos* (lit. overseer, guardian) is applied once to Jesus Christ (1 Peter 2:25). In the Pauline literature it is an alternate for *presbyteros*, "elder" (Titus 1:5–7; 1 Tim. 3:1; 4:14; 5:17, 19). Paul appointed *elders* in all his churches (Acts 14:23), but in writing to the Philippians he also mentions *bishops* and *deacons* (Phil. 1:1). *Elders* and *deacons* probably refer to the same persons who exercised functions of oversight and care (Acts 1:20; 20:28).

In the second century Ignatius of Antioch advanced the understanding of ministerial offices when he referred to a gradation in the church hierarchy among bishops, presbyters, and deacons. "Everyone must show the deacons respect. They represent Jesus Christ, just as the bishop has the role of the Father, and the presbyters are like God's council and an apostolic band. You cannot have a church without these."[22]

With the threat of Gnosticism, however, the office of the bishop developed even further as an important source of authority. The church was forced to solidify its canon and creeds and also to look to bishops as the ones to guard orthodoxy in an authoritative way. Irenaeus and Tertullian sought to preserve the unity of the faith through their views on apostolic succession. In "mother churches," where the Apostles themselves had labored (Smyrna, Ephesus, Jerusalem, Corinth, Philippi, Thessalonica, and especially Rome), the purity of the apostolic tradition was guarded with special diligence and care.[23] Every bishop was an important part of the church universal, because each was given the task of preserving the integrity of apostolic doctrine in his local area.

Among all the churches, including mother churches, the church at Rome became preeminent for a number of reasons. Rome was the capital of the empire, its most populous and wealthy Christian center, and the city where Peter and Paul taught and died. According to tradition Peter, who was perceived as the chief of the Apostles, had founded the church at Rome. By the middle of the third century, Stephen I, the bishop of Rome (254–57), claimed he held the "see of Peter" (*cathedra Petri*) by succession. Therefore, as bishop of Rome and according to apostolic succession, he could speak in the name of Peter. In the Western church many, though not all, acknowledged this claim as legitimate.[24]

Thus in the early church three major sources of authority were most significant. The church was guided through its sacred texts, the canon of Scripture. It understood itself and its teachings through the development of creedal statements and rules of faith. And it was governed and administered through bishops who, as spiritual and liturgical leaders, guarded the "deposit of faith" entrusted to them (1 Tim. 6:20; cf. 2 Tim. 1:12; 14). Through the coming centuries, the hierarchical structure of the church developed along with its theological understanding. As the ecclesiastical structures took shape, further questions about the relationships of the various elements of church authority also arose.

Authority in the Middle Ages

Growth of the Papacy

The bishop of Rome assumed considerable stature as a source of authority in the early church, and this position developed into the Roman Catholic papacy. The bishop of Rome's claim of primacy among other bishops is based on an interpretation of New Testament texts concerning Peter and the "Petrine function." The main text is Matthew 16:18, where Jesus says to Peter, "And I tell you, you are Peter [Gr. *Petros*], and on this rock [*petra*] I will build my church, and the powers of death [lit. gates of Hades] shall not prevail against it." Other important texts are John 21:17 and Luke 22:31, 32.

The primacy of the bishop of Rome as pope underwent a long and tangled historical development. Not all theologians agreed with the interpretation of Matthew 16:18 given by Pope Gregory I (d. 604):

> To all who know the Gospel it is obvious that by the voice of the Lord the care of the entire church was committed to the holy apostle and prince of all the apostles, Peter. . . . Behold, he received the keys of the kingdom of heaven, the power to bind and loose was given to him, and the care and principality of the entire church was committed to him. . . . Am I defending my own cause in this matter? Am I vindicating some special injury of my own? Is it not rather the cause of Almighty God, the cause of the universal church? . . . Certainly, in honor of Peter, the prince of the apostles, [the title "universal"] was offered to the Roman pontiff by the venerable Council of Chalcedon.[25]

An early interpretation by Origen was that *Peter* referred to every Christian. While Cyprian said that Peter was the symbol of the unity of the church, he had a more collegial conception of the episcopate when he wrote, "The other apostles were all that Peter was, endowed with equal dignity and power, but the start comes from him alone."[26] Other ways of interpreting the passage played off the name *Peter* against the word *petra* (rock). The rock on which the church is built may be the person of Peter, as the proponents of the primacy of Peter argued. It may be Peter, the other Apostles, and their successors. The church may be built upon the faith that Peter confessed, or the rock may be Christ himself as apprehended by faith. Each of these interpretations, as well as others, came to the fore at some point.[27]

A strong theoretical justification for the preeminence of the bishop of Rome based on the biblical texts emerged only after the middle of the third century. Pope Damascus (366–84) began the custom of using the term *apostolic see* to describe the Roman church, in order to elevate Rome among the other apostolic churches and to protest Constantinople's new status as capital of the empire (by the decree of the Emperor Constantine), since that city had no claim to apostolic foundation. Damascus also argued that the unique authority of the Council of Nicaea (325) was due to the fact that its decisions had been approved by one of his predecessors, Pope Sylvester (314–35). The theological groundwork for papal supremacy was laid by fifth-century popes such as Innocent I (402–17), who claimed in 416 that the gospel had spread to other Western provinces from Rome alone and referred to the Roman bishop as the "head and apex of the episcopate."[28] By this time the bishop of Rome had already gained the right to review conciliar decisions, and Roman popes had begun issuing their letters in the form of decretals, so that a greater uniformity in church discipline could be established in the West.

Pope Leo I (440–61), called Leo the Great, consolidated the gains made in the sixty years since Pope Damascus. Leo saw himself as more than just the historical successor to Peter. By virtue of the succession of Roman bishops going back to Peter, Leo believed that he spoke and wrote for Peter and that his office included the fullness of Peter's power, which was universal in scope. The authority of other bishops is derived from Christ but mediated through Peter and thus through the Roman pontiff, who is the living incarnation of Peter. When Leo's *Tome* was read at the Council of Chalcedon as orthodox Christian belief (see chap. 2), the cry went up, "Peter has spoken through Leo."[29]

The Eastern church did not accept the broad claims made for the bishop of Rome. In the twenty-eighth canon of the Council of Chalcedon, Constantinople, the "new Rome," was granted special privileges and authority alongside the "old Rome." Eastern theologians argued that Peter had been bishop not only in Rome but prior to that also in Alexandria and Antioch. Indeed, some theologians, such as Nilus Doxopatres, argued that the patriarch of Constantinople should be the highest authority, since he is "called archbishop of New Rome because he has taken over the privileges and prerogatives of Rome."[30] A sharp polemic also claimed that Andrew, brother of Peter, brought Peter to Jesus, and Andrew, according to legend, was the founder of Byzantium (later Constantinople) and the first of Jesus' disciples to be called. Thus "if Rome seeks the primacy on account of Peter, then Byzantium is first on account of Andrew, the first to be called and the brother senior in birth."[31] Controversies about the authority of the pope continued and eventually contributed to the schism between the Eastern and Western churches in 1054, when the pope and the patriarch of Constantinople excommunicated each other.

Papal authority continued to grow in the West. Emperor Valentinian III (423–55) decreed by "perpetual edict that it shall not be lawful for the bishops of Gaul or of the other provinces . . . to do [anything] without the authority of the venerable Pope of the Eternal City."[32] By the year 800 the pope's power and prestige had progressed to the point that Leo III (795–816) crowned Charlemagne emperor of the West on Christmas Day. Through the early Middle Ages (600–1050) the pope as "vicar of Christ" was acknowledged as head of the church in the West, while Eastern churches rarely consulted him. During the high Middle Ages (1050–1500), the papacy gave unity and continuity to the church. It reached the peak of its powers under Innocent III (1198–1216), who established church reforms that also led him into political arenas. As pope, Innocent saw himself "above peoples and kingdoms" and holding "the authority by which Samuel anointed David." He thus believed he had the power to depose a ruler and give the throne to another. Popes Bernard and Boniface VIII continued these emphases. Lather the medieval papacy faced numerous crises and tensions with the secular state. There were reform attempts by church councils, a schism, and a period of three rival popes (the "Babylonian Captivity"). Further reform movements arose in the wake of the Protestant Reformation. At the Council of Trent (1545–63) the issue of the pope's authority, and thus the church's authority, was thoroughly considered.

Scripture and Tradition

In the Middle Ages various reform movements within the Roman Catholic church questioned where ultimate authority in the church is to be found. The growing power of the papacy had meant that the pope was heir to the supreme authority of the Apostle Peter and was the "vicar of Christ" who exercised the fullness of power that belonged to the Lord. Canon lawyers such as Johannes Andreae (d. 1348) could say, "The Pope is wonderful, for he holds the power of God on earth: he is the vicar of him to whom the earth and the fullness of the universe belong." William de Amidanis said, "The Pope is like God." Panormitanus wrote, "The Pope may do whatever God may do. . . . Whatever is done by the authority of the Pope is done by the authority of God."[33]

In the fourteenth century, during a controversy over poverty in the Franciscan Order, the teaching authority of the pope, or *magisterium*, was first described as "infallible." A Carmelite theologian named Guido Terreni writes of the infallible truth of the pope when he speaks on matters of faith. "In matters pertaining to faith and morals, the church has always been directed by the counsel of the Holy Spirit when it made its definitions." Terreni states also that "where the supreme pontiff with the college of the lord cardinals or with a general council are gathered together in the Lord's name and on behalf of his faith, there is Christ, who is the truth without error." Here Terreni is expressing the usual Catholic belief. But he goes on to declare that "in the determination of the things that pertain to faith the pope is directed by the Holy Spirit and the Holy Spirit speaks in him." From biblical and patristic statements about the faithfulness of the church to the apostolic tradition (*indefectibility*), Terreni claims that "the immutable and invariable authority of the catholic church . . . resides universally, after Christ, solely in the supreme pontiff and not in any private person." The conclusion is that "the lord pope, to whose authority it belongs to determine and declare the propositions that belong to the faith, cannot err." Thus the term *infallibility* takes on a highly technical meaning.[34]

This emerging view of the pope's authority was questioned by various medieval theologians and churchmen. Essentially, the issue was where authority for the church is to be found. This was the question of how the authority of Scripture is related to the authority of church traditions. One can trace two medieval streams that answer the question Where is authority? in opposing ways. Both lines are concerned with the authority of tradition, but their ways of conceiving tradition were quite different.[35]

In one stream, labelled *Tradition I*, Holy Scripture is upheld as canon and the standard of revealed truth, and Scripture and church tradition are not seen as contradictory. The gospel message is preached by the church, and the whole message is found in written form in the books of the canon. Church tradition is not an addition to the gospel but a "handing over" of the gospel message in a living form. The whole gospel is found in Scripture and in the living tradition. Thus Scripture can be understood only within the church. Church leaders have been the interpreters of Scripture, and the tradition of the church is its own faithful interpretation of Scripture. In this view Scripture and church totally coincide.[36]

A second stream of understanding authority in the Middle Ages, called *Tradition II*, developed into a wider concept. After the time of Basil the Great and his work *On the Holy Spirit*, there emerged a view that Christians are to obey both written and unwritten church traditions, whether these are found in the pages of Scripture or in the oral tradition "handed over" by the Apostles through their successors. Here it is claimed that the Apostles did not record everything they learned from Christ, especially during the period of "forty days" between his resurrection and ascension, on which the scriptural record is silent. The oral tradition that emerged from this period is seen as a complement to the Scriptures the church later received. In this view tradition is a second source of revelation.[37]

The view of Scripture and tradition portrayed in Tradition I is found in the works of Thomas Bradwardine (1290–1349) of Oxford, John Wycliffe (d. 1384), Wessel Gansfort (d. 1489), and John Huss (d. 1415). For them Holy Scripture is the exclusive and final authority. They do not deny the importance or validity of the succession of church leaders who preserve the truth as their sacred task. But their emphasis in authority is on the succession of the doctors of the church who faithfully interpret Scripture and hand over the faith—not on the succession of bishops who guarantee an ecclesiastical continuity for the church.

Tradition II, on the other hand, stresses the function of the bishops over the doctors. Here the church hierarchy has its own oral tradition with its apostolic origins, but these are not limited to what is in the canon of Scripture. The ecclesiastical traditions—including those of canon law, which by the fourteenth century had become quite strong—were invested with the same apostolic authority as the Scriptures themselves. Leading adherents of this position were William of Occam (d. 1347), Pierre d'Ailly (d. 1420), Jean Charlier de Gerson (d. 1429), Gabriel Biel (d. 1495), and Ambrosius of Speier (d. 1490). These writers could appeal especially to John 20:30: "Now Jesus did many other signs in the presence of the disciples, which are not written in this book."[38]

At issue between the two views was the fundamental question of authority, as noted by the fifteenth-century theologian John Brevicoxa (or Courtecuisse, as he was called in France; d. 1423):

> Some say that only those truths which are asserted explicitly in the canon of the Bible or which can be deduced solely from the contents of the Bible are Catholic truths and should be believed as a condition for salvation. For example, the assertion "Christ is true God and true man," falls directly into this category because it follows necessarily from the contents of Sacred Scripture. [Tradition I] Others say that many truths not found in Sacred Scripture, nor necessarily deducible from its contents alone, ought to be assented to as a condition for salvation. [Tradition II][39]

According to Tradition II there are five categories of truth to which Catholics must assent: (1) truths found in Scripture or deduced from it, (2) truths that have come down from the Apostles but are not in Scripture or deducible from it, (3) truths about faith in chronicles and histories, (4) truths that can be deduced from one of the first three categories that are in combination with truths from one of the first two categories, and (5) truths that God has revealed to persons other than the Apostles or has more recently revealed or inspired and that have reached the universal church.[40]

Both of these positions view apostolic tradition as that to which Christians must adhere, and both agree that Scripture is the primary source from which articles of faith derive. Neither view sanctions a Scripture-alone position, as certain heretics were said to be spreading. The crux of the issue in the late Middle Ages was whether the church could promulgate beliefs not explicitly found in Scripture or deduced from Scripture but which were supposed to have "come down to us through the successive transmission of the apostles and others, as equivalent to the canonical Scripture" in their authority and apostolic authenticity.[41]

Turning Point: Calvin and Catholicism

The issues surrounding the question Where is authority? were fundamental to the Protestant Reformation. In the emerging theology of Martin Luther and the developed theology of other Protestant Reformers, such as John Calvin (1509–64), Ulrich Zwingli (1484–1531), and Heinrich Bullinger (1504–75), the issue of authority was of primary concern. In particular these theologians focused on the question of the relation of Scripture to tradition as tradition was defined and practiced by the Roman Catholic church. This led the Reformers to consider thoroughly their views of the nature of Scripture, as well as how and by whom it should be interpreted in the church.

In his writings Martin Luther rejects the various theological positions of the Roman Catholic church, as well as claims by the popes "that the Roman Church is superior to all others."[42] Luther rejects the interpretation of Matthew 16:18 that says Christ founded the papacy with Peter. Instead, he believed the church was founded on God's Word, the gospel of Jesus Christ. In 1517 Luther states, "The true treasure of the church is the most holy gospel of the glory and grace of God."[43] This means that all obedience must be given, not to the pope or the hierarchy, but to Christ who heads the church. For, Luther writes, "we obey the apostles and the church insofar as they bear the seal of that man [Christ]." "If they do not bear this seal," he continued, "we do not pay any more attention to them than St. Paul did to Peter in Galatians 2."[44] At the Diet of Worms in 1521 Luther affirmed the primary authority of Scripture in the church by maintaining that his conscience was "captive to the Word of God."[45] This means for Luther that neither the pope nor church councils nor the church fathers alone can be the true basis of authority, for "we can neither rely nor build very much on the life and works of the fathers but only on God's word." It also means that Luther rejects the fifth-century principle of Vincent of Lérins that the Christian faith is established only on the basis of what has been believed "everywhere, always, and by all." For this locates the authority for faith in the church and in the church's interpretation of Scripture. Luther contends instead that Scripture interprets itself through the work of the Holy Spirit. So his differences with Rome concerns biblical versus ecclesiastical authority.[46]

Calvin and Authority

The writings of John Calvin present in a sustained way a Protestant alternative to Roman Catholic views of authority. For Calvin, Holy Scripture is God's divine revelation. It is the "Word of God" (*Inst.* I.7.1), which has "flowed to us from the very mouth of God by the ministry of men" (I.7.5).[47] For this reason, Scripture gains its authority for believers who receive the Scriptures as "having sprung from heaven, as if there the living words of God were heard" (I.7.1). This Scripture is superior to all human wisdom, for in the Bible "the sublime mysteries of the Kingdom of Heaven came to be expressed largely in mean and lowly words" (I.8.1).

For Calvin the authority of Scripture for the church and individual Christians is based on its nature as the Word of God and on how it functions by the work of the Holy Spirit. He considers the truth of Scripture self-evident: "Indeed, Scripture exhibits fully as clear evidence of its own truth as white and black things do of their color, or sweet and bitter things do of their taste" (I.7.2). Calvin rejects the Roman Catholic view that the church confers authority to the Scriptures. On the contrary, he claims the church is grounded upon Scripture. He cites Ephesians 2:20, which speaks of the church as "built upon the foundation of the apostles and prophets," and goes on to argue against Rome.

> If the teaching of the prophets and apostles is the foundation, this must have had authority before the church began to exist. Groundless, too, is their subtle objection that, although the church took its beginning here, the writings to be attributed to the prophets and apostles nevertheless remain in doubt until decided by the church. For if the Christian church was from the beginning founded upon the writings of the prophets and the preaching of the apostles, wherever this doctrine is found, the acceptance of it—without which the church itself would never have existed—must certainly have preceded the church. It is utterly vain, then, to pretend that the power of judging Scripture so lies with the church that its certainty depends upon churchly assent. Thus, while the church receives and gives its seal of approval to the Scriptures, it does not thereby render authentic what is otherwise doubtful or controversial. But because the church recognizes Scripture to be the truth of its own God, as a pious duty it unhesitatingly venerates Scripture. As to their question—How can we be assured that this has sprung from God unless we have recourse to the decree of the church?—it is as if someone asked: Whence will we learn to distinguish light from darkness, white from black, sweet from bitter? Indeed, Scripture exhibits fully as clear evidence of its own truth as white and black things do of their color, or sweet and bitter things do of their taste (I.7.2; cf. I.7.3).

In Calvin's view the conviction that Scripture is the Word of God and has God as its author is established by the work of the Holy Spirit. The internal testimony of the Holy Spirit is the way by which the church and individuals become certain about the origin and authority of Scripture. "We ought to seek our conviction in a higher place than human reasons, judgments, or conjectures, that is, in the secret testimony of the Spirit" (I.7.4).[48] The "highest proof of Scripture derives in general from the fact that God in person speaks in it," and the "testimony of the Spirit is more excellent than all reason" (I.7.4). Scripture has a self-authenticating quality for Calvin. "The only true faith" in Scripture, he writes, "is that which the

Spirit of God seals in our hearts" and which all believers experience within themselves (I.7.5).

These views of the nature of Scripture as God's Word and of scriptural authority in the church led Calvin, like Luther, to reject Roman Catholic claims about the authority of the church and the primacy of the pope.[49] He rejects Rome's interpretation of Matthew 16:18: "But as Peter had received the command from the Lord, so he exhorts all other presbyters to feed the church. We must infer from this that by those words of Christ's nothing has been given to Peter above the rest; or that Peter equally shared with others the right that he had received" (IV.6.3). Calvin is willing to call Peter "the first of all believers," but he insists, "I shall not allow them to deduce from this that he has primacy over the others. . . . As if we might not more plausibly infer that Andrew is above Peter in rank because he preceded him in time and brought him to Christ!" (IV.6.5; cf. John 1:40, 42). For Calvin the true head of the church is Jesus Christ (Eph. 4:15-16), "under whose sway all of us cleave to one another, according to that order and that form of polity which he has laid down" (IV.6.9). This means for Calvin that while he venerates and accepts the teachings of ancient church councils as authoritative, he does not see them or the pope as invested with infallibility.[50] Thus on the issues of papal authority and the relation of Scripture and tradition, Calvin and the other Reformers reject the positions of Rome. For them the supreme authority is Jesus Christ, whose word and will for the church is made known through the Scriptures, which are the primary authority for the church's life. All other human authorities—whether creeds, church councils, or other church teachings—have a subsidiary and derivative authority in the church. As Calvin summarizes the positions, "The difference between us and the papists is that they do not think that the church can be 'the pillar of the truth' [1 Tim. 3:15] unless she presides over the word of God. We, on the other hand, assert that it is because she reverently subjects herself to the word of God that the truth is preserved by her and passed on to others by her hands."[51]

Catholicism and Authority

The Roman Catholic church attempted to unify its theology and practice at the Council of Trent (1545-63). Among the major issues to be considered was the question of authority, particularly the relationship between Scripture and church tradition. This issue was given new urgency by the cries of Luther and Protestants for *sola Scriptura* (Scripture alone) as the source of the church's authority.

The bishops at Trent began to debate the issue of Scripture on February 8, 1546, and continued until April 8. During this time various parties emerged, ranging from those who wished to put church traditions as much as possible on a par with Scripture to those who completely refused to treat apostolic traditions in the same way as Scripture, with those in between seeking to combine the authorities of Scripture and tradition.[52]

The Decree on Scripture adopted by the council on April 8, 1546, lists the canonical books of Scripture and recognizes the Apocryphal books as canonical, while decreeing that the Latin Vulgate is the sacred and canonical text of Scripture. The decree also states that the gospel is the "source" of "all saving truth and rules of conduct," which are "contained in the written books and in the unwritten traditions, which, received by the Apostles from the mouth of Christ Himself, or from the Apostles themselves [2 Thess. 2:14], the Holy Ghost dictating, have come done to us, transmitted as it were from hand to hand."[53] The decree goes on to say that both the books of Scripture and the traditions preserved in the Catholic church should be received with "a feeling of piety and reverence." On the interpretation of Scripture the council said the church has the authority to be the "judge of their true sense and interpretation." In a later session the council said its method of proceeding was to draw its teachings "from Sacred Scripture, the apostolic traditions, the holy and approved councils, the constitutions and authorities of the supreme pontiffs and holy fathers, and the consensus of the Catholic Church."[54]

The answer of Trent to the question of whether all of God's revelation is contained in Scripture and what is the relationship of Scripture to tradition, while clear at face value, also led to varying interpretations. It can be construed to mean two things. On the one hand it could mean what an earlier draft document states, namely that the "truth of the gospel is contained partly [partim] in written books, partly [partim] in unwritten traditions." This view led to the position that Scripture and tradition are equal sources of authority for the church's theology.[55] On the other hand, Trent could also mean that the truth of the gospel is wholly contained in the books of Scripture, which the church's subsequent tradition has made clear.[56]

The Council of Trent's teachings on authority were also developed later in regard to the issue of the authority of the pope. Throughout the Middle Ages those who wished to locate the primary authority for the church in councils (conciliarists) struggled with those who stressed the primacy of the pope as the "vicar of Christ." Tensions in the church continued for centuries until 1869, when Pope Pius IX convened the first Vatican Council. On July 18, 1870, by a vote of 533 to 2, it gave an official definition of the dogma of papal infallibility. The canon of the council declared that

> the Roman Pontiff, when he speaks *ex cathedra*—that is, when in the discharge of the office of Shepherd and Teacher of all Christians, he defines

> in virtue of his supreme Apostolic authority a doctrine of faith or morals to
> be held by the universal church—enjoys, through the divine assistance
> promised to him in Blessed Peter, the infallibility with which the divine
> Redeemer willed to equip his Church when it defines a doctrine of faith or
> morals; and therefore such definitions of the Roman Pontiff are irreform-
> able of themselves, not however from the consent of the Church.[57]

There are a number of conditions defining the use of this power of
infallibility, and since its promulgation only two dogmas have been recognized as originating with a papal pronouncement, the Immaculate Conception (1854) and the Assumption of the Blessed Virgin (1950).[58] Vatican I
also asserted that the pope is "the true vicar of Christ, the head of the whole
Church, the father and teacher of all Christians." It asserted the universal
episcopate of the pope when it decreed:

> And so, if anyone says that the Roman Pontiff has only the office of
> inspection or direction, but not the full and supreme power of jurisdiction
> over the whole Church, not only in matters that pertain to faith and morals,
> but also in matters that pertain to the discipline and government of the
> Church throughout the whole world; or if anyone says that he has only a
> more important part, and not the complete fullness of this supreme power;
> or if anyone says that this power is not ordinary and immediate either over
> each and every church or over each and every shepherd and faithful
> member: let him be anathema.[59]

With this the Roman Catholic church asserted the supremacy of the pope
over all bishops and councils as the primary office of authority for the life
of the church.

Later Developments

The issue of authority has taken on dimensions of even greater
proportion in the centuries since the turning point between the Reformers
and Roman Catholicism. Broadly speaking, three major approaches to
authority have emerged in the church's history. The first, as represented by
Roman Catholicism, appeals to the church as the living custodian of the
gospel and the continuing historical manifestation of Christ's authority on
earth. The second, represented by Protestantism, is *sola Scriptura*; it appeals
to the Bible, the written record of the gospel, as the basic authority for the
church. A third approach has emerged prominently at various stages in
church history and is represented by the Quakers as well as the contemporary charismatic movement, among others; it appeals to the Spirit and
individual revelation as the ultimate form of authority.[60]

Historically, an even broader context for the question Where is authority? can be seen when one considers the great variety of events and
influences that have affected the church and the Western world since the
sixteenth-century ecclesiastical struggles. These include the scientific revo-

lution, rationalism, empiricism, the Enlightenment, Kant, Hegel, Troeltsch, biblical criticism, the "new science," the influence of Eastern religions, and much else.[61] All of this has made the theological question Where is authority? much more complicated, but it has also called the Christian church back to its roots and to the fundamental issues involved in the sources to which the church appeals for authority.

7

Sacramental Controversy

What Are the Sacraments?
What Is Baptism?

Many of the great theological turning points in the church were occasioned by specific controversies. The church's understandings of the sacraments, however, emerged over a long period of time without the intense pressure of numerous disputes. In that sense the church has always been at work on the development of sacramental doctrines. At various points, however, there were controversies, such as the questioned validity of the sacraments in the Donatist schism and the ninth-century dispute between Radbertus and Ratramnus over the nature of the Lord's Supper. Doctrinal decisions were made by the church councils such as the Fourth Lateran Council, which in 1215 proclaimed as dogma the doctrine of transubstantiation. During the Reformation Protestants came to understandings of the sacraments that differed from each other and from those of the Roman church. Thus the history of sacramental doctrine is one of numerous viewpoints vying with each other on issues ranging from the nature to the number of sacraments and who can receive them.

While there were numerous suggestions through the centuries about which actions of the church should be called sacraments and how many should be so designated, two major actions emerged and became the primary sacraments: baptism and the Lord's Supper. In Protestant churches these two are the only sacraments, but Roman Catholics recognize seven sacraments, including these two. Each sacrament has a long and involved history.[1] To keep the following discussion focused, attention will be given first to the nature of the sacraments and related theological questions. Then baptism and (in the next chapter) the Lord's Supper will be examined, along with the major turning points associated with those important sacraments.

The Nature of the Sacraments

Biblical Basis

The New Testament writings portray a number of phenomena in the early church that came to be associated with sacramental actions. Yet each of these has its own name, and they are not mutually associated under a generic name such as *sacrament*. The concept of sacrament, however, is associated with the New Testament term *mysterion* (mystery), a word with a rich heritage in both civil and ecclesiastical tradition. In classical antiquity *mysterion* was used to describe something that touched the center of one's life and raised one into an experience of the divine. In cultic practices and in classical Greek philosophy the term could refer to secret religious rituals and truth-bringing wisdom that dramatically affected the life of a person.

In the Old Testament the term is used in the wisdom tradition as reflected in the book of Daniel and in other texts written in the hellenistic period (such as Wisdom of Solomon, Tobit, Sirach, and 2 Maccabees). *Wisdom* is seen as a person who stands between God and humanity and who reveals the divine secrets of God to the world (Wisd. of Sol. 8:4; 6:22). In Daniel a future *mysterion* appears, consisting of "what will be in the later days" (Dan. 2:28), which will be revealed by God alone (2:47; 2:18–19). In this apocalyptic type of literature the secret councils of God are the mysteries that will finally be revealed at the end of time.

In the New Testament this future-eschatological orientation is often connected with the use of the term *mysterion*. Jesus proclaimed to his disciples, "To you has been given the secret [*mysterion*] of the kingdom of God" (Mark 4:11), thus connecting mystery with the coming kingdom of God, one of Jesus' major theological concepts.

In Paul's writings the mystery of God is associated directly with Jesus Christ, whom Paul wishes to know and proclaim. For in Jesus the mystery of God is revealed (1 Cor. 2:1–2; cf. Col. 2:2). The death of Christ on the cross is the manifestation of God's wisdom, which has been hidden through the ages (Col. 1:26–27) but is now revealed (1 Cor. 2:7–13). This message of Christ has been revealed by the Spirit of God (1 Cor. 2:10–15) and is to be proclaimed by the Apostles, who are "servants of Christ and stewards of the mysteries of God" (1 Cor. 4:1; cf. Eph. 3:2–3; Col. 1:25–26).

The message is God's secret plan of salvation (Eph. 1:9–10) revealed by the Spirit in Jesus Christ (Eph. 3:3–6). This is the open, public message to all the world, both Jews and Gentiles (Eph. 3:7–12).[2]

It was this comprehensive message of salvation made known in Jesus Christ that the church proclaimed as the "mystery of God." The New Testament does not directly connect *mysterion* with the acts of baptism and the Lord's Supper, which eventually became sacraments in the church. But when the Bible was translated into Latin by Jerome at the end of the fourth century (and called the *Vulgate*), the term *mysterion* was translated sometimes as *mysterium* and sometimes as *sacramentum*. This led some medieval theologians who knew no Greek to believe that New Testament passages refer to the Roman Catholic sacraments (e.g., Eph. 5:32, which speaks of marriage).

Sacramental Terminology

Early Christian writers speak of a number of actions and rites of the early church but do not call them sacraments. The second-century apologists use the term *mysterion* both to designate the secret rites of various religious cults and to refer to events in the life of Jesus—such as his birth and crucifixion in which salvation as the plan of God was particularly made known.[3]

Tertullian, the first Western theologian to write in Latin, was also the first to use the term *sacramentum* to indicate a Christian theological reality in the midst of Roman culture. In classical Latin the term *sacramentum* has two meanings. In military matters it refers to the oath of allegiance taken by a soldier, expressing his obligation to leader and to country. In this act the soldier dedicates himself to obey authority. Mystery cults styled their religious rituals after this military oath and entreated the presence of underworld powers. In Roman legal proceedings *sacramentum* referred to the sum of money that plaintiffs in legal cases deposited with a priest as a sign of willingness to be humbled before the "divine judgment," since it was recognized that in some cases only an appeal to the gods could determine guilt or innocence.

Tertullian uses *sacramentum* in reference to baptism, where he sees a connection between conversion from paganism and a new commitment of obedience and service to God in Jesus Christ. Baptism is a religious initiation, an oath of allegiance, and the beginning of a new way of life in fidelity to Christ. The baptismal candidate responds to the mystery revealed by God in Jesus Christ.[4]

Tertullian's followers began to use *sacramentum* for several ritual acts and customs in the church. Their *sacramenta* were such things as making the sign of the cross, anointing with oil, and receiving salt when one is baptized. Since sacraments pointed to the divine mystery revealed in the gospel, Tertullian referred to the Christian religion itself as a sacrament. In the fourth century Hilary of Poitiers saw as *sacramenta* the people and events of the Old Testament that prefigured Christ, and Ambrose of Milan said the Christian *sacramenta* include the feasts of Easter and Pentecost.[5] Thus the term came to have a wide scope in this early period.

The Number of Sacraments

Since *sacramentum* had rather elastic qualities in the early church, various rituals and acts were called sacraments. In the history of the church, there have been proposals to recognize as many as thirty sacraments. Augustine does not set a definite number but at times refers to matrimony, holy orders, exorcisms, circumcision, and other rites as sacraments.[6] In the fifth century Pseudo-Dionysius listed six ecclesiastical "mysteries": baptism, the Lord's Supper, unction, holy orders, monasticism, and rites performed on the dead; but chief attention in this period was given to baptism and the Lord's Supper.

Changes in church liturgical practice took place for the next several hundred years. During that time the rite of confirmation was separated from baptism, penance was recognized as a sacrament, the marriage ceremony became a sacramental rite, ordination to the priesthood took the form of "holy orders," and the anointing of the sick became the anointing of the dying. The number of sacraments varied from five to twelve.

The anonymous work *Sentences of Divinity* (c. 1145) listed the seven sacraments that were eventually to become church practice. These included five that were common to all Christians: baptism, confirmation, penance, the Eucharist, extreme unction, and two others: marriage (for the laity) and ordination (for the clergy). Peter Lombard (d. 1160) used this list in his highly influential *Sentences*, and it was officially adopted by the Council of Florence in 1439 and reaffirmed at the seventh session of the Council of Trent in March 1547.

Alexander of Hales (1186–1245) also recognized the seven sacraments and said that only baptism and the Lord's Supper were instituted by Christ, while the other sacraments were appointed by his Apostles and ministers of the church. The Protestant Reformers later argued that a sacrament had to be directly based on the Bible and instituted by Christ himself to be a true sacrament. Thus they claimed the only true sacraments were baptism and the Lord's Supper.

Thomas Aquinas (1225–74) wrote that baptism and the Lord's Supper are the principal sacraments. The Franciscan theologian and cardinal Bonaventura (d. 1274) connected the seven sacraments with the seven diseases of humanity as antidotes: original sin is counteracted by baptism; mortal sin by penance; venial sin by extreme unction; ignorance by ordination; malice by the Lord's Supper; infirmity by confirmation, and evil concupiscence by matrimony.[7]

The Definition of Sacrament

Augustine was the first to treat the doctrine of the sacraments in a systematic way. He did not write a specific treatise on the sacraments, as did his teacher, Ambrose of Milan (*On the Mysteries; On the Sacraments*). Augustine's views developed, rather, in the context of his controversies with the Donatists and Pelagians (see chaps. 3, 4). His work *On the Teacher*, however, deals with the concept of signs and symbols. For Augustine *sacramentum* is part of the family of symbols that belong "to divine things" in the realm of the sacred.[8]

Augustine defines a sign as "a thing that, apart from its appearance to the senses, causes something more to come to mind."[9] In terms of Christian sacrament, "signs are called sacraments when they have reference to divine things." Sacraments are "visible signs of divine things, but in them are to be honored the invisible things themselves." "They are called sacraments," says Augustine, "because in them one thing is seen, another thing understood. What is seen has a bodily appearance, but what is understood has spiritual fruit."[10]

A sign or symbol for Augustine bears a certain resemblance to what it represents. Thus the water of baptism points to inner cleansing, and the grains of wheat in the eucharistic bread point to the many members in the unity of the body of Christ.[11] A symbol is understood or explained by the words that accompany it. In a sacrament "the word is added to the element, and there results the Sacrament, as if itself also a kind of visible word."[12] A Christian sacrament thus consists of two things: an outward, material element (water or bread and wine) and the elucidating word, which for Augustine is the means of conveying the inner reality of the grace of God. The symbol effects what it symbolizes: in baptism cleansing takes place, and in the Eucharist the unifying power of the body and blood of Jesus Christ is conveyed. In the sacraments the word is the vehicle for faith, and faith, the gift of the Holy Spirit, makes the sacrament efficacious for the Christian in the holy catholic church.[13]

This understanding of the sacraments led Augustine to contend in the Donatist controversy that the schismatic heretics (Donatists) did possess the sacraments of the church and administer them validly. But in such churches the ritual actions did not have "the effect of a sacrament," since the congregation was separated from communion with the Holy Spirit and love.[14] Augustine believed that one must be a member of the universal, catholic church for the sacraments to have a positive effect, for only in the true church is the spirit of love present. "If baptism is the sacrament of grace while the grace itself is the abolition of sins, then the grace of baptism is not present among heretics [although baptism is]. Thus there is one baptism and one church, just as there is one faith." So, for Augustine "the Church's baptism can exist outside the Church, but the gift of blessed life is only found inside the Church."[15]

Augustine's definition of sacrament was predominant in the church until it was given greater precision by medieval theologians. Hugo of St. Victor (d. 1141) spoke of the sacraments as "receptacles of grace" and thus introduced the view that the sacraments are primarily concerned with the moral and spiritual growth of their recipients and with healing.[16] Peter Lombard added that "God instituted the remedies of the sacraments against the wounds of original and actual sin" and that "one speaks of sacraments in their proper sense when a symbol of God's grace, which is a form of invisible grace bearing its likeness and being its source, is present."[17] The sacraments thus not only signify but also sanctify in that they are perceived as vehicles for the grace of God. According to Hugo, "a sacrament is a corporeal or material element, openly [and] sensibly presented, representing by similitude and signifying by institution, and containing by consecration, and some invisible and spiritual grace."[18]

This stress on the sacraments as the conveyors of God's grace is emphasized by Thomas Aquinas; for him the sacraments can actually effect what they signify. Though God is not bound to impart grace only through the sacraments, they are, says Aquinas, the normal way in which the grace of God is given. A sacrament thus is "the sign of a sacred thing, since it is [a means of] sanctifying men."[19] Aquinas uses Aristotelian terminology to speak of God as the *principal cause* and the sacraments as the *instrumental cause* given by God through Christ to the church. A sacrament consists of *material* and *form*, just as all physical substances do, according to Aristotle. The material is the unformed substance of a thing, which can be shaped in numerous ways. The form is the shaping energy. In a sacrament the material is either the visible element (the water in baptism, bread and wine in the Eucharist) or the symbolic action perceived by the senses (the confession of guilt by a sinner in penance). The form of the sacrament is the language used by the administrator to clarify and elucidate the action, such as the priest's words of consecration or absolution.[20]

For Aquinas, when the right material and the right form are combined, the sign infallibly conveys the reality. Grace is conveyed when the words are spoken by the priest who has the "intention" of meaning what the church means when it understands the sacraments as instituted by Christ. It is thus through the rite that grace comes. The spiritual worthiness or unworthiness of the priest does not matter. Neither does the spiritual condition of the recipient, as long as that person does not live in mortal sin or pose an "obstacle" to the sacrament's reception. The technical term for this became *ex opere operato*, which literally means "by the work worked" or "from the doing of the thing done."[21] Thus grace is conferred unless there is a hindrance. The sacrament is effective and, as Aquinas says, "is not accomplished through the righteousness of the one who gives or receives it," but rather "through the power of God." Aquinas approves Hugo's formula: "The sign contains the grace."[22]

The effect of these understandings of the nature of sacraments is to lay heaviest stress on the structure, function, and effectiveness of the sacraments themselves rather than on the "faith and repentance" that Lombard says are necessary to receive the sacraments.[23] The emphasis of Tertullian and others on commitment and personal participation in the sacraments is less prominent in this medieval view: the sacraments bring "justifying grace" (Aquinas). The sacraments serve to restore humanity's original righteousness by imparting the merits of Jesus Christ. Thus grace is transmitted through the instrument of the sacraments.[24] As Aquinas says, the sacraments "not only signify but cause grace."[25] They communicate a "spiritual character" that is an indelible, indestructible mark imprinted on the soul for all time.

The immediate point at issue between Martin Luther and the Roman Catholic church was the matter of indulgences, which were a part of the sacramental system related to penance. By the sixteenth century the practice of issuing indulgences was frequently used to elicit donations to the church in exchange for the promise of a lessened punishment for sin in the life after death. Luther objected to this practice and challenged church theologians to ground it in Scripture. His challenges gradually widened to include other abuses in the church, and by 1520 Luther had been excommunicated by Rome. Gradually the Reformation took hold in Europe, and Luther was followed by other prominent theologians, such as Ulrich Zwingli and John Calvin, in protesting Roman Catholic doctrine.

In his writings Luther follows the medieval theologians in accepting Augustine's formula for a sacrament: "The word is added to the element, and there results the Sacrament, as if itself also a kind of visible word."[26] But Luther emphasizes that the word is the force that gives the sacrament its special status. Baptism is "not merely water, but water used according to God's command and connected with God's word."[27] In the Lord's Supper, it is "not the eating and drinking [that] in themselves produce [the effects of the sacrament], but the words 'for you' and 'for the forgiveness of sins.'"[28] Here Luther argues that the sacraments are "efficacious signs" of grace insofar as they are associated with faith in the word of God, which is supremely a word of promise in Jesus Christ. The sacraments are "signs which help and incite to faith . . . without which faith, they are of no benefit."[29] Luther declares, against the Roman view of *ex opere operato*, that "it is heresy to hold that the sacraments . . . give grace to those who place no obstacle in the way." He also believes, against Rome, that faith can be given apart from the sacraments. In commenting on Romans 1:17 ("the righteous shall live by faith"), Luther says that God "does not say that the righteous shall live by the sacraments, but by his faith, for not the sacraments, but faith together with the sacraments, give life and righteousness." It is the word of God—which for Luther means Jesus Christ and the promises of Scripture that convey Christ—that makes the sacrament a means of grace. "For the word can exist without the sacrament, but the sacrament cannot exist without the word. And in case of necessity, a man can be saved without the sacrament, but not without the word."[30]

Ulrich Zwingli expressed the wish "that the word 'sacrament' had never been accepted in German," yet he went on using it.[31] He believed it was not correctly understood by people and joined together rites that are understood better when considered individually. Zwingli returns to the basic meaning of *sacramentum* as an "oath" related to "an initiatory cere-mony or a pledging."[32] Sacraments are signs "by which a man proves to the church that he either aims to be, or is, a soldier of Christ, and which inform the whole church rather than yourself of your faith. For if your faith is not so perfect as not to need a ceremonial sign to confirm it, it is not faith. . . . For faith is that by which we rely on the mercy of God unwaveringly, firmly, and singleheartedly." Thus Zwingli accepts Luther's view that a sacrament is "the sign of a holy thing" but not Luther's insistence "that when you perform the sacrament outwardly a purification is certainly performed inwardly."[33] Zwingli sharply distinguishes between the sign and what is signified by the sign. If the sign were what it signified, he argued, it could no longer be a sign. God has given "covenant signs"—baptism and the Lord's Supper—which are an "initiatory sign" and a "thanksgiving sign." But these signs cannot convey God's grace because grace is given only by God's Spirit. "Moreover, a channel or vehicle is not necessary to the Spirit, for he himself is the virtue and energy whereby all things are borne, and has no need of being borne."[34] The sacraments "represent" (Ger. *darstellen*) Christ, but they do not "present" (*darreichen*) Christ. Faith is strengthened by the sacraments, which "augment faith and are an aid to it," since the sacraments appeal to the senses. Yet this is ineffective unless faith is there, unless the Spirit is present and active. The sacraments help to confirm faith, but they do not give faith. In the sacraments of the church, people receive the "covenant signs" and pledge their oneness with each other as God's people, while also recognizing God's pledge of faithfulness and love to them.[35]

The dominant terms in Calvin's thought on the sacraments are the images of *signs* and *seals*. He too accepts Augustine's definition of a sacrament as "a visible sign of a sacred thing" or "a visible form of an invisible grace." Yet Calvin defines a sacrament more fully: "an outward sign by which the Lord seals on our consciences the promises of his good will toward us in order to sustain the weakness of our faith; and we in turn attest our piety toward him in the presence of the Lord and of his angels and before men (*Inst*. IV.14.1). From this Calvin sees that "a sacrament is never without a preceding promise but is joined to it as a sort of appendix, with the purpose of confirming and sealing the promise itself, and of making it more evident to us and in a sense ratifying it" (IV.14.3). Sacraments are God's gracious gifts to be an outward sign of God's grace and are needed to strengthen the faith of believers, which is "slight and feeble unless it be propped on all sides and sustained by every means, it trembles, wavers, totters, and at last gives way." But "our merciful Lord, according to his infinite kindness, so tempers himself to our capacity that . . . he condescends to lead us to himself even by these earthly elements, and to set before us in the flesh a mirror of spiritual blessings." The sacraments do not "confirm" God's "sacred Word" but rather "establish us in faith in it" (IV.14.3). For Calvin the word of promise must explain the sign and thus "the sacrament requires preaching to beget faith" (IV.14.4).

The sacraments are also "seals" that gain their power when joined with the word. Seals for government documents are "nothing taken by themselves," yet when added to the writing of the document "they do not on that account fail to confirm and seal what is written" (IV.14.5). The sacraments thus seal the promises of God in the gospel of Christ in the hearts of believers. By the work of the Holy Spirit with the Word of God, faith is confirmed and increased through the sacraments. "If the Spirit be lacking," writes Calvin, "the sacraments can accomplish nothing more in our minds than the splendor of the sun shining upon blind eyes, or a voice sounding in deaf ears" (IV.14.9). Calvin objects to the teachings of "the Sophists" that sacraments "justify and confer grace, provided we do not set up a barrier of mortal sin." Rather, faith is crucial since the sacraments "avail and profit nothing unless received in faith" (IV.14.17). The sacraments have "the same office as the Word of God," says Calvin, "to offer and set forth Christ to us, and in him the treasures of heavenly grace." For God "truly executes whatever he promises and represents in signs," yet these signs do not detract from God's freedom and power (IV.14.17).[36] Thus for Calvin sacraments are signs of God's promise. In the sacraments—by the work of the Holy Spirit through the proclamation of the Word of God received by faith—the promises of God in Jesus Christ are received and "sealed" in the lives of believers and confirm God's grace.

The Council of Trent issued its decree on the sacraments in its seventh session in March 1547. The council saw the sacraments as "the completion of the salutary doctrine on justification," which was settled at the sixth session in January. Because of differences among Catholic theologians, Trent did not produce a positive statement on the sacraments but instead framed its teachings in the form of canons that anathematized the views of the Protestants.[37] The council followed the medieval Council of Florence in its decrees.

Trent states that there are seven sacraments of the "New Law" that were all instituted by Christ (canon 1). These sacraments are all equal to each other (canon 3) and necessary for salvation since without them the grace of justification cannot be secured (canon 4). The sacraments are not given for the nourishment of faith alone (canon 5) and actually contain the grace they signify, provided that no one places any "obstacles" in the way (canon 6). The sacraments always impart grace (canon 7) and confer this grace *ex opere operato*. The sacraments and not "faith alone" bring grace (canon 8). Three of the sacraments—baptism, confirmation, and ordination—confer "a certain spiritual and indelible mark" or character upon the soul. The efficacy of the sacraments is not impaired by ministers who are in mortal sin (canon 12), but the ministers must have "the intention of doing what the Church does" when they confer the sacraments (canon 11).[38]

The effect of Trent's actions was to deny the validity of sacraments administered in Protestant churches, with the exception of baptism. The council's general position was that true sacraments in the Catholic sense could only exist when the persons who performed them maintained the Roman Catholic understanding of the nature of the sacraments. Baptism was the exception, since the formulas used by both Catholics and Protestants were scriptural and in most cases the two traditions shared a common understanding of the New Testament portrayal of both infant and adult baptism. (This did not mean, however, that the theologies of baptism were similar in every respect.) Further reforms in canon law imposed a greater uniformity in the Roman Catholic church. These included the use of the Roman missal as the standard liturgical book for the service of the Mass. The missals included both the prescribed words for the sacraments and the rubrics of how the sacraments were to be carried out. This eventually made it possible for the church to point to a common, worldwide theory and practice of the sacraments among Catholic churches, which, according to the Roman church, attested to the unity of faith. The Council of Trent firmly established the Roman Catholic sacramental understanding. For the following four centuries sacramental theology was refined only on smaller issues.

Baptism

Biblical Basis

The Greek verb *baptizein* is the New Testament term for "baptize." It has the various senses of "immerse," "sink," "drown," "go under," "sink into," and "bathe." The noun form *baptisma* denotes not only the outward action but also the inner meaning and force of baptism.

Baptism has been practiced since the earliest days of Christianity. Though the act of baptism is not often mentioned in the New Testament, it is seen as the expression of a convert's public commitment and obedience to God in Jesus Christ. The baptism of Jesus was the paradigm, or model, for the early church's baptisms. Jesus is portrayed receiving baptism from John the Baptist (Mark 1:9–11 and parallels; John 1:32–34), who announces the imminence of "him who comes" to establish the judgment and kingdom of God, whose "way of righteousness" must be "prepared" (Matt. 3:3; 21:32). John calls on people to repent (Matt. 3:2; Mark 1:4) and "bear fruits that befit repentance" (Luke 3:8) by living a new kind of life (Luke 3:10–14).

The baptism of Jesus marks the recognition of his identity and mission. It joins him in solidarity with sinners and displays the freedom in which he chooses to obey God, even to the point of suffering and death (see Luke 12:50). The heavenly voice and descent of the Spirit (Mark 1:9–11; Matt. 3:13–17; Luke 3:21–22), in connection with the water of baptism, correspond to the vindication of the crucified one in his resurrection (see 1 Tim. 3:16).

The book of Acts begins with the promise of the baptism of the Holy Spirit and the call of the disciples to a worldwide mission (1:5; cf. Matt. 28:16–20). After the day of Pentecost, when the Holy Spirit is received and people repent (2:38, 41), baptism with water is practiced in the church (see 8:38; 9:18; 16:15, 33; 19:5). The gospel message (*kērygma*) evokes a response of acceptance by faith that is represented by baptism (2:37–38, 41; 8:12; 16:14–15). The practice of baptism is joined with the reception of the Holy Spirit (2:38; 9:17–18; 10:47; 11:16).[39] Baptism is done "in the name of Jesus Christ" (2:38; 10:48) or "in the name of the Lord Jesus" (8:16; 19:5).

In the letters of Paul the meanings of baptism are spelled out more formally. In Romans 6:1–4 Paul relates the death and resurrection of Jesus Christ to the dying and rising of people who are in and with him; baptism describes one's union with Christ in his death and one's subsequent rising with Christ in his resurrection. In 1 Corinthians 12:12–13 baptism is seen as the means of incorporation into the Christian community, the body of Christ. Baptism as "putting on" Christ is connected by Paul in Galatians 3:26–29 with the special relation termed *sonship*. Colossians 2:9–13 describes baptism as the Christian counterpart of Jewish circumcision through a dying to sin and a rising again to new life. This union with Christ in baptism provides all that is necessary for salvation. In Ephesians 4:5–6 baptism is related to the unity of Christian faith by the formula, "one Lord, one faith, one baptism, one God and Father of us all."

Other New Testament references to baptism include Hebrews 6:2, 10:22, and 1 Peter 3:21, where baptism is the basis of the Christian's faithful witness to God. Though the term is not used in Titus 3:5, the reference to the "washing of regeneration and renewal in the Holy Spirit" links water and Spirit (cf. John 3:5). Similarly, 1 John 5:6ff. links water and the blood with which Jesus Christ is said to have come (cf. John 19:34; Rev. 7:13; 16:3).

Baptism in the Early Church

The *Didache* of the ancient church prescribes that the church must "not let anyone eat or drink of your Eucharist except those baptized in the Lord's name." According to this document, baptism is administered with the trinitarian formula, and from the earliest times in the church, baptism attests to the forgiveness of sins.[40] It is the doorway into the church family of faith. The candidate descends into the waters of baptism, weighted down with sin, then emerges "bearing fruit in our hearts, having fear and hope in Jesus in the Spirit," according to the *Epistle to Barnabas*.[41] Baptism is connected with receiving the Holy Spirit; thus Clement of Rome speaks of "one God, one Christ, one Spirit of grace which was poured out on us."[42]

Justin Martyr deals with Christian baptism as part of Christian worship in his *First Apology*. Justin appeals to Isaiah 1:16–20 and John 3:3-4 for the practice of baptism, which, when administered in the triune name, brings about regeneration, illumination, and the forgiveness of sin.[43] Irenaeus refers to it as "the seal of eternal life and new birth unto God." "As dry flour cannot be united into a lump of dough, or a loaf, but needs moisture; so we who are many cannot be made one in Christ Jesus without the water which comes from heaven. . . . For our bodies have received the unity which brings us to immortality, by means of the washing [of baptism]; our souls receive it by means of [the gift of] the Spirit."[44]

Tertullian was the only early theologian to write a separate treatise (*On Baptism*), but his clearest statement comes from his polemic against Marcion. Tertullian argues that baptism bestows four fundamental gifts, which could not occur if Marcion's dualism between the Creator and Redeemer were permitted. These gifts are the remission of sins, deliverance from death, regeneration, and the bestowal of the Holy Spirit. Tertullian teaches that baptism is necessary for salvation. He notes that it is administered to children, yet he personally prefers baptism to be postponed until children reach the age of discretion. Baptism is unrepeatable, except in the case of heretics who have not been truly baptized anyway. At different times Tertullian held various views about the relation of the Spirit to baptism.[45]

In the Eastern church Clement of Alexandria writes, "Being baptized, we are illuminated; illuminated, we become sons; being made sons, we are made perfect; being made perfect, we are made immortal." He then cites Psalm 82:6 and says, "This work is variously called gift of grace, illumination, perfection, and washing: washing, by which we wash away our sins; grace, by which the penalties accruing to transgressions are remitted; and illumination, with which that holy light of salvation is beheld, that is, by which we see God clearly."[46] Origen stresses that the primary gift at baptism is the gift of the Holy Spirit, with the convert being "baptized in Christ, in the water and the Holy Spirit," which descends on the Christian as at Christ's baptism, so that the Christian is "pneumatic." Baptism is administered to children who, being defiled with sin, need the forgiveness found therein. Baptism frees one from the power of the devil and brings a person into membership in the church as Christ's body.[47]

The issue of baptism was closely related to the struggles between Cyprian and Novatian over the nature of the church (see chap. 3). Cyprian held that God's grace is given in baptism, which marks the "origin" of faith and "the saving entrance upon the hope of eternal life and the divine regard for the purifying and vivifying of the servants of God." In baptism a "second birth" occurs in which the recipient receives the Holy Spirit, becomes free from the devil, from death and hell and secures health by having inborn sins forgiven.[48] Cyprian denies the validity of baptism administered by heretics or those who have separated from the true church; this he describes as a "sordid and profane bath." When the lapsed return to the true church they need not to be rebaptized but baptized, since it is only in the true church that the Spirit of God is received. "Water alone is not able to cleanse away sins, and to sanctify a man, unless he also has the Holy Spirit. Therefore it is necessary that they [his opponents on the question of rebaptizing heretics] should grant the Holy Spirit to be there, where they say that baptism is; or else there is not baptism where the Holy Spirit is not, because there cannot be baptism without the Spirit." Cyprian's view of sin leads him to urge that children be baptized, not on the customary eighth day, but as soon as possible. The infant "approaches that much more easily to the reception of the forgiveness of sins because the sins remitted to him are not his own, but those of another," by which Cyprian means that the infant had "contracted the contagion of the ancient death" from Adam.[49]

Augustine's views on humanity and sacraments in general led him to put his own distinctive stamp on the doctrine of baptism. For him the primary effect of baptism is to remove the depravity inherited from Adam and the concupiscence that is a person's special and real guilt. "Baptism washes away all, absolutely all, our sins, whether of deed, word or thought, whether sins original or added, whether knowingly or unknowingly contracted." Baptism has a life-long effectiveness: "By that which is given once it comes to pass that pardon of any sins whatsoever, not only before but also afterward, is granted to believers."[50] No amount of prayer, almsgiving, or good works can bring forgiveness without baptism.

In his controversy with the Donatists, Augustine taught that in baptism a person receives a spiritual seal, which is the image of Christ. The seal is imparted in baptism, regardless of the minister's fitness or moral character. In baptism one receives the Holy Spirit and the seal of the Spirit, which mark one who belongs to Christ and who will receive the grace of God. In baptism a person receives the assurance "one may hope for an unending life when he dies," rebirth through "the washing of regeneration," which leads to an eternal regeneration and the gift of the Holy Spirit.[51] Augustine's distinction between the sacrament itself and its effect led him to oppose Cyprian's position on the validity of Donatist sacraments. Baptism is unrepeatable, but it becomes effectual only when one is converted to the unity of the true church.

> He who has received the baptism of Christ, which they have not lost who have separated themselves . . . in any heresy or schism, in which sacrilegious crime his sins were not remitted, when he shall have reformed and come to the fellowship and unity of the church, is not to be again baptized, because in this very reconciliation and peace it is offered to him, that the sacrament which, when received in schism, could not benefit, shall now in the unity [of the church] begin to benefit him for the remission of his sins.[52]

Augustine's heavy stress on the inherited guilt of sin led him to advocate infant baptism very strongly and also to orient the forgiveness of sins in baptism toward the inherited guilt from Adam rather than only toward prebaptismal sins. Augustine says that the effect of baptism in infants becomes evident in later life: "We all know that if one baptized in infancy does not believe when he comes to years of discretion, and does not keep himself from lawless desires, then he will have no profit from the gift he received as a baby." He also distinguishes between the sacrament in itself and true conversion to Christ:

> This all shows that the sacrament of baptism is one thing, the conversion of the heart is another; but the salvation of man is effected by these two. If one is missing, we are not bound to suppose that the other is absent: in an infant, baptism can exist without conversion; in the penitent thief, conversion without baptism . . . there can be conversion of the heart when baptism has not been received, but not when baptism has been rejected.[53]

But those (of the elect) who receive the sacrament of baptism and its full effects receive the graces of illumination and justification, are incorporated into the body of Christ, are released from death, and are reconciled to God.[54]

Baptism in the Middle Ages

The medieval definitions of sacrament, with their reliance on Aristotelian terminology, are reflected in views on baptism. In the mode of *matter* and *form*, Peter Lombard defines baptism as "a dipping or external washing of the body together with a prescribed formula of words." Hugo of St. Victor defines it as "water made holy by the word of God for washing away sins." Pope Eugene IV, speaking of the effect of the sacrament, said that baptism brings "the remission of all original and actual sin, also of every penalty which is due for that sin."[55]

In the early Middle Ages baptism was seen as the key to sacramental theology. Later, however, the Eucharist became more prominent as the model by which sacraments are understood. Baptism was central because it was the one sacrament that was necessary for salvation. It was so crucial that in medieval Catholic theology even the children of believing parents were condemned without the grace of baptism. This led to the provision that in emergencies baptism could be administered by a lay person, a pagan, or even an infidel. This was possible because, as Augustine had argued and Bruno of Segni (d. 1123) recorded, "Baptism is good regardless of who gives it, because it does not depend on the faith of the one giving it."[56] Yet those who desire baptism but—like the thief on the cross—cannot obtain it are not denied salvation.

Thomas Aquinas developed the view that while baptism bestows forgiveness of sins and freedom from "the guilt [liability; *reatus*] of the entire penalty owed for . . . sins," through baptism one also "secures grace and powers." These powers, given with the baptismal character, come from God to enable Christians to rise above their natural abilities and were won for humanity by Christ's incarnation into human life.[57] Among these powers are the power to resist temptation and avoid sin. Adam lost this for the race, but Christ restored it with his sinless life. Another power is the ability to offer perfect worship by living in obedience to God and offering oneself to God in the liturgy. Christians can live in accord with Christ's perfect law of love and in the eucharistic liturgy can be united with Christ's perfect sacrifice on the cross.

Yet the most fundamental powers imparted in baptism and discussed by the medieval theologians are the theological virtues of faith, hope, and love. These enable Christians to believe in God's revelation, hope for what God promised, and love God above all things. Other special powers, termed "gifts of the Holy Spirit," are wisdom, understanding, counsel, fortitude, knowledge, piety, and the fear of God. Aquinas sees clearly that the bestowal of these powers is the reason why Christians should never be rebaptized. Once Christians receive the character and powers of baptism, they can never receive anything new or different by being baptized again.

Aquinas and the medieval theologians knew, however, that there is a distinction between the reception of these powers and their actual use by Christians. The exercise of the virtues is often called "grace." God bestows the powers in baptism, but people have to cooperate and use them along with their own natural powers and God-given abilities. People have to be willing to resist temptation and to cooperate with God's gift of grace. The more they cooperate, the more grace they receive. Then they are willing to cooperate even further. This means salvation is a process of justification and sanctification (see chap. 5), which finally leads to the eternal life of blessed union with God. For all people the beginning of this process is the same: the sacrament of baptism.

The medieval doctrine of baptism was the church's view through the Reformation period and was made official at the Council of Trent. There, in the session on the sacraments, fourteen canons were laid out to condemn Protestant doctrine and reassert the basic teachings of Aquinas and others. Among the views condemned as heretical were the following: that the Roman church does not teach true baptismal doctrine (canon 3), that baptism administered by heretics is not a true baptism (canon 4), that baptism is not necessary for salvation (canon 5), that the baptized cannot lose God's grace through sin but only by lack of faith (canon 6), that the baptized are free to obey only their own consciences and not the law of the church (canon 8), that baptismal grace covers sins committed after baptism and must only be remembered to receive forgiveness (canon 10), that anyone should be rebaptized after having been baptized in the Catholic church (canon 11), that infants should not be baptized (canon 13), and that children should not be compelled to live a Christian life (canon 14).[58]

Baptism in the Reformation

Martin Luther's understanding of baptism is integrally related to his doctrine of justification (see chap. 5). Luther strongly distinguishes the *sign* in baptism from its theological significance. The outward sign, of course, is water, but the inner meaning of baptism embraces two major points. First, through the water of baptism the Holy Spirit brings regeneration. It is "a spiritually-rich water, in which the Holy Spirit is, and in which he works; yea, the entire holy Trinity is present, and the man who is baptized is then called regenerated." The heart is washed clean, the whole nature is transformed, and the Holy Spirit is granted, bringing grace to the believer. In baptism the Holy Spirit begins the work of combating evil, "the unclean spirit." Since the baptized Christian struggles every day against evil and the "old Adam," the whole Christian life for Luther is basically a return to one's baptism, "so that Christian life is nothing else than a kind of daily baptism." For "as we have once obtained forgiveness of sins in Baptism, so forgiveness remains day by day as long as we live."[59]

Second, for Luther baptism is a sign of God's constant readiness to forgive sin and renew the sinner for the sake of Christ. Here Luther finds the answer to his basic question, "How do I find a gracious God?" Believers are "incorporated" by baptism into God's kingdom and assured of God's covenant, through which justification occurs by faith. Because of this sacrament they are made innocent in God's gracious judgment and are "children of grace and justified persons." This is the work of God's forgiving love; "a person is thus pure by the gracious imputation of God, rather than by virtue of his own nature." In baptism there is "death and resurrection; that is, full and complete justification," which is actualized by faith in God's ongoing forgiveness of the one who is "both justified and a sinner."[60]

Consistent with his understanding of the nature of sacraments, Zwingli sees baptism as a pledge to amend one's life and follow Christ. As a sign of the beginning of a new life, it is like the cowl one dons when entering an order and wears before learning the rules of the order: "Baptism in water is an initiatory sign, with which we pledge ourselves to a new life." For Zwingli baptism is analogous to the Old Testament rite of circumcision, which signaled one's incorporation into the nation of Israel. This means that infants most certainly should be baptized. "The children of Christians are no less sons of God than the parents, just as in the Old Testament. Hence, since they are sons of God, who will forbid this baptism? Circumcision among the ancients . . . was the same as baptism with us. As that was given to infants so ought baptism to be administered to infants." Like Luther, Zwingli was eager to defend his views of infant baptism against the Anabaptists who acknowledged only "believer's baptism."[61]

Zwingli's view of the sacraments denies baptism as a "means of grace" or a necessity for salvation. To tie God to such a rite would mean that God is not sovereign, Christ is not central, and the Spirit is not free. Thus Zwingli's whole view of God and salvation is closely related to his view of baptism. His major motif is the "covenant sign" that is initiated by God and acknowledged in baptism. This sign is "given and received for the sake of fellow-believers, not for a supposed effect upon those who receive it." Baptism is given by God and thus is part of Christian faith. To scorn it completely, says Zwingli, is to show a lack of trust in God, but to receive baptism is to attest to one's trust in God, which is a cause for rejoicing.[62]

John Calvin defines baptism as "the sign of initiation by which we are received into the society of the church, in order that, engrafted in Christ, we may be reckoned among God's children" (*Inst. IV.15.1*). It has two fundamental purposes: to serve our faith before God and to serve our confession before others. Baptism is "like a sealed document to confirm to us that all our sins are so abolished, remitted, and effaced that they can never come to his sight, be recalled, or charged against us. For he wills that all who believe be baptized for the remission of sins" (Matt. 28:19; Acts 2:38 —IV.15.1). Calvin says that baptism contributes to the Christian's faith by serving as a token and proof of our cleansing, a token of mortification and renewal in Christ, and a token of our union with Christ (IV.15.1–6).

Calvin rejects the purely symbolic view, which says that baptism is "nothing but a token and mark by which we confess our religion before men, as soldiers bear the insignia of their commander as a mark of their profession" (IV.15.1).[63] Although Calvin acknowledges baptism as a sign of the profession of faith, his major emphasis is on baptism as a seal of God's forgiveness, grace, and salvation given to bless and strengthen the Christian community. The virtue of baptism does not rest with water as the outward sign, since it has no power in itself. Rather, the Word of God is needed along with the sign to interpret the sign. The water does not contain in itself "the power to cleanse, regenerate, and renew," nor is it the "cause of salvation." Instead, one receives in baptism "the knowledge and certainty of such gifts. This the words themselves explain clearly enough" (IV.15.2). "Baptism promises us no other purification than through the sprinkling of Christ's blood, which is represented by means of water from the resemblance to cleansing and washing" (ibid.). Though conferred upon us only once, baptism should not be considered "only for past time, so that for newly committed sins into which we fall after baptism we must seek new remedies of expiation in some other sacraments, as if the force of the former one were spent" (IV.15.3). Rather, "we must realize that at whatever time we are baptized, we are once for all washed and purged for our whole life. Therefore, as often as we fall away, we ought to recall the memory of our baptism and fortify our mind with it, that we may always be sure and confident of the forgiveness of sins" (ibid.).

For Calvin, baptism is a means of grace, but this does not mean God's freedom or sovereignty are surrendered. Instead, God has chosen to confirm faith in believers and has graciously "accommodated" or limited himself to human capacity by giving common signs to nurture faith in those in the covenant of grace.[64]

> It is not my intention to weaken the force of baptism by not joining reality and truth to the sign, in so far as God works through outward means. But from this sacrament, as from all others, we obtain only as much as we receive in faith. If we lack faith, this will be evidence of our ungratefulness, which renders us chargeable before God, because we have not believed the promise given there.

> But as far as it is a symbol of our confession, we ought by it to testify that our confidence is in God's mercy, and our purity in forgiveness of sins, which has been procured for us through Jesus Christ; and that we enter God's church in order to live harmoniously with all believers in complete agreement of faith and love. This last point was what Paul means when he said, "We have all been baptized in one Spirit that we may be one body" [1 Cor. 12:13 paraphrase]. (IV.15.15)[65]

In many ways Protestants and Roman Catholics share similar perspectives on baptism. They both look back to Augustine for their basic understanding of a sacrament and acknowledge baptism to be basic for the Christian life. In that sense they share a common perception of the nature of baptism. Unlike groups such as the Quakers who reject sacraments altogether, they also hold essentially the same views on the general necessity of baptism. They both regard baptism as a means of grace through which God works in a special way. They agree too on the need for infant baptism, as opposed to groups such as the Anabaptists, who rejected this practice. In addition both churches recognize the validity of baptism by the trinitarian formula in the other's communion.

Yet differences are also to be found. Baptismal rituals differ between Protestants and Roman Catholics as well as among Protestants themselves. Different understandings of the efficacy of baptism, its relation to original sin, and the fate of unbaptized children, as well as the capacity of faith in the baptized and the degree of grace conferred in the rite—all of this means that traditional Catholicism and Protestantism are far from agreement on the theology of baptism.

8

Sacramental Controversy

What Is the Lord's Supper?

Biblical Basis

From the earliest times Christians have assembled to celebrate the "Lord's supper" (1 Cor. 11:20). This meal originated with the supper Jesus and his disciples shared in the Upper Room during the last night of Jesus' life. At that time Jesus commanded his followers to share bread and wine "in remembrance of me" (1 Cor. 11:25). Accounts of this supper appear in all four Gospels and in 1 Corinthians 11:23–26; except for the description in the Gospel of John, these accounts are very similar.

Numerous technical questions surround these passages. Among the issues are questions about the antecedents of the supper in the Jewish faith, variations in words and procedure in the Gospels, the dating of the supper and whether it was a Passover meal, the form of the supper, and its theological interpretation—particularly the words of Jesus: "Take, eat; this is my body" (Matt. 26:26; cf. Mark 14:22; Luke 22:19; 1 Cor. 11:24). These are complex questions, and scholarly opinion is widely varied.

In addition to these issues there are broader theological questions about the general meaning of eating and drinking in the Scriptures. In what sense is the Lord's Supper like or unlike the eating and drinking portrayed in other parts of the Bible? What is the relation of the Lord's Supper celebrations to normal eating and drinking by Christians as exemplified in the life of the early church, where believers "devoted themselves to the apostles' teaching and fellowship, to the breaking of bread and the prayers" (Acts 2:42)? These questions set the supper in the context of other human actions and ask What are the similarities and differences between these and the Lord's Supper?

Biblical and theological questions also surround Jesus' words about eating and drinking in relation to himself. Particularly in the sixth chapter of John, Jesus is shown feeding a large multitude and then discoursing about "food which perishes" compared to "food which endures to eternal life, which the Son of man will give to you" (6:27). He speaks of *signs* (6:26, 30) and a *seal* (6:27) and proclaims himself as the *bread of life* (6:35, 48), so that whoever comes to Jesus "shall not hunger," and whoever "believes in me shall never thirst" (6:35). "I am the living bread which came down from heaven; if any one eats of this bread, he will live for ever; and the bread which I shall give for the life of the world is my flesh" (6:51). This language of eating in relation to Jesus continues as Jesus says, "Unless you eat the flesh of the Son of man and drink his blood, you have no life in you; he who eats my flesh and drinks my blood has eternal life" (6:53–54; cf. 6:55–58). Jesus links this eating with believing and indicates that "it is the spirit that gives life, the flesh is of no avail; the words that I have spoken to you are spirit and life" (6:63). These passages have been the source of considerable debate about whether Jesus himself is eaten in the Lord's Supper, or whether this is no more than eating, drinking, and remembering Jesus in faith—in other words, a "spiritual eating and drinking."

Other dimensions of the Lord's Supper include terms and concepts such as *new covenant* (1 Cor. 11:25), *remembrance* (11:25), proclamation of "the Lord's death until he comes" (11:26), and *kingdom* (Matt. 26:29; Mark 14:25). In addition, the Lord's Supper can be seen in relation to broader biblical motifs such as sacrifice, the marriage feast, judgment, the Holy Spirit, faith, hope, love, resurrection, and the unity of the church.

The Lord's Supper in the Early Church

The *Didache* was the first document to use the term *Eucharist* (Gr. *eucharistia*, "thanksgiving") for the Lord's Supper. In the ancient church the supper took place in the evening as part of a Christian fellowship meal called an *agape*, or love feast.[1] As the church grew, however, these two experiences became separated. The Eucharist began to precede the agape, and soon the Eucharist was celebrated in the morning and the fellowship meal in the evening. By the end of the fourth century, the agape was held in private homes and eventually discontinued.

Liturgies from the ancient church, such as the Eucharist discussed in the *The Apostolic Tradition*, by Hippolytus (c. 215), follow the outline described earlier by Justin Martyr. The prayers are not set, except for the words of institution, and generally follow the pattern of earlier Jewish thanksgiving prayers. The distribution of the elements takes place with the words, "The Body of Christ, the Blood of Christ, the Cup for eternal life," and those who receive the elements answer, "Amen."[2]

The beginning church possessed no unified theology of the Lord's Supper, just as it had no view of the nature of a sacrament, but two major ways of understanding the nature of the supper developed very early. In the first view the consecrated elements of bread and wine undergo a transformation. This is called the *realist* theory. The other way is the *symbolic* view, which says the elements are symbols of the body and blood, which are the sacramental realities.

The transformation view is stated by Justin:

> For we do not receive these things as common bread or common drink; but as Jesus Christ our Saviour being incarnate by God's word took flesh and blood for our salvation, so also we have been taught that the food consecrated by the word of prayer which comes from him, from which our flesh and blood are nourished by transformation is the flesh and blood of that incarnate Jesus.[3]

The *Didache* sees the bread and wine as "holy" and as "spiritual food and drink and eternal life."[4] Ignatius of Antioch speaks of the Eucharist as "the flesh of our Saviour Jesus Christ," which is "the medicine of immortality, and the antidote which wards off death but yields continuous life in union with Jesus Christ."[5] Irenaeus—in arguing against the Gnostics, who rejected everything related to the "earthly"—contends that when the bread, "which comes from the earth, receives the invocation of God," it is "no longer common bread but Eucharist." After partaking of the Eucharist, our bodies "are no longer corruptible, having the hope of the eternal resurrection."[6] In the elements of the supper, heaven and earth are united as they are united in the person of Jesus Christ himself. Further, Irenaeus draws the parallel that bodies receiving the Eucharist are no longer subject to corruption, just as the bread that receives the consecration is no longer "common."

This realist view continued in the Western church through Tertullian, who speaks often of the bread as the "body of the Lord" and says, "The flesh feeds on the body and blood of Christ that the soul may be nourished on God."[7] Cyprian, in commenting on the Lord's Prayer, says that Christ is our bread "because He is the bread of us who touch his body."[8] Athanasius is said to have written, "So long as the prayers and invocations have not yet been made, it is mere bread and a mere cup. But when the great and wondrous prayers have been recited, then the bread becomes the body and the cup the blood of our Lord Jesus Christ. . . . The Word descends on the bread and cup and it becomes his body."[9]

Cyril of Jerusalem spoke most clearly of this transformation view in

340, stating that the same miracle of change in elements happens in the Eucharist as occurred when Jesus turned the water into wine at the wedding in Cana.

> Once, in Cana of Galilee, he changed water into wine (and wine is akin to blood); is it incredible that he should change wine into blood? . . . Therefore with complete assurance let us partake of those elements as being the body and blood of Christ. For in the symbol of bread his body is given to you, and in the symbol of wine his blood; so that by partaking of the body and blood of Christ you may be made of the same body and blood with him. For in this way we become Christ-bearers, since his body and blood is distributed in the parts of our body. Thus, as blessed Peter says, we "become partakers of the divine nature."[10]

In the liturgy, according to Cyril, "after sanctifying ourselves with those spiritual hymns, we call upon the compassionate God to send out his Holy Spirit on the gifts that are set out; that he may make the bread the body of Christ, and the wine the blood of Christ. For whatever the Holy Spirit has touched is assuredly sanctified and changed.[11] Gregory of Nyssa speaks of this change as being a "transelementing" of "the nature of the visible things into the immortal body," so that they acquire the "form" of Christ's body and blood with their corresponding properties.[12] Chrysostom describes the elements as being "refashioned" or "transformed," and Ambrose of Milan says Christ's words "have the power to change the character of the elements."[13] Thus the realist or materialist description of the changes in the elements in the Eucharist had strong adherents in both the Western and the Eastern churches.

The alternative view of the elements was proposed most strongly by the Alexandrine theologians, though traces of it can be found alongside realist statements in writers such as Tertullian and even Cyril. In this view the elements are signs of realities that are truly apprehended only by faith. This view is integrally related to Platonic tendencies in these theologians and is also revealed in their use of allegory when interpreting Scripture, as they attempted to find the spiritual reality behind the outward or physical manifestation.

One proponent of this view of the Eucharist was Clement of Alexandria. "The flesh and blood of the Word are the apprehension of the divine power and essence. . . . For thus he imparts himself to those who partake of this food in a more spiritual manner; for then, as the truth-loving Plato says, 'the soul nourished itself' [*Protagoras* 313c]. For the eating and drinking of the divine Word is the knowledge of the Divine essence." For Clement, "My flesh is an allegory for the Holy Spirit, for the flesh is his handiwork. 'Blood,' by analogy, stands for the Word, for the Word is like rich blood poured into our life."[14] Origen continued this view: "Bread which

God the Word proclaims as his body is the word which nourishes our souls.
. . . That drink which God the Word proclaims as his blood is the word
which 'so wonderfully refreshes and inebriates' [Ps. 22 (23):5]. . . . For the
body and blood of God the Word can be nothing else than the word which
nourishes and the word which 'makes glad the heart' [Ps. 104:15]." In the
Eucharist Origen distinguishes between the corruptible matter that the
communicant receives and the incorruptible reality that sanctifies.[15]

Heirs of the Origen tradition interpreted John 6, in which Jesus speaks
about eating his flesh and drinking his blood, in a spiritual sense. The flesh
and blood the disciples are to eat and drink are the teachings of Jesus rather
than his physical body. As Evagrius Ponticus puts it, "We eat His flesh and
drink His blood, becoming partakers through the incarnation both of the
sensible life of the Word and of His wisdom. For by the terms 'flesh' and
'blood' He both denoted the whole of His mystic sojourning on earth, and
pointed to His teaching, consisting as it did of practical, natural and
theological insights."[16]

In Augustine's writings on the Eucharist both a realistic and a symbolic
strand can be found. In a sermon he says, "That bread which you see on the
altar, sanctified by the Word of God, is Christ's body. That cup, or rather
the contents of that cup, sanctified by the word of God, is Christ's blood. By
these elements the Lord Christ willed to convey His body and His blood,
which he shed for us."[17] Augustine even speaks of a "chewing" of the flesh
of Christ and a drinking of his blood. Augustine's identification of the
eucharistic elements with the "body and blood of Christ" is so complete at
times that he is able to write that Judas, as well as other "unworthy"
recipients, receives "the body of the Lord and the blood of the Lord
nonetheless." Speaking of the incarnate Christ, Augustine says, "He
walked here in the flesh, and he gave this flesh to us to eat for our
salvation."[18]

Yet there is also a symbolic side in Augustine. He says that Christ, "in
explaining what it means to eat his body and to drink his blood," intended
that "to eat this food and to drink this drink means to abide in Christ and to
have Christ abiding in him." Christ's words in John 6:53, Augustine asserts,
are to be interpreted in a figurative way; and when Jesus says, "He who eats
of this bread will not die" (John 6:50), he means "the one who eats what
belongs to the power of the sacrament, not simply to the visible sacrament;
the one who eats inwardly, nor merely outwardly; the one who eats the
sacrament in the heart not just the one who crushes it with his teeth."[19]
Thus in answer to the question, "Why are you preparing your teeth and
your stomach?" Augustine replies with his famous formula, "Believe, and
you have already eaten." In a broader sense the body of Christ is the church

or the "mystic body," and Jesus "wishes the food and drink to be understood as the fellowship of his body and of his members, which is the holy church."[20]

Other important dimensions of the Lord's Supper were also developing in the early church. These include the question of how the Lord's Supper is a sacrifice. In this the church moved from the eucharistic sacrifice as the offering of the congregation to God—as a sacrifice of praise for the once-for-all sacrifice of Christ on the cross—to the offering by the priest of the elements dedicated for use in the Eucharist. As Cyprian wrote, "The bishop now imitates that which Christ did, and he offers the true and full sacrifice in the Church to God the Father."[21] Thus the sacrifice possessed an objective efficacy. This issue and the major question of whether there was a symbolic or a "real participation" in the body and blood of Christ were to be crucial issues in the centuries to come.

The Lord's Supper in the Middle Ages

From the fourth century on, there were increasing changes and additions in the eucharistic liturgy of the church. The eucharistic prayer, or canon of the Mass, grew much longer than the early prayers in Hippolytus's form. Throughout there were many references to the Eucharist as "the offering of the church," with the prayer that this offering be acceptable to God. In addition, growing emphasis was put on the role of the clergy in offering the Mass, which, after the era of Charlemagne, was said throughout the empire in Latin.[22]

Two medieval debates focused attention on the nature of the presence of Christ in the Eucharist. Around the year 832 the French abbot Paschasius Radbertus (c. 790–865) wrote a book *On the Body and the Blood of the Lord*. In it he tried to combine Augustine's symbolic view with the idea that there is a change in the elements of the Eucharist. On Radbertus's symbolic side the Eucharist is not a bodily meal but a spiritual feast. By partaking, the Christian shows a living union with Christ. Only those who believe receive this spiritual benefit. Thus there is a distinction between the visible and the invisible in the sacrament.

On the other side, Radbertus claimed that after the elements are consecrated in the Eucharist, they are the flesh and blood of Christ in the same way as Christ's physical body and blood in the days when he lived. This change cannot be perceived physically, but only inwardly as a divine mystery. Only believers can receive this body.

Two opponents challenged Radbertus's views. Rabanus Maurus (780–856) became archbishop of Mainz in 847 and emphasized strongly that the bread and wine are symbols. The claim by Radbertus that they were changed into the body and blood of Christ was obnoxious to him. For Rabanus the body and blood of Christ are to be received mystically or sacramentally only.

Radbertus was also challenged by the Benedictine monk Ratramnus (d. 868), who was asked by Charles the Bald to answer two questions about the Eucharist. (1) Are the body and blood of Christ present in such a way as to be seen only with the eyes of faith (*in mysterio*), or are they real (*in veritate*), so that the human eye actually sees the body and blood? (2) Are the body and blood of Christ that are present in the Eucharist the same as what "was born of Mary, suffered, died, and was buried and ascended to the heavens to the right hand of the father"?[23]

Ratramnus responded with a book of the same title as Radbertus's *On the Body and the Blood of the Lord*. His answer to the first question is that Christ is present in the supper only "figuratively," not "in truth." This meant for Ratramnus that Christ could not be perceived externally, by the senses, but only by the eyes of faith. Both ways of perception are real and true, but it is only by faith and not through the eyes of flesh that Christ is perceived in the sacrament. To the second question Ratramnus responded that the body of Christ present in the Eucharist is not the same body that was "born of Mary," since that body is in heaven at the right hand of God. There is only a spiritual presence of Christ in the Eucharist, which is perceived spiritually by believers. The Lord's Supper is not just an act of remembrance, since Christ is truly present in the elements. But the presence of Christ is perceived only by faith not by sight.

This controversy marked the first time that major views on the nature of the Lord's Supper were precisely formulated. The two streams from the early church were now clarified with a realistic doctrine featuring a transmutation of the elements on one side and on the other a symbolic interpretation in which the elements are basically signs and the Eucharist is a spiritual communion with Christ.

Two centuries later the development of medieval eucharistic doctrine was furthered by another controversy. Berengar of Tours (d. 1088), following the views of Ratramnus, stressed the difference between the "sacramental sign" and the "sacramental reality" and held that the body and blood of Christ are consumed purely in a spiritual sense.[24] Berengar relied heavily on the use of reason and argued that there is no change of substance in the elements, for it is impossible for something to lose its substance. Even after consecration by the priest, the elements look the same because they are the same. To explain how the elements can be the body and blood of Christ after the consecration, Berengar argued that while there is no change in the elements, there is a new dimension added. This is the whole, heavenly Christ, who—though in heaven—adds the saving power of his death and spiritual presence to the Eucharist. Neither the bread nor the wine is raised to heaven, nor does the body of Christ descend to earth. The bread and wine are merely signs. Only in figurative sense as pledges of salvation are they the body and blood of Christ, and this only for believers.

Berengar's views stirred further controversy. In 1050 a synod condemned his teachings and excommunicated him, but his doctrine continued to be influential. In 1059 he signed a formula prepared by Cardinal Humbert (d. 1061), which contradicted his views. It said that the bread and wine after consecration are "not only a sacrament, but they are also the true body and blood of our Lord Jesus Christ, and they are not merely sacramentally, but sensibly and in truth held by the hands of the priest, and thus they are broken by the faithful and masticated with their teeth."[25]

Berengar soon renewed his opposition. In 1079 a synod at Rome forced him again to recant. This time the formula stressed the identity between the original body of Christ and the eucharistic body: "The bread and wine, which are placed on the alter, through the mystery of the sacred prayer and the words of our Redeemer are substantially changed into the true, proper, and life-giving flesh and blood of our Lord Jesus Christ."[26]

In this eucharistic controversy the Roman church established firmly that there is a change of the elements into the body and blood of Christ and that Christ is present in the host. While there is a change in substance, there is no change in the outward appearance of the elements. The controversy also led to the development of the concept of *sacramental reality*, in which the eucharistic bread and wine could be called both a sacrament and a reality.

The scholastic theologians of the twelfth century, particularly Peter Lombard, explored the issue of *how* the elements in the Eucharist could be called the "body and blood of Christ" in a real and substantial way. In about 1140 Rolando Bandinelli, who became Pope Alexander III, used the term *transubstantiation* to say that the reality or substance of the elements changes while they still appear to be bread and wine. This view became official church teaching at the Fourth Lateran Council in 1215 and was reaffirmed at the Council of Lyons in 1274. The council in 1215 asserted that "the body and blood [of Christ] are truly contained in the Sacrament of the Altar under the species of bread and wine, transubstantiated by the divine power—the bread into his body and the wine into his blood" when the words of consecration are spoken.[27]

The theory of transubstantiation was further developed by Thomas Aquinas, who, with the help of Aristotelian philosophical concepts, made the theory more precise. Aquinas taught that the *substance* of the bread and wine is changed into the body and blood of Christ, while the *accidents*, or outward characteristics, of the elements remain the same. The transformed substance is perceived by faith, which recognizes the inner reality of the bread and wine. The change in the substance, said Aquinas "is perceptible neither by sense nor by imagination, but only by the mind, which is called 'the eye of the soul.'" The mind is aided by faith, which is crucial, and in faith the real recognition of the substance of the body and blood of Christ is possible. The connection between the body of Christ in heaven and the elements on earth occurs through the miracle of the transformation of the substance.[28]

The Council of Trent solidified the teachings of Aquinas and later scholastic theologians on the Eucharist and particularly on transubstantiation. On October 11, 1551, the council issued its decree on the Eucharist stating that "after the consecration of bread and wine, our Lord Jesus Christ, true God and true man, is truly, really and substantially contained in the august sacrament of the Holy Eucharist under the appearance of those sensible things." This does not contradict Christ's "natural mode of existing," which is in heaven, but in the Eucharist Christ is "sacramentally present to us in His own substance by a manner of existence which, though we can scarcely express in words, yet with our understanding illumined by faith, we can conceive and ought most firmly to believe is possible to God" (Matt. 19:26; Luke 18:27). Trent's chapter on transubstantiation states that "by the consecration of the bread and wine a change is brought about of the whole substance of the bread into the substance of the body of Christ our Lord, and of the whole substance of the wine into the substance of His blood."[29]

The Eucharist, then, became the major sacrament in the Roman Catholic church. By virtue of its "excellence" it is superior to all other sacraments, because the other sacraments have "the power of sanctifying when one uses them, while in the Eucharist there is the Author Himself of sanctity before it is used."[30] In the Eucharist it is God who is present in Jesus Christ.

The Lord's Supper in the Reformation

The streams of thought inherited from the early church and clarified in the Middle Ages form the context of Reformation teachings about the Lord's Supper. The symbolic stream—which may also be called *significationist,* since it stresses the elements in the supper as signs signifying the body and blood of Christ—was clarified by Berengar of Tours, Ratramnus, and Rabanus Maurus and stemmed from Augustine and Origen. The other stream, the realist, or *transformationist,* became dogma at the Fourth Lateran Council as the outgrowth of the views of Radbertus and theologians who began this approach in the early church.[31]

The views of Luther emerged from these currents and developed along two major fronts. Until 1524 Luther set his views on what happens in the Mass over against the teachings of Rome. In 1524 he engaged in controversies over the real presence of Christ in the Eucharist, and from then on he opposed the "Enthusiasts," who had no use for the Lord's Supper, and the Swiss Reformers—particularly Zwingli—who were advocates of an essentially symbolic view.

In Luther's *Babylonian Captivity of the Church* (1520) he claims the Roman Catholic church holds the Lord's Supper in a threefold captivity. First, it withholds the cup from the laity. Second, it teaches transubstantiation, which Luther says is a concept captive to Aristotelian metaphysics. And third, the church teaches that the Mass is "a good work and sacrifice." Against these and other views Luther developed his own.

Four stages can be identified in Luther's view of the Eucharist. The first (1518–22) stresses the sacrament as the sign of the benefits of the Word of God. The second (1523–24) sees in the sacrament the sign of the benefits given along with the Word. In the third stage (1524–25) Luther speaks of the supper as the vehicle through which the Word gives the benefits. In the fourth (1526–29) Luther emphasizes that the Eucharist is the vessel in which the Word gives the benefits.[32]

Stage 1. In Luther's 1518–22 writings he refers to the bread eaten and the wine drunk as *signs*. The significance or effect of the supper is the "fellowship of all the saints," and receiving the sacrament is a "sure sign of this fellowship and incorporation with Christ and all his saints." Here Luther stresses the aspect of *seeing*, for the supper shows believers they are in fellowship with each other and incorporated into the body of Christ.[33]

Luther goes on to emphasize a *hearing* dimension as well. This concerns the words of institution, which are joined with the elements and constitute the signs of God's promise. Luther emphasizes the spoken promise of forgiveness, which is Christ's "testament": "Everything depends . . . on the words of this sacrament. These are the words of Christ." For Luther "it is as if [the priest] were saying to us, 'Behold, this is the seal and sign of the testament in which Christ has bequeathed to us the remission of all sins and eternal life.'"[34]

In 1521 Luther expanded his concept of the Eucharist as a sign even more when he emphasized a *receiving* dimension. In the sacrament salvation is received, and the supper, including especially the body and blood of Christ, is given as a pledge of the promise made by Christ in his death. "Body and blood are given in order that we whose sins are forgiven may have salvation."[35]

Stage 2. From 1523–24 Luther's emphasis was on the Word of God in the words of institution, which produce the real presence of Christ in the supper. For Luther, then, the "body and blood" in the supper *are* the body and blood of Christ, and the Word "brings with it everything of which it speaks, namely, Christ with his flesh and blood and everything that he is and has." Through the words of institution, the bodily reality of the sign of the supper is made present. Luther writes, "For me it is enough to know that the Word which I hear and the body which I receive are truly the Word and body of my Lord and God."[36]

Stage 3. During 1524–25 Luther entered major eucharistic controversies with his colleague Andreas Carlstadt (d. 1541) and with the Swiss Reformers, especially Zwingli. These led him away from his emphasis on *sign*—since his opponents insisted that this is all a sacrament is—to a description of the supper as a vehicle of God's grace in communicating the real presence of Christ. In the supper the benefit of Christ's death as forgiveness is communicated through the bread and wine. "Christ has achieved it on the cross, it is true. But he has not distributed or given it on the cross. He has not won it in the Supper or Sacrament. There he has distributed or given it through the Word, as also in the gospel where it is preached."[37] The supper is the vehicle for divine comfort; it presents Christ's crucified body to those who believe.

Stage 4. From 1526–29 Luther emphasized the body and blood as the content of the sacrament in which forgiveness is "contained" and distributed. This note is captured in his *Large Catechism*, where he relates the words of institution to Christ's body:

> These and no other are the treasure through which forgiveness is obtained. This treasure is conveyed and communicated in nothing other than in the words, "given and poured out for you." For here you have both truths, that it is Christ's body and blood and that these are yours as your treasure and gift. Christ's body can never be an unfruitful, vain thing, impotent and useless. Yet however great the treasure may be in itself, it must be comprehended in the Word and offered to us through the Word, otherwise we could never know of it or seek it.[38]

In this description Luther equates the sacrament itself (the sign) with the gift, the forgiveness of sins. Forgiveness comes in and through the sacramental body of Christ made present by the words of institution.

Throughout these stages Luther became more and more concerned with the issue of the *real presence* of Christ in the supper. This meant for him that Christ is *bodily present* in the sacrament. As to the mode of this presence, Luther rejects the Roman Catholic view of transubstantiation and speaks instead of Christ's body and blood being present in the untransformed elements of bread and wine. For Luther there is an exact analogy with Christology. In confessing that "the Word became flesh" (John 1:14), the church proclaims that God became a human being. In the

Lord's Supper the church proclaims that God dwells "in" and "under" the elements of the bread and wine. "Thus," says Luther, "what is true in regard to Christ is also true in regard to the sacrament." The Christ who is communicated in the supper is the risen, ascended Lord, the "ubiquitous" Christ who is present in both his divine and human natures at all times everywhere.[39]

This view of the real and personal presence of Jesus Christ in the Lord's Supper marks the sharpest point of divergence between Luther and Zwingli. Luther's acceptance of a real presence in the sacrament is close to that of medieval theology—without the notion of transubstantiation.[40] But Zwingli, consistent with his understanding of the sacraments, forthrightly rejects this dimension of Luther. Zwingli's controversies with the Lutheran view began in 1525 and escalated through fierce disputes in 1527–28, which led to the Marburg Colloquy in 1529. During this time also, Zwingli was contending with Roman Catholic theologians, such as Cajetan (d. 1534) and Johann Eck (d. 1543).

Before Marburg, Zwingli had responded to Luther's views four times. The main idea he attacked was Luther's placing "the chief point of salvation in the bodily eating of the body of Christ," which Luther saw as strengthening faith and forgiving sins. Zwingli rejected Luther's views on the ground that it conflicts with the understanding and use of faith as well as with the testimony of Scripture.

For Zwingli faith means belief and trust in God and not—as Luther has it—a belief about the body of Christ in the bread. The Eucharist is just what its name implied, "the thanksgiving and common rejoicing of those who declare the death of Christ."[41] Zwingli declares that John 6 is the place to turn first in discussing the Eucharist, and he appeals to verses like John 6:63 and 3:6 to make a sharp contrast between mind and flesh. Like Erasmus he interprets Jesus' saying, "It is the spirit that gives life, the flesh is of no avail; the words that I have spoken to you are spirit and life" (John 6:63), to mean that the earthly, visible, and material world cannot be the bearer of the salvation that comes by God's Spirit. All of the material world—including spoken words and the elements in the Lord's Supper—point beyond themselves to a higher, salvation-bringing reality, which is the Spirit of God. "For body and spirit are such essentially different things," says Zwingli, "that whichever one you take it cannot be the other." When Jesus speaks of eating his flesh, this must be a metaphor for believing in Christ, since "he is a means of salvation to us not by being eaten, but by being slain."[42]

Zwingli interprets the words of institution, "this is my body," not literally, but as a metaphor. The word *is*, says Zwingli, means "signifies" here, as it does in many other parts of Scripture, such as when Christ says he is the door, the shepherd, or the way.[43] Zwingli's liturgy for the Lord's Supper includes the reading of John 6:47–63, but he maintains that whenever Jesus speaks of "eating his flesh and drinking his blood he simply means believing in the worth of that suffering which he bore for our sakes."[44] Zwingli interprets Augustine like this and says he meant that "when you partake of the two elements of bread and wine, all that you do is to confess publicly that you believe in the Lord Jesus Christ."[45] To put it another way, "eating is believing" (*edere est credere*).

Zwingli acknowledged Christ's spiritual presence at the supper in the heart, "in contemplation, faith, hope, and love alone." But Christ is not physically present in the Eucharist, for the bread and wine are only signs and not what the signs signify.[46] Zwingli also questioned Luther's Christology and his view of ubiquity—that Christ is present everywhere in both his human and divine natures at all times. Zwingli claimed the body of Christ can be in only one place at a time—namely, at the "right hand of God"—and not on earth in the bread and wine. If this were not so, Christ's human nature would be completely different from anyone else's, and this would contradict the gospel.

At Marburg in October 1529, Luther, Zwingli, and such supporters as Melanchthon, Oecolampadius, and Bucer produced an agreement on fourteen articles, modeled after Luther's formulas, on such issues as the Trinity, Christology, original sin, faith, and justification. The fifteenth article, on the Eucharist, had five points of agreement and one of disagreement over "whether the true body and blood of Christ are bodily in the bread and wine."

As the discussion began, Luther drew a circle with chalk on a table and wrote, "*Hoc est corpum meum*" (this is my body). Oecolampadius said this must be interpreted in a metaphorical sense, since the flesh profits nothing, and the body of Christ has ascended to heaven. Luther asked why the ascent into heaven should not be interpreted metaphorically too. Zwingli said that flesh and spirit are incompatible, and therefore the presence of Christ was only spiritual. Luther replied that flesh and spirit can be conjoined, and the spiritual does not exclude the physical. Therefore, "Christ is truly present, that is, substantively, essentially, though not quantitatively, qualitatively or locally." This was rejected by the Swiss as not clearly safeguarding the spiritual character of the Lord's Supper, for how, they asked, could something be present but not locally present? Luther said that geometrical conceptions could not be used to describe the presence of God. At the end Zwingli, with tears in his eyes, extended his hand to Luther, but Luther withheld his hand, saying, "You have a different spirit." This ended the colloquy, and future reunion efforts came to nothing.[47]

John Calvin's doctrine of the Lord's Supper is often seen as taking a "middle way" between the positions of Luther and Zwingli. In essence, Calvin remained closer to the Lutherans than to the Zwinglians, since he was convinced that both he and Luther had the same fundamental convictions and differed only on the mode of Christ's presence in the supper. Calvin accepted the revision of article 10 (on the Eucharist) of the Augsburg Confession (1530), prepared by Melanchthon and called the "Variata," which says, "With the bread and wine the body and blood of Christ are truly presented to those who eat the Lord's Supper." In this Calvin said he found "not a single word contrary to our doctrine" of the Lord's Supper.[48]

Calvin criticized Zwingli and his colleague Johann Oecolampadius for not emphasizing that although the bread and wine in the supper are signs, they are "the kind of signs with which reality" is joined. On the other hand, said Calvin, though Luther rejected transubstantiation, he still wrote as if he "intended to assert the sort of local presence that the papists dream about."[49]

Calvin emphasizes that the Lord's Supper was given by God through Jesus Christ to the church as a "spiritual banquet, wherein Christ attests himself to be the life-giving bread, upon which our souls feed unto true and blessed immortality."[50] The signs of the supper are the bread and wine, which "represent for us the invisible food that we receive from the flesh and blood of Christ." This food is continually supplied to us "to sustain and preserve us in that life into which he has begotten us by his Word." For Calvin "Christ is the only food of our soul" (*Inst.* IV.17.1). But since Christ's union with believers "is by nature incomprehensible," God "shows us its figure and image in visible signs best adapted to our small capacity. Indeed, by giving guarantees and tokens he makes it as certain for us as if we had seen it with our own eyes." Thus the Lord's Supper for Calvin is a gracious gift of God, in which God adapts "to our small capacity" in order to strengthen and nourish faith. When believers partake of the elements, "we may assuredly conclude that the power of his life-giving death will be efficacious in us." In this act God "renews, or rather continues, the covenant which he once for all ratified with his blood (as far as it pertains to the strengthening of our faith) whenever he proffers that sacred blood for us to taste" (IV.17.1).

Therefore, says Calvin, union with Christ is the special fruit of the Lord's Supper. Believers can "gather great assurance and delight from this Sacrament" and can assure themselves eternal life, the kingdom of God, and all the benefits of Christ (IV.17.2). Calvin speaks of the "wonderful exchange" Christ has made with us, which includes our iniquity for his righteousness (similar to Luther's description—see chap. 5, n. 66).

Calvin speaks of a true spiritual presence of Christ in the Lord's Supper. "We have such full witness of all these things that we must certainly consider them as if Christ here present were himself set before our eyes and touched by our hands" (IV.17.3). The "entire force" of the sacrament lies in these words: "which is given for you," "which is shed for you," says Calvin.

> From the physical things set forth in the Sacrament we are led by a sort of analogy to spiritual things. Thus, when bread is given as a symbol of Christ's body, we must at once grasp this comparison: as bread nourishes, sustains, and keeps the life of our body, so Christ's body is the only food to invigorate and enliven our soul. When we see wine set forth as a symbol of blood, we must reflect on the benefits which wine imparts to the body, and so realize that the same are spiritually imparted to us by Christ's blood. (ibid.)

These benefits are given to "nourish, refresh, strengthen, and gladden." For this purpose, "we shall clearly perceive that those qualities of bread and wine are, according to such an analogy, excellently adapted to express those things when they are communicated to us" (ibid.).

Calvin clearly rejects a literal reading of the words of institution and recognizes them as being figurative in force and pointing beyond themselves to the one who uttered them, Jesus Christ (see IV.17.22–23). Christ himself is the gift who is given in the supper, where there is a spiritual imparting of the benefits Christ has acquired. "The Lord Jesus is the content and the substance of the sacraments."[51] The bread and wine are "visible signs, which represent the body and the blood to us and to which the name and title of the body and blood is attributed."[52] They "represent" and even "present" the body and blood of Christ. Yet as signs they are not empty but have a "reality and efficacy joined" with them.[53] Calvin said:

> I indeed admit that the breaking of bread is a symbol; it is not the thing itself. But, having admitted this, we shall nevertheless duly infer that by the showing of the symbol the thing itself is also shown. For unless a man means to call God a deceiver, he would never dare assert that an empty symbol is set forth by him. Therefore, if the Lord truly represents the participation in his body through the breaking of bread, there ought not to be the least doubt that he truly presents and shows his body. And the godly ought by all means to keep this rule: whenever they see symbols appointed by the Lord, to think and be persuaded that the truth of the thing signified is surely present there. (IV.17.10)

Calvin does not equate the sacrament with the reality. "It is not, therefore, the chief function of the Sacrament simply and without higher consideration to extend to us the body of Christ. Rather, it is to seal and confirm that promise by which he testifies that his flesh is food indeed and his blood is drink [John 6:56], which feed us unto eternal life [John 6:55]" (IV.17.4). "To do this," says Calvin, "the Sacrament sends us to the cross of Christ, where that promise was indeed performed and in all respects fulfilled. For we do not eat Christ duly and unto salvation unless he is crucified, when in living experience we grasp the efficacy of his death" (ibid.).

The benefits of the supper according to Calvin are received by faith. He does not wish either to have "too little regard for the signs, divorce them from their mysteries, to which they are so to speak attached" nor did he wish to be "extolling them immoderately" (referring to Zwingli and the Lutheran theologians; IV.17.5). Against the Zwinglians Calvin writes, "For them to eat is only to believe; I say that we eat Christ's flesh in believing, because it is made ours by faith, and that this eating is the result and effect of faith." To put it more clearly, "For them eating is faith; for me it seems rather to follow from faith" (ibid.). Faith, which imparts the benefits of the supper, is a "true partaking" of Christ, so that "his life passes into us and is made ours—just as bread when taken as food imparts vigor to the body" (ibid.). By faith, says Calvin, "we embrace Christ not as appearing from afar but as joining himself to us that he may be our head, we his members" (IV.17.6).[54] Faith is given by the "secret power of the Holy Spirit" who "truly unites things separated in space" (IV.17.10). When faith is present by the Holy Spirit, the benefits of the supper are received. When faith is absent, however, all that is received is the empty sign; thus unbelievers "go away empty after outward participation in it" (IV.17.33).

Calvin goes on to reject the Roman Catholic theory of transubstantiation (IV.17.11–15), in which the "bread is made Christ, so that thereupon Christ lies hidden under the appearance of bread" (IV.17.13). While the Catholic theologians say that Christ "is so contained in the Sacrament that he remains in heaven," Calvin says, "we maintain no other presence than that of a relationship" (ibid.).

Calvin also rejects the Lutheran doctrine of the ubiquity of Christ's body as being narrowly literal and canceling the true corporeality of Christ (IV.17.16–31). The risen, ascended Christ is in heaven, according to Calvin: "Not Aristotle, but the Holy Spirit teaches that the body of Christ from the time of his resurrection was finite, and is contained in heaven even to the Last Day" (IV.17.26). Calvin claims the Lutheran view leaves "nothing to the secret working of the Spirit, which unites Christ himself to us. To them Christ does not seem present unless he comes down to us. As though, if he should lift us to himself, we should not just as much enjoy his presence! The question is therefore only of the manner, for they place Christ in the bread, while we do not think it lawful for us to drag him from heaven" (IV.17.31).

Calvin, then, stands over against Roman Catholic views on the one hand, the views of the Zwinglians on the other, and the views of the Lutherans in between.[55] He affirms the Augustinian view of the nature of a

sacrament and presses that definition in distinguishing between the outward elements and the inner spiritual realities. God's gracious gifts in the
supper are given through the signs and are sealed in the hearts of believers.
But the gifts are not to be confused with the instruments, or "signs,"
through which they are imparted. For Calvin there is a true presence of the
risen Christ who presents himself to those with faith and who by the work
of the Holy Spirit imparts the benefits and nourishment of salvation. "In his
Sacred Supper he bids me take, eat, and drink his body and blood under
the symbols of bread and wine. I do not doubt that he himself truly
presents them, and that I receive them" (IV.17.32; cf. 17.10). The manner of
Christ's presence in the supper is "spiritual because the secret power of the
Spirit is the bond of our union with Christ" (IV.17.33). Christ himself is "the
matter of the Supper; and the effect follows from the fact that by the
sacrifice of his death we are cleansed of sins, by his blood, we are washed,
and by his resurrection we are raised to the hope of heavenly life" (ibid.).

9

Eschatological Controversy

What Is the Kingdom?

The church has always recognized, though not often emphasized, a future dimension in the Lord's Supper. The Gospel accounts show Jesus looking to the future: "Truly, I say to you, I shall not drink again of the fruit of the vine until that day when I drink it new in the kingdom of God" (Mark 14:25; cf. Matt. 26:29; Luke 22:16, 18, 29–30). In Paul's account the Lord's Supper is a proclamation of the Lord's death "until he comes" (1 Cor. 11:26). The links between Eucharist and eschatology are very strong.[1]

Eschatology is also a dominant note in the proclamation of Jesus throughout his ministry. He inherited from Judaism a strong future orientation, especially from the prophetic and apocalyptic writings of the Old Testament. Jesus' teachings about the coming kingdom of God form the keystone of his preaching and teaching. Hence many New Testament writers and later the theologians of the church have offered their views of the divine and human dimensions involved in the "last things" and the coming kingdom of God.

Eschatology embraces a wide range of concepts derived from both the Old and New Testaments, including the second coming of Christ (Gr. *parousia*), the resurrection of the dead, the final judgment, and the end of the world. Related to these are more specific questions dealing with the biblical interpretation of the millennium or thousand-year reign of Christ (Rev. 20:4–6), the nature of the resurrection body (1 Cor. 15:35ff.), the "tribulation" period (Dan. 12:1; Mark 13:19; Rev. 7:14), Antichrist (2 Thess. 2:10; Rev. 13; 16:12–16; 17; 19:19–21), the battle of Armageddon (Rev. 16:16), hell, and eternal life.

Eschatological controversies have been numerous and protracted in the history of Christianity. Some church groups have come into existence solely because of their own eschatological understanding and their time table of specific future events. Of course, a final assessment of such views lies in the future!

One way to focus on eschatology, however, is to ask, What is the kingdom? This question is broad, but the answers show the important ways eschatology has been understood by church theologians. More specifically, we must ask, What is the relationship between the kingdom and the church—that is, How is the future related to life in the present? What is the relationship between salvation as future expectation and salvation as present reality?

In a sense this question brings together the doctrines considered in earlier chapters, for it concerns the work of the triune God in Jesus Christ for the salvation of humanity in the church, which is sustained by the authority of Scripture and nourished by the sacraments. The eschatological kingdom looks to the future for the culmination of the work of God begun in history and continued through history into the present day. Those conscious of God's will and work in history and in the church also look forward to the culmination and ultimate completion of God's work. In this way present and future are joined, and God's word is fulfilled.

Biblical Basis

The phrase *kingdom of God* is not used in the Old Testament, but the concept is found throughout, particularly in the writings of the prophets. It points basically to God's rule over God's people and especially to the glorious vindication of God's rule and people at the end of history.

God is described in the Old Testament as King both of Israel (Exod. 15:18; Num. 23:21; Deut. 33:5; Isa. 43:15) and of all the earth (2 Kings 19:15; Isa. 6:5; Jer. 46:18; Pss. 29:10; 99:1–4). God is King in the present and will also be King in the future (Isa. 24:23; 33:22; 52:7; Zeph. 3:15; Zech. 14:9ff.).

The prophets portray their vision of the form of the future kingdom in various ways. The prophetic hope of the Hebrew prophets looks for the kingdom to arise out of history and be ruled by a descendant of David here on earth (Isa. 9, 11). After the return from the Exile in Babylon, this hope of a kingdom to be established in history is replaced with a kingdom that will break into history. A heavenly "son of man" will establish a kingdom beyond history (Dan. 7). For the prophets the "day of the Lord" is a coming day of judgment on which all the nations of the world will be judged, including Israel (Amos 5:18–20; Zeph. 1:14–18). Beyond this day the prophets look for God to establish a new and glorious age marked by universal peace (*shālōm*) and harmony (Isa. 2:2–4; 22:6–9; Mic. 4:1–4). This prophetic hope is celebrated in apocalyptic literature (Joel; Isa. 24–27; Zech. 9–14), where God is seen as victorious over all powers of evil at the final consummation. The future salvation in the coming reign of God is marked by exquisite enjoyment of God's presence, great feasting, and rejoicing in the context of the abolition of death (Isa. 25:6–9).

In Jewish apocalyptic literature some writers emphasize the historical and earthly aspect of the kingdom (Enoch 1–36; Pss. of Sol. 17–18), while others look to his suprahistorical dimensions (Enoch 37–71). The focus, however, is always on the future. Sometimes the kingdom is seen as directly established by God with no mediator (As. Mos. 10:1), while at other times the kingdom is connected with the figure of a "messiah," or "anointed one" (Bar. 73). In Daniel the kingdom is given to the "saints of the Most High" (7:27) represented by "one like a son of man" (7:13), after the world empires that have dominated Israel since the Exile (represented by beasts) are taken away (7:18, 22, 25, 27). By the time of Jesus pious Jews prayed in the words of the Kaddish, "May he establish his kingdom during your life and during your days, and during the life of all the house of Israel" (cf. Mark 15:43; Luke 23:51; 2:25, 38).[2]

In the New Testament the kingdom of God (or "kingdom of heaven") is the central theme of the public proclamation of Jesus. His message is, "Repent, for the kingdom of heaven is at hand" (Matt. 4:17), and he goes through all Galilee preaching "the gospel of the kingdom" (4:23; 9:35; Luke 4:43; 8:1). In the Synoptic Gospels the phrase *kingdom of God* is used fourteen times in Mark, thirty-two in Luke, and four in Matthew; *kingdom of heaven* appears thirty-three times in Matthew.[3] In the summary of Jesus' ministry in the Gospel of Mark, Jesus says, "The time is fulfilled, and the kingdom of God is at hand; repent, and believe in the gospel" (Mark 1:15).

Basic to Jesus' kingdom teaching is the arrival of a new age and order. In this Jesus reflects the Old Testament picture of God as already King and as becoming King. The term *kingdom of God* (Gr. *basileia tou theou*; Heb. malkūth) and the synonymous *kingdom of heaven* refer to the reign of God that is established by God and not by human efforts.[4] The terminology that emerges in the Gospels is related to Jewish teachings about two ages, this age and the age to come. The present age is a time of sinfulness and rebellion against God. The coming age is the time of the perfect will and rule of God, when all sin, evil, and rebellion will be no more. The thrust of Jesus' teaching about the kingdom is that the rule of God will come fully in the future and that the new age has already dawned in the present with Jesus himself.

The tension between the present and the future dimensions of the kingdom of God is the tension between the "already" and the "not yet." The coming of the kingdom (Matt. 6:10), or its "appearing" (Luke 19:11), brings the old age to an end and inaugurates the new age. The kingdom means both God's reign and the realm of that reign, which includes the whole cosmos. The preaching of Jesus makes its clear that inheriting eternal life is the same as entering into the new age (Mark 10:17–31; cf. Dan. 12:2). When God's eschatological kingdom comes, the power of evil will be destroyed (Matt. 25:41), society will not be mixed with sin and evildoers (Matt. 13:36–43), a new fellowship with God will be established (Matt. 5:8; 25:21, 23), and eating and drinking in the messianic feast will be a reality (Luke 13:28–29; 14:16–24; 22:30; Matt. 8:11). The eschatological kingdom will feature God as ruler of all.

The new note in Jesus' kingdom teaching, beyond what was already common in Judaism, is the fulfillment of the Old Testament promise of the kingdom in his own life and ministry.[5] This is clear at the beginning of his ministry when he reads in the synagogue at Nazareth from Isaiah 61:1–2 and asserts, "Today this scripture has been fulfilled in your hearing" (Luke 4:21). Jesus cites the prophecy of Isa. 35:5–6 to reassure John the Baptist that in Jesus himself this prophecy is being fulfilled (Matt. 11:2–6). When he is accused of casting out demons by the power of Satan, Jesus claims that his power is from God and is proof that the kingdom of God has become a reality here and now (Matt. 12:28; cf. Luke 11:20). Jesus tells his audience that they themselves are witnessing what the people of old longed to see (Luke 10:23–24; Matt. 13:16–17). Jesus proclaims that the kingdom is in the midst of his contemporaries, yet in an unexpected form (Luke 17:20). The many kingdom parables of Jesus (Mark 4; Matt. 13) portray facets of the "secret of the kingdom" (Mark 4:11). Many of these parables concern growth. As an image, growth captures the two dimensions of the kingdom in Jesus' teachings, since there is both the anticipated consummation and present activity. The kingdom is likened to the act of sowing in the parables of the Seed Growing Secretly (Mark 4:26–29) and the Tares (Matt. 13:24–30); it is also like mustard seed and leaven (Luke 13:18–21). The kingdom is present in Jesus and his ministry, but its final consummation is still to come.

Jesus himself cannot predict when the future consummation would take place (Mark 13:32). In the Synoptic Gospels there are three different types of sayings about the time of the coming kingdom. One group stresses the imminence of the kingdom; for example, Jesus says to his disciples embarking on a preaching mission, "You will not have gone through all the towns of Israel, before the Son of man comes" (Matt. 10:23). Other sayings include Mark 9:1; 13:30; Matthew 16:28; Luke 9:27. A second group shows the delay of the kingdom. Here parables such as the Ten Maidens (Matt.

25:1–13) and the Talents (Matt. 25:14–30) sound a note of waiting for the kingdom (cf. Luke 17:22; 19:11). Third, there are Synoptic texts that point to the uncertain time of the coming of the kingdom. Jesus says that neither he nor anyone, except the Father, knows "when the time will come" (Mark 13:32–33). This theme is repeated when Jesus commands his followers to "watch, therefore, for you do not know on what day your Lord is coming" (Matt. 24:42; cf. 24:30, 44; 25:13; Luke 12:40).

The rest of the New Testament, reflecting the early church's preaching, uses the term *kingdom of God* relatively rarely. The book of Acts records several conversations about the kingdom (1:3; 1:6; 8:12) and reports that Paul in Ephesus "spoke boldly, arguing and pleading about the kingdom of God" (19:8; cf. 20:25), which is portrayed as a future kingdom (14:22).

The double reality of the *already-but-not-yet* is found in Paul's writings, where he speaks of the life to be lived by those in the community under the rule of God (Rom. 14:17; 1 Cor. 4:20) as well as of the vices that bar entrance to the kingdom (1 Cor. 6:9–10; Gal. 5:21; Eph. 5:5). The kingdom to come is one of glory (1 Thess. 2:12) and is also called the kingdom of Christ (Eph. 5:5; 1 Cor. 15:24–28; Col. 1:13).

The Johannine writings use *eternal life* as a synonym for the kingdom of God (see John 5:24, 1 John 3:14; 5:12); the two are linked, however, by Jesus in his conversation with Nicodemus (John 3:3, 5). Jesus is called the "King" (John 1:49; 6:15; 12:13, 15; 18:33, 37, 39; 19:3, 12) and says, "My kingship is not from the world" (18:36). The book of Revelation looks forward to the consummation and the coming glory: "The kingdom of the world has become the kingdom of our Lord and of his Christ, and he shall reign for ever and ever" (Rev. 11:15; cf. 1:9; 12:10).

Early Eschatology

The Millennial Kingdom

The eschatology of the early theologians regarding the kingdom of God is marked by the development of *chiliasm*, a term that refers to the thousand-year reign of Christ (Rev. 20:1–10) connected with his second coming, the resurrection of the dead, and the final judgment. Very early Papias (d. 130) connected this thousand-year reign with an earthly rule of Christ. The historian Eusebius records that Papias believed on the basis of an "unwritten tradition" that "there will be a millennium following the resurrection of the dead, when the kingdom of Christ is to be established physically on this earth."[6] Papias uses the "thousand" image to speak of the coming days when "vines will be produced, each one having a thousand branches, and in each branch ten thousand twigs, and on each twig ten thousand shoots, and on each shoot ten thousand clusters, and in each cluster ten thousand grapes, and each grape when pressed will give twenty-five metretes of wine."[7] In speaking of the transformation of the cosmos and the animals, Irenaeus quotes Papias on this point.

Other early writings describe the end of the world as near. The *Epistle of Barnabas* proposes that since there were six days of creation, God will work in history six thousand years till the end comes, for "with the Lord one day is as a thousand years, and a thousand years as one day" (2 Peter 3:8). The universe, says Barnabas, must last for six thousand years, most of which has past. Then will follow the return of Christ to renew the world and the righteous while judging the wicked during a seventh millennium, which corresponds to God's rest on the seventh day of creation, the şabbath. The "eighth day" begins another world. Yet none of the early writers tried to establish a precise date for Christ's return.[8]

The millennial picture in the early church stands alongside other descriptions of Christ's reign that do not map out a timetable to the kingdom. Justin Martyr believed Christ will return to Jerusalem, where he will begin a thousand-year reign; the city will be rebuilt and enlarged, and Christians and Old Testament saints will share perfect happiness with Christ. But Justin acknowledged that there were other pious and orthodox Christians who did not share such a view.[9]

Irenaeus's eschatology focuses on refuting the scheme of salvation and the future propounded by the Gnostics. Believing that matter is naturally evil and the flesh cannot be part of salvation, the Gnostics argued that the resurrection must be purely spiritual. Irenaeus counters by citing the resurrection of Christ and the indwelling of the Spirit in our bodies as well as in the Eucharist, in which the body and blood of Christ nourishes our physical flesh. He defends chiliasm against the Gnostics and holds that the end will come when Satan in the form of "Antichrist" has "recapitulated" all sins since the fall and "tyrannically attempts to prove himself God."[10] Then Christ will appear. The six thousand years of the world will be followed by the first resurrection and the "seventh day, which is sanctified, in which God rested from all his works which he made." This, says Irenaeus, is "the true Sabbath of the just, in which they will have no earthly work to do, but will have a table prepared before them by God, who will feed them with dainties of all kinds."[11]

Tertullian also furthers millenarian hope. "A kingdom has been promised to us on earth, but before [we attain] heaven: but in another state than this, as being after the [first] resurrection. This will last for a thousand years, in a city of God's making, Jerusalem sent down from heaven." In the thousand-year kingdom "the saints will rise sooner or later, according to their degrees of merit, and then when the resurrection of the saints is completed, the destruction of the world and the conflagration of judgment will be effected; we shall be 'changed in a moment' into the angelic substance, by the 'putting on of incorruption' [1 Cor. 15:52–53], and we shall be transferred to the celestial kingdom."[12] In other places, however, Tertullian leans to a more figurative interpretation, for example, when he speaks of the new Jerusalem as signifying Christ's flesh. He also focuses the kingdom in a direct, christological way: "In the gospel Christ Himself is the kingdom of God."[13]

Millenarianism is also defended by Hippolytus (d. 236) in his *Commentary on Daniel* and *Antichrist*. Yet he argues that since the prophecies of Daniel have not yet been fulfilled, the end of the world is not imminent. Hippolytus spiritualizes his interpretation of Revelation 20:2–5: against Irenaeus he says the thousand years is not the literal length of the kingdom, but is used as a symbolic term indicating the kingdom's greatness and splendor.[14]

This tendency toward a figurative reading of the thousand years is prominent in Origen's eschatology. He examines the millenarianists' exegesis of promises related to the kingdom of Christ and concludes that their interpretations are "unworthy of the divine promises." To interpret these passages "in accordance with the understanding of the apostles," he says, leads to the conclusion that it is not the body but the soul that receives these promises. Therefore, the promised kingdom will be a purely spiritual one. The kingdom of God is interpreted by Origen as the apprehending of divine truth and spiritual reality, as the indwelling of the Logos, or as "the spiritual doctrine of the ensouled Logos imparted through Jesus Christ."[15] Most clearly, Origen says that the kingdom of God is *autobasileia*, a "self-kingdom"–that is, Jesus Christ himself.[16]

In Cyprian's writings there are frequent references to the coming end and strong expressions of a desire to escape from the present world. The resurrection is a central facet of faith, from which a reward for good works will follow. God "declares that they shall be permitted to see the kingdom who have performed works in his church."[17] The sufferings of the present age, and especially the persecutions under the rule of the Antichrist (Nero) are contrasted with the joys of the millennial kingdom. Therefore, the kingdom is primarily in the future and a long distance away from the visible church of the present world.

The Kingdom in Augustine

Augustine united both streams of millennial interpretation, the literal and the figurative, but ultimately decided against a literal view. Initially Augustine held that the kingdom is the result and goal of the church's development,[18] but later he claimed that the thousand-year period when Satan is bound, according to Revelation 20, is not a future millennium but the present age. It is the time of the history of the church. Between the resurrection and the last judgment, the church "militant," the church on earth, "even now is the Kingdom of Christ and the kingdom of heaven."[19] The church "triumphant" (the saints already dead) now reigns with Christ but not in the way it will in the future. At the last day the righteous and the wicked will be separated for blessedness or eternal punishment.[20]

Augustine's view coincides with his overall position on history and eschatology. In his *City of God*, written in twenty-two books over a thirteen-year period (413–26), Augustine develops the view that running through history are two cities, the city of God and the city of the world, or the city of the devil. These two cities are actually two great loyalties that are inextricably mixed in the world throughout history yet will ultimately be separated at the last judgment. In one city God is served; in the other the devil is obeyed.

The difference is the object of one's love. Scripture enjoins love, says Augustine, which is the affection of the mind that aims at the enjoyment of God for God's own sake. Scripture condemns desire, which is the affection of the mind aimed at enjoying one's own self without reference to God.

> The two cities were created by two kinds of love: the earthly city was created by self-love reaching the point of contempt for God, the Heavenly City by the love of God carried as far as contempt of self. In fact, the earthly city glories in itself, the Heavenly City glories in the Lord [2 Cor. 10:17]. The former looks for glory from men, the latter finds its highest glory in God, the witness of a good conscience. The earthly lifts up its head in its own glory, the Heavenly City says to its God: "My glory; you lift up my head" [Ps. 3:3]. In the former, the lust for domination lords it over its princes as over the nations it subjugates; in the other both those put in authority and those subject to them serve one another in love, the rulers by their counsel, the subjects by obedience. The one city loves its own strength shown in its powerful leaders; the other says to its God, "I will love you, my Lord, my strength" [Ps. 18:1].[21]

Therefore, "in one city love of God has been given first place, in the other, love of self."[22]

For Augustine the two cities represent the elect and the non-elect. These two cities are "interwoven, as it were, in this present transitory world, and mingled with one another"; there may be those in the city of the world who will become citizens of the heavenly city, and among those of the heavenly city there may be some who share the sacraments but, nevertheless, will not share the "eternal destiny of the saints."[23] Thus one cannot make a hasty decision about who is in which city.

Yet while the two cities represent a distillation of Augustine's anthropology, ecclesiology, and views of God's eternal election and judgment in the coming kingdom, only rarely does he identify the city of God with the universal Christian church. At times he speaks of "the City of God, that is, God's Church,"[24] but since the two cities are two "loves," they are ultimately inward and spiritual conditions that cannot be completely identified with outward or political distinctions.

The Kingdom after Augustine

Through the centuries the kingdom concept continued to have appeal, and millennial impulses did not die. Near the year 1000 chiliastic fever was especially strong, since many believed in the view of Augustine and others that a millennium would occur between Christ's first coming and his *parousia*. Joachim of Fiore (c. 1135–1202)—a Cistercian monk from Calabria, Italy, who founded a society of hermits—teaches in his commentary on Revelation that a new third age will soon appear. He sees history as periods of revelation during which the three persons of the Trinity are revealed. The period of the Father was marked by law and fear. The time of the Son, up to the year 1260, was a period of grace and faith. The third period will be dominated by love and the Spirit. Later followers appropriated Joachim's threefold schema and "eternal gospel," with overtones that ranged from criticism of the church to completely secular applications.[25]

Nevertheless, Augustine's view of the kingdom, as seen in the images of the two cities, had immense influence. Eusebius of Caesarea (d. 340), in his church history, had interpreted the victory of the church during the reign of Constantine as the beginning of the millennium.[26] The subsequent growth of the papacy and the identification of the church with the kingdom, which developed out of Augustine's two cities, became a powerful theological tool for the medieval church as it asserted its own position in history. This was especially true in relation to the state. Pope Gregory the Great (d. 604) asserts, "The present church is called the kingdom of heaven—for the congregation of the saints is said to be the kingdom of heaven."[27] To accomplish its work the church (kingdom) can enlist the aid of the state, even if it is unchristian, says Gregory. "The holy church, because she is not sufficient in her own strength, seeks the assistance of that rhinoceros." The city of earth must then submit to the city of God. By the time of Pope Gregory VII (Hildebrand, 1073–85), the city of God had absolute dominion over the city of the world. In his *Dictations of the Pope* Gregory claims that the pope as "vicar of Christ" has the power to depose emperors who do not act righteously. Thus the kingdom that was eschatological and other-worldly also became highly political and this-worldly.[28]

Reformation Eschatology

Luther

Martin Luther had a strong sense of the nearness of the last day. In 1530 he wrote that he was afraid God's kingdom would come before he finished translating the Scriptures: "The world runs and hastens so diligently to its end that it often occurs to me forcibly that the last day will break before we can completely turn the Holy Scriptures into German."[29] He went so far in 1541 and again in 1545 to calculate that since A.D. 1540 was 5,500 years after creation, there was still 500 years to go before the eternal sabbath. Since God had promised, however, to shorten the time for the sake of the elect, and since Christ did not stay three full days and nights in the grave, the day of the church's resurrection might indeed be hastened. There might be no more than one hundred years left till Christ's return.[30]

Luther's concept of the kingdom of God (and its related description as the kingdom of Christ) stands in contrast to what he variously describes as the kingdom of the world or the kingdom of earth, Caesar, works, etc.[31] Luther's doctrine of the two kingdoms is related to Augustine's two cities. Luther emphasizes the personal and social dimensions of the struggles between the two cities, which are seen in the spiritual authority of the church and the priest vis-à-vis the temporal authority of the state and the prince.

For Luther the two kingdoms are intermingled and move back and forth with each other. The two realms must be distinguished, though not ultimately separated. Luther sees this as part of his preaching task.

> I must always drum and hammer and force and drive in this distinction between the two kingdoms, even if it is written and spoken so often that it becomes tiresome. For the Devil himself never ceases cooking and brewing up the two kingdoms together. The secular authorities always seek, in the name of the Devil, to teach and instruct Christ how he should conduct his Church and his spiritual rule. Similarly, the false priests and sectaries, not in the name of God, always seek to teach and instruct people how they should conduct secular rule. Thus the Devil is unrestrained on either side and has much to do. May God defend us from him, amen, if we are worthy of it.[32]

For Luther the two kingdoms are two overlapping aspects of the one invisible reign of God. The kingdom of God has two mutually dependent forms in this world.

> There are two kinds of regiment in the world, as there are also two kinds of people, the believing and the unbelieving. Christians yield themselves to the control of God's Word; they have no need of civil government for their own sake. But the unchristian portion require another government, even the civil sword, since they will not be controlled by the Word of God. Yet if

all were Christians and followed the Gospel, there would be no more necessity or use for the civil sword and the exercising of authority; for if there were no evil doers there certainly would be no punishment. But since it is not to be expected that all of us should be righteous, Christ has ordained magistracy for the wicked, that they may rule as they must be ruled. But the righteous He keeps for Himself, and rules them by His Word.[33]

This means both of the kingdoms concern humanity's relations with God, who is Creator and Redeemer. In the spiritual realm the relationship with God is direct; in the secular realm it is indirect. "It is the Kingdom of God's left hand," says Luther, "where God rules through father, mother, Kaiser, king, judge, and even hangman, but His proper Kingdom, the Kingdom of His right hand, is where God rules Himself, where He is immediately present and His Gospel is preached."[34] Both kingdoms can be confounded either when the spiritual kingdom is subordinate to the worldly (as among the Turks) or when the worldly kingdom is subordinate to the spiritual (as in the papacy).[35] God encounters the world in two ways: in the gospel and in the law, in which the evil consequences of sin are checked in society. Since the Christian is "both righteous and a sinner" (*simul justus et peccator*), the Christian needs both forms of rule.[36] The outward realm is also under Christ ultimately, and thus princes and rulers of this world must listen to the word of God's kingdom proclaimed in the gospel. Christ's kingdom is inward and spiritual and hence has no right to seek to dominate the corporeal realm or assert authority. That would confound the kingdoms again. Hence the two kingdoms are distinct for Luther, yet they are involved with each other and should not be separated. They are differentiated yet unified under the all-encompassing kingdom of God.[37]

Calvin

The eschatology of John Calvin is biblically grounded and takes human history very seriously. It stresses the great acts of God in history and supremely in Jesus Christ; the church witnesses to these acts and responds in obedience and joy. Through the victory of Christ the church participates in the kingdom—though the church itself is not the kingdom—and thus receives assurance of final victory. Yet the church works in history under tribulations and sorrows. Because of Christ's victory the Christian can both "meditate on the future life" and be actively involved on earth in extending the kingdom.[38]

For Calvin the turning point of history is the coming of Jesus Christ. The kingdom of God has two great "eschatological moments." These are the beginning and the completion of salvation. Christ is the one through whom salvation is begun, and it is accomplished in his death and resurrection.[39] The kingdom of Christ for Calvin has two senses: (1) "the teaching of the Gospel by which Christ gathers the Church to Himself, and by which He governs it when it has been gathered," and (2) "the actual fellowship of the godly (*societas piorum*), who, having been united among themselves by the sincere faith of the Gospel, are truly regarded as the people of Christ (*populus Christi*)."[40]

In one sense this means the kingdom of Christ is already complete. By his death, resurrection, and ascension Christ has won the victory over sin and death and rules the world from the right hand of God.[41] All else in history must be seen in relation to that "renovation of the world which took place at the advent of Christ." Yet in a second sense the world has not yet arrived at the victory that is won. The renewing of all things is still in the process of being completed.[42] In his victory and through the Holy Spirit, Christ has called out the church to be the people of God and to live by faith in union with him. Through this union of Christ and the church, the people of God actually and continually participate in the new humanity of the resurrection and in the kingdom of God through Christ. Those gathered in the church (the elect) reach forward to the "society of divine glory" in history. The church grows and increases on earth until the final coming of Christ. The fullness of the kingdom is "delayed," according to Calvin, "to the final coming of Christ when, as Paul teaches, 'God will be all in all'" (1 Cor. 15:28).[43]

Calvin sees the time between the beginning of salvation and its completion in terms of two ages, the old world and the new world. Since these two ages overlap,[44] Calvin rejects the idea of a literal millennial kingdom. This belief taught that Christ would reign outwardly for a limited time on an earth that is not yet renewed. For Calvin the perfected kingdom is already a reality in Christ. It is eternal and includes within it the renovation of the world. When Christ returns, this can mean only God's final revelation of the perfected kingdom. Calvin calls the teaching of chiliasts, "who limited the reign of Christ to a thousand years," a "fiction" that is "too childish either to need or to be worth a refutation." The number one thousand (Rev. 20:4) "does not apply to the eternal blessedness of church, while still toiling on earth." Prophecies are intended to evoke hope and patience. They are not intended to give specific time tables and dates for divine occurrences.[45]

Since the two ages overlap and the last days have already come in the resurrection of Christ and the gift of the Holy Spirit to the church, then the "last day" can be looked for every hour.[46] In commenting on the phrase "he has appeared once for all at the end of the age" (Heb. 9:26), Calvin relates this to the "fulness of time" of which Paul speaks in Galatians 4:4 (KJV): "Paul declares in 1 Cor. 10:11 that the ends of the ages are come upon us, by which he means that the kingdom of Christ has brought fulfillment to everything."[47] The church now looks to the future consummation with hope. "Not that the glory and majesty of Christ's Kingdom will only appear at His final coming, but that the completion (*complementum*) is delayed till that point—the completion of those things that started at the resurrection, of which God gave His people only a taste, to lead them further along on the road of hope and patience."[48] While Calvin can say that "the Kingdom of God increases, stage upon stage, to the end of the world," he does not believe in a gradual, evolutionary growth of the kingdom of God through the structures of the present world.[49] The kingdom is not ours to win; it's God's to give. The Christian church and Christians themselves live "between the times" in a life of discipleship. The present reign of God is found where people both by denial of themselves and by contempt of the world and of earthly life, pledge themselves to God's righteousness in order to aspire to a heavenly life.[50]

Later Developments

The question What is the kingdom? has continued to be important for the church. Luther and Calvin defended their views against others— particularly the *Schwärmer* (enthusiasts), the Anabaptists, and the chiliasts—on a variety of eschatological issues. In post-Reformation times, especially in England, millenarianism in a variety of forms was prominent throughout the sixteenth and seventeenth centuries.[51] Attempts to predict when the kingdom of God would come, or even to force its coming, have occurred regularly through the centuries.

How the kingdom of God has been conceived since the period of the Enlightenment is summarized by the twentieth-century theologian Karl Barth (1886–1968). Barth saw the Enlightenment view of the kingdom as a "brotherhood" or community Jesus intentionally founded, which became international in outreach with the purpose of establishing a harmony between morality and nature. Immanuel Kant (1724–1804), says Barth, saw the kingdom of God as a world where rational beings dedicate themselves completely to the moral law and where the world is ordered by this law. In J. G. Herder (1744–1803) the kingdom was the elevation of the whole race to its true humanity in accord with the law of nature, which is the power, goodness, and wisdom of God. Friedrich Schleiermacher (1768–1834) saw the kingdom as the fulfillment of the moral life, which rises from the redemption effected in Jesus. This represents human nature at its highest as each person's will acts in accord with this nature. Richard Rothe (1799– 1867) envisioned the kingdom as the fellowship of redemption, initially established by the church but then growing into a merger of sacred and profane that leads to fulfillment in the life of the state. Albrecht Ritschl (1822–89) saw the kingdom as coming through joint human activity where a fellowship of love works towards God's ultimate goal for humanity and the world.[52]

Barth himself, in his exposition of the petition "Thy kingdom come" in the Lord's Prayer, says, "The kingdom of God defies expression. It is real only as God himself comes as King and Lord, establishes righteousness in our relationship to him and to one another, and thus creates peace on earth."[53] Barth's emphasis on God as the one who comes and establishes the kingdom is a key emphasis in his theology as a whole. This he sees as setting his views of the kingdom over against the emphases prominent from the Enlightenment onwards and expressed especially in the theologies of Schleiermacher, Ritschl, and, in Barth's day, Adolf von Harnack (1851–1930). In Barth's view they emphasize a basic continuity of the human with the divine and thus stress human achievement and potential.[54]

For Barth, however, the kingdom of God "escapes all intellectual systematizing." While humans "can and may attempt many things," they "cannot bring in the kingdom of God." The kingdom is to be sought above all else (Matt. 6:33; 13:45), but like the treasure hid in the field (Matt. 13:44), the kingdom is "there even before it is sought or found by anybody." The kingdom is "God's own action, which does not merge into the best of human action," either that of the Christian faith or that of the Christian church. It does "not mingle with it let alone identify itself with it." The kingdom remains "free and independent" and "in its purity and freedom is God's gracious, reconciling, and finally redeeming action." As such, says Barth, the kingdom is to be

> gratefully, joyfully, and humbly affirmed in Christian faith and boldly and strongly proclaimed by the Christian church, but without being equated with either the work of faith or that of the church. Conversely, then, it is not a divine work for whose commencement, continuation, and completion some human cooperation has to be considered and postulated and which could have no standing or being without the assistance of certain people. It is God's work alone, which as it is revealed to them can be known by people in faith, gratefully hailed and extolled by them, and then attested and proclaimed, but which cannot in any circumstances be made their own operation or promoted, augmented, or perhaps improved by their action.[55]

In this emphasis Barth sees himself "parting company with an imposing ecclesiastical consensus." He cites theologians including Origen, Chrysostom, Augustine, Luther, and Calvin, whom he believes "constantly suppressed the point that the kingdom of God is a unique entity or factor not only in relation to the world but also in relation to the Christian world." The issue here for Barth is the need to stress the kingdom as Jesus Christ himself. For "the proclamation of the kingdom of God by Jesus . . . is not the proclamation of a reality and truth differing from himself as its Proclaimer, from his being and life."[56] The difference between Barth and Calvin is summarized in Barth's interpretation of "Thy kingdom come":

> What is to be asked for, according to Calvin, is God's gradual seizure of power and final triumph *within* this history, in the changing of bad persons into good, the glory of the people, and the removal of the opposition of some definitively bad persons. The second petition, however, looks to a mighty act that limits and determines from outside the whole of human history with its brighter and darker elements, its advances, halts, and setbacks. It looks to an unequivocal act of the grace of God, to the mystery of the kingdom of God which encounters all that history and limits it in its totality as its hope.[57]

For Barth the kingdom of God is Jesus Christ. The reign of God is Jesus Christ, and the key to all understandings of the kingdom is to recognize that "Jesus is Victor!"[58]

10

Theological Turning Points Today

A lot of theology has come and gone through the centuries. The previous chapters have dealt with some of it, but by no means all. Each of the controversies has gone through further phases with many proposals that have often set theological issues on new footings. The following brief discussion indicates for each of the doctrines some of the major trends in contemporary theology and the areas where significant turning points are occurring today.

Who Is God Today?

The doctrine of the Trinity has recently received major attention. Karl Barth examines it in his *Church Dogmatics* (I/1). He argues that this doctrine must be the presupposition with which all biblical teachings about God are read. Instead of three "persons" Barth speaks of three "modes of being" in order to guard against what he considers the dangers of tritheism, the belief in three Gods.

Jürgen Moltmann has rooted the doctrine of the Trinity in the relationships between Father, Son, and Holy Spirit. He begins with the "threeness" of God as God is experienced in the world and particularly in the cross of Jesus Christ. Moltmann sees his approach as having very practical and political implications, for the God of the Bible is a God who suffers and who stands over against all forms of domination—political, sexual, and ecclesiastical.[1]

Contemporary discussions of the Trinity often center on the meaning of the word *person*. Instead of this term, however, Karl Rahner speaks of a "distinct manner of subsisting": the Trinity may be understood as Father, Son, and Spirit, each subsisting in a different and distinct manner. For Rahner the members of the Trinity should not be considered separate persons, since "in God there is only one essence, hence one absolute self-presence."[2]

Process philosophers and theologians such as Alfred North Whitehead and John Cobb have spoken of God as evolving along with the world in a process of "becoming." For Whitehead God is the one "actual reality" who acts with the world and leads it into what it can be in the future. God thus gives a unity and direction to the world's evolution. God is very personal, but not tripersonal. God is "social" and related to creatures by bonds of love and sympathy.[3]

Some feminist theologians have written of the need to "resymbolize" God and to find ways of speaking of a "feminine dimension of the divine." Not all of them agree on the nature of this task nor the extent to which it should be carried out in relation to traditional theological formulations about the Trinity. But they have put new emphasis on biblical and theological images of God that are directly related to feminist experience.[4]

These turning points raise serious issues regarding the social nature of the Trinity, the community of the divine persons, the question of divine "suffering," and the relationship of God to the world and to both men and women in it. In all, they continue to probe the mystery in the question Who is God today?

Who Is Jesus Christ Today?

Christology has also been a prominent theological focus in recent years. Some theologians have criticized traditional orthodox teaching concerning the two natures of Christ. As with the doctrine of the Trinity, some have claimed that traditional teachings have been too heavily influenced by Greek philosophy and have too firmly absolutized the place of Jesus in relation to other world religions. As one critic puts it, "The eternal God, and an historical man, are two beings of quite different ontological status. It is simply unintelligible to declare them identical." The Christ of the Gospels is not one who embodies God but one "who with the whole of his passionate nature witnesses *to* God."[5]

There are a number of different ways of speaking about Jesus Christ on the current theological scene. One writer has grouped these around various "models" of Jesus: the incarnation of the second person of the Trinity, the mythological Christ, the ethical liberator, the human face of God, the man for others, and personal Savior.[6] Process and feminist theologians have also been active in writing about Christology.[7]

Another way to view contemporary Christology is through the distinctive emphases of major writers. Wolfhart Pannenberg stresses the idea of universal history and tries to integrate God's revelation in Jesus into God's revelation in history and within the history of other religions without losing its distinctiveness.[8] Schubert Ogden has proposed an existential Christology in which "the only meaning that the event Jesus Christ has is a purely existential meaning," so that to believe in and understand Jesus is to understand oneself authentically.[9] John Hick speaks of the "myth of the incarnation" and prefers dynamic language rather than language about "substance" or "essence."[10] When John A. T. Robinson speaks of the "provisional Christ," he agrees with Hick that in the life of Jesus there was "not divine substance injected into a human frame, but divine action taking place in and through a human life," so that the "incarnation" is a mythic expression of the Christian's attitude toward God.[11] For Hans Küng it is the Jesus of history who matters, since he served as God's "representative" and acts as the universal norm for humanity's relationship with God, neighbors, and society.[12] Karl Rahner has popularized the term *anonymous Christianity* to describe persons who are related to Christ, who has acted on their behalf and has thus become related to them, though they are presently unaware of it.[13]

Insofar as it is critical of traditional Christology, contemporary Christology tends to be a "Christology from below." It emphasizes the humanity of Jesus and describes Christ's divinity in light of it. The issues surrounding current-day Christology are many; theological language, history, biblical criticism, and much more are involved in wrestling with the question Who is Jesus Christ today?

What Is the Church Today?

The twentieth century has been marked ecclesiologically by the ecumenical movement. More attention has been paid to the nature of the church in these years than at any other time. Sweeping social changes as well as renewed theological reflection have brought the issue of the nature of the church into the spotlight. The World Council of Churches, formed in 1948 as "a fellowship of churches which accept our Lord Jesus Christ as God and Saviour," has sought to be an instrument for church unity, both inward and outward.[14] In the Roman Catholic church, the Second Vatican Council (1962–65) opened new doors to ecumenical cooperation and broke new ground with its pronouncements in the "Dogmatic Constitution on the

Church," the "Pastoral Constitution on the Church in the Modern World," and the "Decree on Ecumenism."

A number of significant discussions of ecclesiology have emerged during the past years. These works deal in various ways with the fundamental aspects of ecclesiology that were set in motion by the Scriptures and have received concrete expression in writings and controversies throughout the history of the church.[15] What has emerged strongly in these works by both Roman Catholic and Protestant writers is that the nature of the church cannot be separated from the mission of the church, and vice versa. The church expresses what it is by what it does, and what the church does emerges naturally and directly from what it is. This note was struck by Dietrich Bonhoeffer, writing in a Nazi prison camp: "The Church is the Church only when it exists for others."[16]

Other Protestant theologians who have significantly contributed to answering the question What is the church today? include Karl Barth and Paul Tillich. Barth stresses that the church's existence stems from the divine act of God's revelation as the Word in Jesus Christ. The church is the true church only insofar as Jesus Christ, its risen Lord, is present and acting in and through its members.[17] This happens when the Holy Spirit creates in history the one, holy, catholic, and apostolic church, which is a servant community of Jesus Christ existing for the world. Tillich refers to the church as the "spiritual community" that is based on "the appearance of the New Being in Jesus as the Christ." The church is both a spiritual reality as the body of Christ and a social reality in history.[18] It is constituted by faith and love, which are always related to the source of the spiritual community's existence, the original revelation of Jesus as the Christ.

Two years after the end of Vatican II, Hans Küng published his major work, The Church. Küng sees Vatican II as having achieved "a powerful breakthrough in terms of freedom, openness and flexibility on behalf of the Catholic Church. . . . A fresh era was opening out, heralding new relationships between the Catholic Church and other Christian Churches, new attitudes to Judaism and the other world religions—in fact a new approach to the world in general."[19] What followed then is Küng's own treatment of the doctrine of the church in terms of its nature, marks (dimensions: one, catholic, holy, and apostolic), and structures (offices). Küng constantly stressed that the church should be defined primarily as "the people of God" rather than as an outward institution that is heavily clericalized, private and exclusive, hypostasized, and idealized.[20]

In these writers and many others, issues about the nature of the church, its unity, its mission, and function in society take place. All of these discussions look back to the basics of ecclesiology considered above, as the people of God struggle with the question What is the church today?

What Is Humanity Today?

More than any other of the theological turning points, the question What is humanity? attracts the attention of people both inside and outside the church. This ancient issue lives on in contemporary writing and engages opinions from people in numerous field committed to all types of ideologies. This means that biblical portrayals of humanity have been judged by an array of critics and in certain dimensions have been both accepted and rejected.

In particular, the twin issues of sin and freedom of the will, which occupied the attention of early church and Reformation theologians, continue to be foci of discussion in many quarters. Christian theologians of the eighteenth and nineteenth centuries often rejected the Augustinian theology that was elaborated by seventeenth-century Calvinism and clarified most fully at the Synod of Dort (1618–19) in the controversy between Calvinism and Arminianism.

In addition, the impulses of the eighteenth-century Enlightenment were toward a stress on human autonomy and the powers of the human mind. In many ways these run counter to the emphases of the Augustinian tradition on sin and free will. Of course, other major issues also emerged in the relationship of Christianity to the philosophies of Descartes (1596–1650), Locke (1632–1704), Hume (1711–76), and Kant (1704–84). Insofar as their pictures of humanity were later developed by other philosophers such as Nietzsche (1844–1900) and Sartre (1905–80), the stress is on human autonomy and freedom as opposed to sin and dependence on God.[21]

Some Christian theologians have heavily stressed the place of sin in their portrayals of humanity. Karl Barth, Paul Tillich, and Reinhold Niebuhr have in various ways defined and redefined what sin is and how it accords with the phenomenon of humanity as it appears in the contemporary world. Reinhold Niebuhr, for example, was reportedly fond of quoting the *London Times*, which once said, "Original Sin is the most empirical of all Christian doctrines."[22] The dialogue with modern philosophers about the nature of humanity is taken up by John Macquarrie, who is influenced by existentialism and draws most frequently from Nietzsche, Kierkegaard, Marx, and Sartre. For Macquarrie "creative freedom is at the very heart of our humanity," and this freedom is a "presupposition of the moral life." In support of his views, Macquarrie turns to the works of Irenaeus and early Eastern theologians for the meaning of the image of God and the expectation of an "ever new enhancement of being" and potentiality for humanity.[23] Wolfhart Pannenberg thoroughly engages contemporary thought, especially psychology and sociology, in his works on anthropology. He starts with their insights as the way to begin a contemporary portrait of humanity. For Pannenberg the image of God in humans is their "closeness to the divine reality," while sin is the "factual separation from God." This means that the image of God is expressed as an "openness to the world which is lost when humans turn from their true identities (sin) and attempt to gain control over all things."[24]

Thus the complicated issues surrounding sin, freedom, the image of God, and human communities are all raised by this topic. Further turning points will doubtless arise as theologians turn to the Scriptures Christian tradition, and current understandings to come to grips with the question What is humanity today?

What Is Salvation Today?

Many contemporary ecumenical discussions between Roman Catholics and Protestants have highlighted ways in which the two churches can speak more clearly of the points of convergence in their traditions. For example, in the dialogues held between Lutherans and Roman Catholics, an extensive "Common Statement" was issued, which included many places where the two traditions found common ground. Cited as a most helpful affirmation for the discussions was the mutually agreeable statement, "Our entire hope of justification and salvation rests on Christ Jesus and on the gospel whereby the good news of God's merciful action in Christ is made known; we do not place our ultimate trust in anything other than God's promise and saving work in Christ."[25] The Common Statement recognizes that the two churches did not come to full agreement on justification by faith, but it also raises the question "whether the remaining differences on this doctrine need be church-dividing."

Contemporary theology recognizes that the issue of salvation includes many biblical and theological images that are variously stressed by theologians and movements. Thus on the issue of salvation there are numerous theological options today. Karl Barth's doctrine of salvation stresses the objective work of God in Christ in providing reconciliation for the whole world. In Tillich's thought salvation means healing, or becoming whole, and is the overcoming of the gulf between God and humanity through the reuniting of that which was estranged—namely, humanity—from its *ground of being*, which is God. For Pannenberg the goal of salvation is the restoration of community, the reintegration of individuals into the community, the removal of alienation, the 'purification' of conscience." Thereby "individuals recover their identity through reintegration into the community; they recover a freedom which they neither possess nor can exercise for themselves in isolation, but which they possess only as recognized members of the shared world."[26] In liberation theology salvation occurs through the struggle for liberation in political and economic life in the cause of establishing justice.[27] Process theology, with its emphasis on creative evolution within nature, sees salvation as the continuing realization of a higher degree of harmony and integration toward the ideals of the great masters of religion (such as Jesus, Buddha, and Plato).[28] Many feminist theologians see salvation as "the affirmation and promotion of the full humanity of women" which leads to "wholeness and well-being," integration with nature, and "participation in the restoration of wholeness, peace, and justice in the world."[29]

The multiple descriptions of salvation in contemporary theology are intimately related to the specific theological systems under consideration. Their accounts of salvation are also bound up with their perceptions of humanity, sin, the character of God, the nature of Jesus, and other theological issues. In the area of soteriology a host of assumptions and presuppositions are thus implied. All of this means that there are many different answers to the question What is salvation today?

Where Is Authority Today?

The question of authority has been an important one for theologians and churches of all persuasions. The divisive issue of Scripture and tradition, which was crucial in the Reformation debates, is still present, though it now takes different forms. In general Roman Catholicism has tended in recent years to turn more to Scripture in its scholarship, while Protestantism has noted more clearly the complexities of interpreting Scripture and thus the complications involved in speaking of *sola Scriptura*. As one observer put it, "Catholics see tradition as deeply rooted in Scripture and as an on-going interpretation of Scripture, but no longer treat tradition as a source for theology equal to Scripture. Protestants have recognized the legitimacy of tradition; they have become more sensitive to the intellectual heritage of the Church prior to the Reformation."[30]

In Roman Catholicism Vatican II addressed the question in its "Constitution on Divine Revelation." It rejects the two-source view of Scripture and tradition, which holds that each contains a certain portion of divine revelation, in favor of a view that sees them as a unified whole. Tradition (instead of *traditions*, as in Trent) is seen as a living and dynamic process that is constantly changing and developing. It is a handing on of the Word of God, which is present in both Scripture and tradition. Thus "both Scripture and Tradition must be accepted and honored with equal feelings of devotion and reverence."[31]

In Protestantism theologians like David Kelsey argue that Scripture and tradition should not be seen as competing authorities. There is an awareness that the Scriptures arose out of communities of faith that felt free on occasion to use older materials in new ways and to engage in the ongoing interpretation of "the will of God as that is illumined in a new time by earlier traditions."[32]

One issue related to authority has been the nature of the Bible. In particular, debates have raged over various ways of saying what the Bible is. These have centered at some points around the terms *infallibility* and *inerrancy*.[33] These words have implications for describing the nature of the inspiration of Scripture and appropriate means for interpreting it. Thus *hermeneutics*, or the rules for interpreting Scripture, is also a prime concern in the ongoing work of theologians.[34]

Since the issue of authority is an underlying and crucial concept, controversies over authority will continue. These debates will range over a number of points and have far-reaching implications. They have affected and will continue to affect how churches understand their lives and ministries in terms of church government and structures. The various church polities of today are examples of the exercise of authority through structure, whether hierarchical, presbyterial, or congregational. But turning points will also be made where theologians find the sources of their authority for doing theology itself. In that sense, perhaps the most important question for this time and every time is Where is authority today?

What Are the Sacraments Today?

A number of important developments have occurred in sacramental theology, especially in the Roman Catholic church in recent decades. Vatican II opened doors to liturgical renewal within Catholicism, and the sacraments were areas of focus. The council called for a complete reexamination of the church's liturgy and an updating of its sacramental practices. As a result of this and also a renaissance in biblical studies within the Roman church, there have been major reinterpretations of the religious significance of the sacraments within Catholicism by many of the church's leading theologians.

In the context of a Catholicism that has tended to define the sacraments as *causes* rather than *signs* of grace, the Dutch theologian Edward Schillebeeckx suggests that the sacraments focus on Jesus Christ, who is the one, true sacrament, and that in Jesus the mystery of God is encountered. In the church's seven sacraments Christ is himself a sacrament of God for humanity. By highlighting this personal dimension Schillebeeckx attempts to translate the ideas of traditional scholastic sacramental theology into contemporary terms.[35] Karl Rahner does the same thing but speaks of sacraments as symbolic actions of the church. These actions symbolize the new embodiment of the community in terms of what it is and what it is becoming. The meaning of the sacraments transcends the persons who participate in them; they are a means by which people may acknowledge, experience, and incorporate grace into their lives.[36] Alexandre Ganoczy has proposed a "communications theory" of the sacraments in which he understands them as "systems of verbal and non-verbal communication through which those individuals who are called to Christian faith enter into the communicative process of the ever concrete faith-community, participate in it, and in this way, borne up by the self-communication of God in Christ, progress on the path of personal development." The sacraments are thus "events of encounter between grace and the faith of individual members of a concrete faith-community in their personal and particularly oriented individuality."[37]

Protestant theologians likewise have tried to articulate the meaning of the sacraments for the present day. Ecumenical dialogues have been held with Roman Catholics to see if some agreement could be reached. Protestants have also held conversations among themselves about the sacraments and the enduring legacies of the Protestant tradition. Recently the World Council of Churches sponsored discussions on the sacraments and produced the document "Baptism, Eucharist and Ministry." In many churches an era of sacramental renewal has arrived.

At the same time some segments of Protestantism have been influenced by Karl Barth's treatment of the sacraments. Barth looks to the Reformers and finds himself closest to Zwingli's views about the nature of sacraments and the fundamental meaning of baptism and the Lord's Supper. He grew into this understanding from an earlier period of his life when his views were closer to Calvin's. In the final stages of working on his *Church Dogmatics*, Barth came to the position that the sacraments should be seen as vehicles, not of God's action, but of human actions. The sacraments are a witness and sign of the one sacrament, or means of grace, namely, Jesus Christ. Participation is the human acknowledgement of who Jesus is and a response in faith to him.[38]

Since the sacraments are so central to the life and worship of the church, they will draw attention from a variety of theologians. The contemporary concern to show the meaning of the sacraments for church members indicates creativity in theology. As this is expressed, further dialogue among the churches can take place, as they all consider What are the sacraments today?

What Is the Kingdom Today?

Jürgen Moltmann's *Theology of Hope* has helped establish an important theological viewpoint since its publication in 1964 (Eng. trans. 1967). Moltmann argues that the biblical theme of hope is a primary doctrine of Christianity, and thus Christianity is thoroughly eschatological in nature. With the resurrection of Christ as a "history-making event," all other history is enlightened, questioned, and transformed. In the cross and resurrection the future kingdom of God is promised, and this promise is the pull toward the future. The world can be transformed by this hope, which can mold it for good or ill. Thus Christian eschatology is not confined to the "last things" but possesses a revolutionary power that pervades all phases of the Christian life. The church works for the kingdom, according to Moltmann, through "the realization of the eschatological *hope of justice*, the *humanizing* of man, the *socializing* of humanity, *peace* for all creation."[39]

The future as a key theological category is also employed by Pannenberg. The future is present (proleptically) in Jesus Christ, who as God's revelation gives meaning to history and is the "final measure of all subsequent history."[40] God's lordship in Christ has not yet fully been revealed; it will only be revealed at the end of time. But this end of history gives present history its drive and meaning, since the end has already appeared in Jesus Christ. God is thus the "power of the future," and "God in his very being is the future of the world." The church is "an eschatological community pioneering the future of all mankind."[41]

Process theology with its "emerging" views of God and the world has also had much to say about the future. In process thought God is, as Charles Hartshorne put it, "perpetually growing in content by virtue of additions from the world, each addition being strictly permanent, once for all."[42] Humans are co-creators with God, who with them is evolving into the new possibilities of the future. Each moment is a new creation and thus is pregnant with possibilities as humans progress together with God into a more unified and harmonious coming day. The kingdom and the church are both in the process of evolving.[43]

Liberation theologies of various kinds also deal with the eschatological message of Scripture. Influenced by theologies of hope and revolution, many liberationists apply the eschatological symbols of the Bible to present situations and thus seek a historical transformation of the conditions of life here and now.[44]

Eschatological thought has been renewed in the twentieth century through a variety of theological paths. Some thinkers still carry on the traditional debates over eschatology, including the issues of millennialism, life after death, and judgment. Others, however, have more directly related the "last things" to the "present things" and find eschatology to be the driving force behind their various social and ethical objectives for society. Thus the issues are still open, and the mysteries still many, surrounding the question What is the kingdom today?

Turning Points Today

Christian theology has come a long way, zigging and zagging from its earliest days through many expressions of faith. The path has not always been smooth or straight. Through theological debate and dialogue new forms of expression arise and new answers are given to old questions. Yet new answers inevitably raise new questions, and so it goes.

The Christian church and Christian theology can only turn new corners, however, when critical and sustained attention is given to all the issues raised by adherents. While the main figures in the history of theology are often considered "superstars," theology at its best is done through the open participation of people in all arenas and cultures, so that what results can resonate with truth and touch the lives of people in many contexts. As theology today becomes open to more and more people with varying accents and experiences, the tapestry of Christianity can be increasingly enriched. New contexts, methods, issues, and conclusions will come. New turning points will arise, and from these new resources the continuing history of Christian doctrine will emerge.

Abbreviations

AIB   Jack B. Rogers and Donald K. McKim. *The Authority and Interpretation of the Bible: An Historical Approach*. San Francisco: Harper & Row, 1979.

CC   Richard A. Norris, Jr. *The Christological Controversy*. Philadelphia: Fortress, 1980.

CCT   Aloys Grillmeier. *Christ in the Christian Tradition*, translated by John Bowden, 2d ed. Atlanta: John Knox, 1975.

CD   Karl Barth. *Church Dogmatics*, translated by G. W. Bromiley et al. Edinburgh: T. & T. Clark, 1936–75.

Creeds J. N. D. Kelly. *Early Christian Creeds*, 3d ed. London: Longman, 1972.

CT   *The Christian Tradition: A History of the Development of Doctrine*, edited by Jaroslav Pelikan, 4 vols. Chicago: Univ. of Chicago Press, 1971–84.

Doct.   J. N. D. Kelly. *Early Christian Doctrines*, rev. ed. San Francisco: Harper & Row, 1978.

Early   *The Early Christian Fathers*, edited and translated by Henry Bettenson. London: Oxford, 1969.

ECF   *Early Christian Fathers*, edited and translated by Cyril C. Richardson. New York: Macmillan, 1970.

FPEC   Carl A. Volz. *Faith and Practice in the Early Church*. Minneaplis: Augsburg, 1983.

HCT   One of the following works:
        Justo González. *A History of Christian Thought*, 3 vols. Nashville: Abingdon, 1970.
        Otto W. Heick. *A History of Christian Thought*, 2 vols. Philadelphia: Fortress, 1965.

IDB   *The Interpreter's Dictionary of the Bible*, edited by G. A. Buttrick, 4 vols. Nashville: Abingdon, 1962. Supplement (*IDB* Sup.), 1976.

Inst.   John Calvin. *Institutes of the Christian Religion*, translated by Ford Lewis Battles. Philadelphia: Westminster, 1960.

ISBE   *International Standard Bible Encyclopedia*, edited by G. W. Bromiley, 3 vols. Grand Rapids: Eerdmans, 1979–86.

Later   *The Later Christian Fathers,* edited and translated by Henry Bettenson. London: Oxford, 1970.

LCC   *Library of Christian Classics*

LW   Martin Luther. *Luther's Works,* edited by Jaroslav Pelikan and Helmut Lehmann. Philadelphia: Fortress; St. Louis: Concordia, 1955–.

NPNF   *Nicene and Post-Nicene Fathers*

POHT   Herman Ridderbos. *Paul: An Outline of His Theology,* translated by John Richard De Witt. Grand Rapids: Eerdmans, 1975.

Rise   W. H. C. Frend. *The Rise of Christianity.* Philadelphia: Fortress, 1984.

SHCD   Bernhard Lohse. *A Short History of Christian Doctrine from the First Century to the Present,* translated by F. Ernest Stoeffler. Philadelphia: Fortress, 1966.

ST   Thomas Aquinas. *Summa Theologica.*

Story   Justo González. *The Story of Christianity,* 2 vols. San Francisco: Harper & Row, 1984.

TDNT   *Theological Dictionary of the New Testament,* edited by G. Kittel and G. Friedrich, translated by G. W. Bromiley, 10 vols. Grand Rapids: Eerdmans, 1964–76.

THD   Reinhold Seeberg. *A Text-Book of the History of Doctrines,* translated by Charles E. Hay, 2 vols. 1952; rpt. Grand Rapids: Baker, 1966.

TSP   D. E. H. Whiteley. *The Theology of St. Paul.* Philadelphia: Fortress, 1964.

WA   Martin Luther. *Werke,* Weimarer Ausgabe (Weimar edition). Weimar: Bohlau, 1883–.

Notes

INTRODUCTION

1. See Peter Toon, *The Development of Doctrine in the Church* (Grand Rapids: Eerdmans, 1979), xiii.
2. See Jaroslav Pelikan, *Historical Theology: Continuity and Change in Christian Doctrine* (New York: Corpus, 1971), 4ff.
3. Toon, *Development*, 68.
4. Toon notes that the Westminster Confession of Faith, which represents the Reformed faith to which Orr adhered, does not exactly follow the sequence Orr outlined (ibid., 69–70).
5. More recent mini-histories of doctrine include the following. Carl Volz (*FPEC*) traces the doctrines of God, humanity, salvation, worship and sacraments, authority, and church and society through the early church period only. In *A Short History of Christian Thought* (New York: Oxford Univ. Press, 1986) Linwood Urban treats scriptural sources, the Trinity, incarnation, atonement, the fall and original sin, natural theology, authority, and revelation; he does not deal with the church, sacraments, Christian ethics, and life after death. M. Eugene Osterhaven has covered many topics, primarily through the Reformation period, in *The Faith of the Church: A Reformed Perspective on Its Historical Development* (Grand Rapids: Eerdmans, 1982). William C. Placher's *History of Christian Theology: An Introduction* (Philadelphia: Westminster, 1983) takes a historical approach by time periods.
6. My chapter on authority does not deal with the historical development of the doctrine of Scripture, on which I have written in Rogers and McKim, *AIB*.

CHAPTER 1

1. On Paul's theology see Ridderbos, *POHT*; Whiteley, *TSP*; Günther Bornkamm, *Paul*, trans. D. M. G. Stalker (New York: Harper & Row, 1971). Cf. 1 Peter 1:2; Jude 20.
2. See Justin, *I Apology* (32.8; 5.4; 46; 59; 63; 64.5); *II Apology* (8.1; 10.1; 10.2; 6.3). Cf.

Kelly, *Doct.*, 96; Edmund J. Fortman, *The Triune God* (1972; rpt. Grand Rapids: Baker, 1982), 44–50; William G. Rusch, ed., *The Trinitarian Controversy* (Philadelphia: Fortress, 1980), 3–6; González, *HCT* 1, chap. 4.

3. See *I Apol.* 6.32; *Dialogue with Trypho*, 63; *I Apol.* 14, 32, 60; Christopher Kaiser, *The Doctrine of God* (Westchester, Ill.: Crossway, 1982), 56.

4. See Tatian, *Dial.* 7,1 in Kelly, *Doct.*, 98–99.

5. See Theophilus of Antioch, *To Autolycus* 2,10 as in Kelly, *Doct.*, 99.

6. Ibid., 2, 15.

7. See Justin, *I Apol.* 61.3–12; Athenagoras, *Supplication for the Christians* 24, 6; Kelly, *Doct.*, 101–4.

8. See Irenaeus, *Against Heresies* 2.1.1; 2.30.9; Rusch, *Controversy*, 6–7; Kelly, *Doct.*, 104–8; Fortman, *Triune God*, 101–7; González, *HCT* 1, chap. 6.

9. See *Ag. Her.* 4.20.2ff.; 5.1; 3.6.1; 5.12.1; *Demonstration of the Apostolic Preaching* 47, in Kelly, *Doct.*, 107.

10. On Monarchianism see Rusch, *Controversy*, 8–9; Kelly, *Doct.*, 115–23.

11. Tertullian, *Apol.* 21.12–13 in Kaiser, *Doctrine of God*, 64. Cf. Fortman, *Triune God*, 107–15.

12. On Tertullian's use of *persona* see Kelly, *Doct.*, 114–15; Rusch, *Controversy*, 10.

13. On Origen see González, *HCT* 1:210–33. For the effects of Platonism on his biblical interpretation, see Rogers and McKim, *AIB*, 11–16.

14. See *Comm. on John* 2.2.16; 2.10.75; *On First Principles* 1.2.4; *Against Celsus* 2.64. Cf. Kelly, *Doct.*, 128.

15. *Principles* 1.2.6.; *Discussion with Heraclites* 3.

16. See *Frag. on the Letter to the Hebrews* 24.359 in Fortman, *Triune God*, 55. Cf. Kelly, *Doct.*, 130ff.

17. See *Comm. on John* 2.6. Rusch notes that "originally *hypostasis* and *ousia* were synonyms, the former Stoic and the latter Platonic, meaning real existence or essence. Although *hypostasis* has this original sense in Origen, it is often used in the sense of individual subsistence" (*Controversy*, 14).

18. *Against Celsus* 5.39; *Comm. on John* 6.39.202. Cf. *On Prayer* 15.1–16.1. See Kelly, *Doct.*, 128.

19. On the Arian controversy see González, *HCT* 1, chap. 11; Frend, *Rise*, 492–97; and below, chap. 2.

20. See Athanasius's *Orations against the Arians* 1.5, 6, and Arius's letters in Rusch, *Controversy*. Cf. Kelly, *Doct.*, 226–31; Lohse, *SHCD*, 48–50.

21. See Alexander of Alexandria's *Letter to Alexander of Thessalonica* in Rusch, *Controversy*, chap. 4.

22. See Jack Rogers et al., *Case Studies in Christ and Salvation* (Philadelphia: Westminster, 1977), 22.

23. From Rusch, *Controversy*, 49. On Nicaea see Frend, *Rise*, 498–501; Lohse, *SHCD*, 50–55; Kelly, *Creeds*, 211ff.; Philip Hughes, *The Church in Crisis: The Twenty Great Councils* (London: Burns & Oates, 1961), chap. 1.

24. *Dial. c. Lucif.* 19, in Kelly, *Doct.*, 238.

25. See Frend, *Rise*, 635–39; Hughes, *Church in Crisis*, chap. 2.

26. This work (cited as *Ar.*) is in Rusch, *Controversy*, chap. 10. On Athanasius's theology see González, *HCT* 1, chap. 13.

27. *Ar.* 3.15. Cf. Kelly, *Doct.*, 240ff.

28. *Ar.* 1.14 in Rusch, *Controversy*, 77.

29. See *Ar.* 2.36; 3.66–67; 1.9; Kelly, *Doct.*, 244.

30. Athanasius wrote his *Letters to Serapion* against this group from Egypt who

interpreted certain biblical texts as "tropes" or figures of speech. See Kaiser, *Doctrine of God*, 60; *Letters to Serapion* 1.17; 1.10; 1.2; 1.21, as well as Kelly, *Doct.*, 255ff.

31. *Letters to Serapion* 1.14, in Kelly, *Doct.*, 258.
32. On the Cappadocians see Fortman, *Triune God*, 75–83; Kelly, *Doct.*, 258ff.; González, *HCT* 1, chap. 14.
33. Gregory of Nazanzius, *Orations* 39.11.
34. This creed omits the Nicene phrases "of the substance of the Father" and "God from God" as an explanation of *homoousios*. It says, "true God from true God, begotten not made, of one substance with the Father." It also did not explicitly name the Holy Spirit as "God," as did the later "Athanasian Creed" (c. 430–500). See Fortman, *Triune God*, 158–61; Kelly, *The Athanasian Creed* (London: A. C. Black, 1964).
35. These emphases are drawn from Kelly, *Doct.*, 271ff.
36. See Augustine, *On the Trinity* 5.9; 8.1; 6.9.
37. See Kelly, *Creeds*, 358–67; Dietrich Ritschl, "Historical Development and Implications of the Filioque Controversy," *Interegini Parietis Septum (Eph. 2:14)*, ed. Dikran Y. Hadidian (Pittsburgh: Pickwick, 1981), 285–308.
38. *On the Trinity* 11.1.
39. See *On the Trinity* 9.2–8, 17–19; 14.15–20; Fortman, *Triune God*, 148–49.

CHAPTER 2

1. See Oscar Cullmann, *The Christology of the New Testament*, rev. ed. trans. Shirley C. Guthrie and Charles A. M. Hall (Philadelphia: Westminster, 1963); Edward Schweizer, *Jesus*, trans. David E. Green (Atlanta: John Knox, 1971); Günther Bornkamm, *Jesus of Nazareth*, trans. Irene and Fraser McLuskey (New York: Harper & Row, 1965).
2. See Reginald H. Fuller, *The Foundations of New Testament Christology* (London: Collins, 1965), 204–27; George E. Ladd, *A Theology of the New Testament* (Grand Rapids: Eerdmans, 1974); *TDNT*; Grillmeier, *CCT*, 17ff.; *ISBE* 3:781–801.
3. See Ridderbos, *POHT*, 86ff.; Whiteley, *TSP*, 99–123; Schweizer, *Jesus*, 73ff.; Ladd, *Theology*, 415–17. Cf. other non-Pauline passages such as James 1:1; 2:1; 1 Peter 1:3; 3:15; 2 Peter 1:2; 8; Jude 4, 17, 21, 25; Heb. 7:14; Rev. 17:14; 19:16.
4. On the Ebionites see Grillmeier, *CCT*, 76ff.; Lohse, *SHCD*, 73–74; Kelly, *Doct.*, 139ff.
5. *De res.* 2, in Kelly, *Doct.*, 141. Cf. Grillmeier, *CCT*, 78–79; Lohse, *SHCD*, 74.
6. See *Ep. to the Trallians* 10; *Ep. to the Smyrneans* 2; *Gospel of Peter* 4, 11 in Kelly, *Doct.*, 141.
7. On Gnosticism see Kelly, *Doct.*, 142; Grillmeier, *CCT*, 79–84 and passim; *ISBE* 2:484–90; *IDB*, 2:404–6; *IDB* Sup., 364–68.
8. See Justin Martyr, *Dialogue with Trypho* 87.2; *I Apology* 46.5; 10.1; Kelly, *Doct.*, 145; Norris, *CC*, 6.
9. *I Apol.* 66.2; 71.2. See *II Apol.* 10.1; Grillmeier, *CCT*, 93.
10. See Melito, "A Homily on the Passover," 8: 9–10 in Norris, *CC*, chap. 2. Cf. Grillmeier, *CCT*, 96.
11. See *Ag. Her.* 3.16.8; 4.6.7; 5.14.2–3; Kelly, *Doct.*, 147–48.
12. See *Ag. Her.* 5.1, where Irenaeus writes of Christ "bringing God down to human beings through the Spirit and, conversely, bringing humanity up to God by his own incarnation" (Norris, *CC*, 58; cf. p. 10; Grillmeier, *CCT*, 101).

13. *Ag. Her.* 3.16.6 in Kelly, *Doct.*, 172. Cf. Norris, *CC*, 12, 47. On Tertullian see Kelly, *Doct.*, 150ff.; Grillmeier, *CCT*, 117ff.; Lohse, *SHCD*, 77–78; Norris, *CC*, 12–14.
14. Origen, *On First Principles* 2.6.2 in Kelly, *Doct.*, 154–55. Cf. Grillmeier, *CCT*, 138ff.
15. On this period see Grillmeier, *CCT*, 167–218.
16. Arius, *Thaleia.* See Athanasius, *On the Synods of Ariminum and Seleucia* 15, in Grillmeier, *CCT*, 224.
17. Athanasius, *Orations Against the Arians* (cited as *Ar.*) 1.6. See Kelly, *Doct.*, 228.
18. *Ar.* 1.6. See Kelly, *Doct.*, 229.
19. See Philip Hughes, *The Church in Crisis: The Twenty Great Councils* (London: Burns & Oates, 1961), chaps. 2, 4.
20. *Ar.* 3.30, in Norris, *CC*, 88. Cf. Kelly, *Doct.*, 284ff.; Grillmeier, *CCT*, 308–28; Norris, *CC*, 18–21.
21. *Ar.* 2.8; *On the Incarnation of the Logos of God* 17; 8; 9; 10; cf. 4; 16; 54. For Athanasius, to "become" flesh means that "the Logos *is* man." See Grillmeier, *CCT*, 327. Cf. *Epist. to Epictetus* 8 in Kelly, *Doct.*, 285.
22. *Ar.* 3.55, 31 (in Norris, *CC*, 89).
23. See Grillmeier, *CCT*, 329ff.; Kelly, *Doct.*, 289ff.; Lohse, *SHCD*, 80–84; Norris, *CC*, 21–23.
24. In Lohse, *SHCD*, 82.
25. *Fragment* 2, in Kelly, *Doct.*, 292. Cf. Grillmeier, *CCT*, 333ff.
26. Gregory of Nazianzus, *Orations* 38.13. See Kelly, *Doct.*, 297.
27. See *Epist.* 101.4; Kelly, *Doct.*, 297; Grillmeier, *CCT*, 369.
28. On the two schools see Lohse, *SHCD*, 84ff.; Norris, *CC*, 23–26; Grillmeier, *CCT*, 417ff.; Kelly, *Doct.*, 301ff.; R. V. Sellers, *Two Ancient Christologies* (1940; rpt. London: SPCK, 1954). On their differences in biblical interpretation, see Rogers and McKim, *AIB*, 11ff.
29. See *On the Incarnation* 15 and *Cathechetical Homilies* 8, 13 in Kelly, *Doct.*, 304–5.
30. *Cathechetical Homilies* 8, 14.
31. In Kelly, *Doct.*, 306. Cf. Grillmeier, *CCT*, 433ff.
32. *On the Incarnation* 8. Cf. Norris, *CC*, 120. On Theodore see also Richard A. Norris, Jr., *Manhood and Christ: A Study in the Christology of Theodore of Mopsuestia* (Oxford: Clarendon, 1963).
33. See Norris, *CC*, 26, as well as Lohse, *SHCD*, 87ff.; Grillmeier, *CCT*, 451ff.; Kelly, *Doct.*, 310ff.
34. See his "First Sermon" in Norris, *CC*, 130.
35. In Kelly, *Doct.*, 314.
36. Norris speaks of Cyril's "Christological monism" (*CC*, 28). On Cyril see also Lohse, *SHCD*, 88ff.; Grillmeier, *CCT*, 473–83; Kelly, *Doct.*, 317–23.
37. In Kelly, *Doct.*, 319. Cf. Grillmeier, *CCT*, 480ff.
38. Cyril of Alexandria, *Anathema* 12. See Kelly, *Doct.*, 322; Volz, *FPEC*, 32.
39. See Norris, *CC*, 131–35. On the Council of Ephesus see Grillmeier, *CCT*, 484–87; Hughes, *Church in Crisis*, chap. 3; Frend, *Rise*, 758–61.
40. On Eutyches see Kelly, *Doct.*, 330–34; Grillmeier, *CCT*, 523–26; Frend, *Rise*, 764–66.
41. These are drawn from Kelly, *Doct.*, 337. The quotations are from Norris, *CC*, 148–51. Cf. Grillmeier, *CCT*, 526–39; Frend, *Rise*, 766–70; Norris, *CC*, 29–31, 145–55.
42. Leo, *Sermon* 27.1, in Kelly, *Doct.*, 338.
43. See Grillmeier, *CCT*, 543–50. Cf. Kelly, *Doct.*, 338–43; Hughes, *Church in Crisis*,

chap. 4; Frend, *Rise*, 770–73; R. V. Sellers, *The Council of Chalcedon* (London: SPCK, 1953).
44. In Norris, *CC*, 159.
45. The definition uses *hypostasis* and *prosopon* to express the concept of "person" and *physis* for "nature."
46. See Hughes, *Church in Crisis*, 117. The major emphases of the conciliar decisions on Christology can be summarized as follows:

325	Nicaea	Christ is divine
381	Constantinople	Christ is human
431	Ephesus	Christ is one person
451	Chalcedon	Christ is two in nature

CHAPTER 3

1. See *TDNT* 3:504. The term is not found in Mark, Luke, John, 2 Timothy, Titus, 1 Peter, 2 Peter, 1 John, 2 John, or Jude. Cf. ibid., 517 for parallel expressions for *ekklēsia*.
2. The Septuagint translation is almost always from *qāhāl*. This term can also be rendered by the Greek *synagogē* (synagogue). See Hans Schwarz, *The Christian Church* (Minneapolis: Augsburg, 1982), 20; *TDNT* 3:527ff.; Eric G. Jay, *The Church: Its Changing Image through Twenty Centuries* (Atlanta: John Knox, 1980), 5ff.
3. See Paul Minear, *Images of the Church in the New Testament* (Philadelphia: Westminster, 1960); *IDB* 1:609–15.
4. See Ignatius of Antioch, *Smyrnaeans* 8.2.
5. *The Martyrdom of Polycarp* 8.1. See Jay, *The Church*, 29; Kelly, *Doct.*, 189.
6. Shepherd of Hermas, *Similitudes* 9.17.
7. Justin Martyr, *Dialogue with Trypho* 63.5.
8. *Epistle of Barnabas* 3.6; 5.7; Aristides, *Apology* 2. See Kelly, *Doct.*, 190; Clement of Alexandria, *Stromata* 6, 5, 41.
9. *Epistle to Diognetus* 5. See Jay, *The Church*, 41.
10. See *Ag. Her.* 1.10.1; Jay, *The Church*, 44.
11. *Ag. Her.* 4.33.7; 3.24.1; 5.20.2.
12. Ibid., 3.3.1. Cf. Jay, *The Church*, 45.
13. See *Apology* 39.1; Kelly, *Doct.*, 200.
14. See Frend, *Rise*, 253–56.
15. See Origen, *On First Principles*, Preface, 2.; Jay, *The Church*, 61.
16. *Hom. on Ez.* 1.11; *Hom. on Ex* 9.3 in Kelly, *Doct.*, 202.
17. *Hom. on Jeremiah* 20.3, in Jay, *The Church*, 62.
18. See *Exposition of the Song of Solomon* 2; 1; 3. On Origen's Platonism see Frend, *Rise*, 376–84.
19. See González, *Story*, 82–85.
20. In Frend, *Rise*, 321, and his *Martyrdom and Persecution in the Early Church* (Garden City, N.Y.: Doubleday, 1967), 304, from Eusebius, *Ecclesiastical History* VI.41.10–12.
21. *Epist.* 68.8; See Jay, *The Church*, 67–68.
22. *Epist.* 73.21 and *On the Unity of the Church* 6. Cyprian recognized the preeminence of Rome among the sees. See Heick, *HCT* 1:104.
23. See *Epist.* 75.15. Cf. W. H. C. Frend, *The Donatist Church* (Oxford: Clarendon, 1952), chap. 10.

24. The Latin *trado* means "hand over." The English *traitor* is from *traditor*, meaning "betrayer." See Frend, *Rise*, 489; González, *Story*, 152.
25. In Augustine, *On Baptism Against the Donatists* 7.31.60. See Pelikan, *CT* 1:309.
26. Augustine, *Ag. the Letters of Petilian* 2.105, 240.
27. Optatus of Milevis, *Ag. Parmenianus the Donatist* 2.1. See Pelikan, *CT* 1:311.
28. See Augustine, *Ag. the Writings of Petilian* 3.68; *Epist.* 29.11; and *Ag. Cresconius* 2.7.9. cf. *Epist.* 43.2; Frend, *Donatist Church*, 240–42; Heick, *HCT* 1:136.
29. See *Epist.* 34:3; *Serm.* 22.9; *Epist.* 141.5. Cf. Kelly, *Doct.*, 412.
30. See Augustine, *On Baptism* 1.12–18; 5.8–9; 6.5–7; 4.24; 7.87.
31. See *Epist.* 93.23; 49.3; 185.5; *Serm.* 46.32–33; Kelly, *Doct.*, 413.
32. See Augustine, *On Christian Doctrine* 3.45; *On Baptism* 1.26; 3.26; 4.4; 7.100; *Ag. the Writings of Petilian* 2.247; *On the Unity of the Church* 74.
33. See *Expos. on the Psalms* 2 on Psalm 32.21; *On the Trinity* 15.33–37; Kelly, *Doct.*, 414.
34. See Augustine, *City of God* 18.50.1, in Kelly, *Doct.*, 414, and *Ag. Cresconius* 1.34.
35. See *Letters* 61.2; Jay, *The Church*, 86–87.
36. See *On Baptism* 3.19.26; *City of God* 10.6; Kelly, *Doct.*, 416, 368. For Augustine the "elect" continue as true members of the church through the gift of perseverance. They include some who do not belong to the Catholic church. See *On Rebuke and Grace* 9.22; *On the Gift of Perseverance* 2; Heick, *HCT* 1:137.
37. *Expos. of the Gospel of John* 45.12. This is cited by John Calvin, who continued Augustine's emphases. See *Inst.* IV.1.8.
38. See *Expositions on the Psalms* 56.13; 56.1; *Ag. Faustus the Manichean* 28.2; *Letters* 93.7.23; Jay, *The Church*, 89.
39. See *On Baptism* 6.10.15, in Pelikan, *CT* 1:311.
40. Ibid., 3.14.19.
41. See *Letters* 61.2; Jay, *The Church*, 87.

CHAPTER 4

1. H. Wheeler Robinson coined the phrase "corporate personality" in a 1935 essay. See *Corporate Personality in Ancient Israel* (Philadelphia: Fortress, 1964); cf. *Inspiration and Revelation in the Old Testament* (1946; rpt. Oxford: Clarendon, 1967), 70ff.; H. H. Rowley, *The Faith of Israel* (1950; rpt. London: SCM, 1970), chap. 4.
2. See A. R. Johnson, *The One and the Many in the Israelite Conception of God* (1942; rpt. Cardiff; Univ. of Wales Press, 1961).
3. See Whiteley, *TSP*, 41ff.; W. D. Stacey, *The Pauline View of Man* (London: Macmillan, 1956); Ridderbos, *POHT*, 115–26.
4. See Justin, *I Apology* 10.4; 28.3. See Kelly, *Doct.*, 166ff.
5. See González, *HCT* 1:50–52; J. Patout Burns, ed. and trans., *Theological Anthropology*, (Philadelphia: Fortress, 1981), 1–2.
6. See *I Apol.* 43; *II Apol.* 7, as well as *I Apol.* 44.11; *Dial. with Trypho* 141.2. Cf. Tatian, *Oration to the Greeks* 7.2; Kelly, *Doct.*, 166; Pelikan, *CT* 1:281–82.
7. *Dial. with Trypho* 124. Cf. H. D. McDonald, *The Christian View of Man* (1981; rpt. Westchester, Ill.: Crossway, 1985), 53; Kelly, *Doct.*, 167.
8. See Theophilus of Antioch, *To Autolycus* 2.24–25, 27, in Kelly, *Doct.*, 168.
9. Ireanaeus, *Against Heresies* 4.38.1, in Burns, *Anthropology*, 23.
10. See *Ag. Her.* 4.39.1; 3.18.1; 5.2.1; 3.18.7. Cf. Volz, *FPEC*, 42.
11. On "recapitulation" see Kelly, *Doct.*, 170ff.

12. Tertullian, *The Resurrection of the Flesh* 14. Tertullian cited the creation story and Matt. 5:29–30 to support his views. See McDonald, *View of Man*, 51.
13. *On the Flesh of Christ* 12.
14. *The Resurrection of the Flesh* 7. Cf. McDonald, *View of Man*, 51.
15. See *On the Soul* 27, in *Early*, 109. Tertullian's view that the soul derives from one's parents is called *traducianism*, as opposed to the view that God creates each human soul fresh, which is called *creationism*. See Volz, *FPEC*, 43.
16. See *On the Soul; Resurrection* 49. Cf. *Early*, 115; Kelly, *Doct.*, 175.
17. *On the Soul* 41. See *Early*, 117.
18. *On the Soul* 21. See *Early*, 110. In upholding free will, Tertullian was reacting against the determinism of Gnosticism and Marcion. See Volz, *FPEC*, 44; Kelly, *Doct.*, 175.
19. Clement, *Stromateis* 2.14.60; 2.15.66. See *Early*, 174.
20. Origen, *Against Celsus* 4.40; *Homilies on Leviticus* 6.2. Cf. *Early*, 206–7. Cf. *Sel. in Genesis*; Kelly, *Doct.*, 182.
21. See Origen, *On First Principles* 1.8.1; Kelly, *Doct.*, 181–82. Origen believed that while Adam represents each human, each person is expelled from paradise because of personal sin. Cf. Volz, *FPEC*, 46–47.
22. See *Principles* Pref. 5; cf. 1.8; 1.6; 3.1. Cf. McDonald, *View of Man*, 54; *Early*, 209–10.
23. This discussion is drawn from Burns, *Anthropology*, 3–6.
24. Athanasius, *On the Incarnation* 3. See *Early*, 274–75; Kelly, *Doct.*, 346–48.
25. John Chrysostom, *Sermon 10 on Romans* in Volz, *FPEC*, 50–51.
26. Calvin mentions these citations in *Inst.* II.2.4.
27. See Ambrose, *A Defense of the Prophet David* 2.12.71, in *Later*, 177; *An Oration on the Death of His Brother Satyrul* 2.6; Volz, *FPEC*, 52; Kelly, *Doct.*, 354.
28. See *A Defense* 56–57; Kelly, *Doct.*, 354–55. Ambrose holds that Christ was born of a virgin so as to escape original sin. Ambrose was the first to suggest that "the sexual act of procreation, even within marriage and by Christians, carries with it a stigma which is transmitted to the child" (*A Defense* 52–53). Cf. *Later*, 178.
29. Ambrose, *De Jacobo et vita beata* 1.1. Cf. *De Poenit.* 2.9.80, in Seeberg, *THD* 1.330.
30. On Pelagius see Frend, *Rise*, 673–83; González, *HCT* 2:27–31; Lohse, *SHCD*, 106–10; Peter Brown, *Augustine of Hippo: A Biography* (1967; rpt. Berkeley and Los Angeles: Univ. of California Press, 1969), passim; as well as Robert F. Evans, *Four Letters of Pelagius* (New York: Seabury, 1968) and *Pelagius Inquiries and Reappraisals* (New York: Seabury, 1968).
31. Pelagius's *Letter to Demetrias* is in Burns, *Anthropology*, 39–55. On his controversy with Jerome see J. N. D. Kelly, *Jerome* (New York: Harper & Row, 1975), chap. 26. Cf. Frend, *Rise*, 677–79. On the Synod of Orange, see Burns, *Anthropology*, chap. 7; and on "Semi-Pelagianism" see Kelly, *Doct.*, 370ff.; Pelikan, *CT* 1:318–31; Heick, *HCT*, 1:206ff.
32. *On the Grace of Christ* 1.28, 29; 2.14. See *Later*, 193.
33. See Augustine, *Confessions* 10.40; *On the Perseverance of the Saints* 53. Cf. Kelly, *Doct.*, 357.
34. Augustine, *On the Career of Pelagius* 20 (*Later*, 194).
35. Augustine, *On the Career* 22. See *Later*, 194.
36. Pelagius, *Letter to Demetrias* 8, in Burns, *Anthropology*, 50. Pelagius argued for the power of free will to preserve the goodness of God against the Manichees.
37. See *On the Grace of Christ* 1.27–30; *On the Life of Pelagius* 16. Cf. Burns, *Anthropology*, 81–82; Kelly, *Doct.*, 359–60.

38. See Roy W. Battenhouse, ed., *A Companion to the Study of St. Augustine* (1955; rpt. Grand Rapids: Baker, 1979), 219; Pelagius, *Letter to Demetrias* 17, in Burns, *Anthropology*, 54.

39. See Augustine, *Confessions* 4.1.1; Brown, *Augustine*, 352.

40. See Augustine, *Genesis According to the Letter* 6.36; and *On Condemnation and Grace* 33, 34. Cf. *Later*, 194–95; Kelly, *Doct.*, 362; Augustine, *On Rebuke and Grace* 31, in Burns, *Anthropology*, 101.

41. Augustine, *On the Trinity* 14.6. See *Later*, 195.

42. See Augustine, *The City of God* 14.13; *On Marriage and Concupiscence* 2.58; *On Nature and Grace* 33; *On Corruption and Grace* 12.33 (Burns, *Anthropology*, 103); Pelikan, *CT* 1:299–301; González, *HCT* 2:42–44; Heick, *HCT* 2:299ff.; Kelly, *Doct.*, 363.

43. See *Genesis According to the Letter* 11.5; *On the Nature of the Good Against the Manicheans* 35; *On the Reward and Remission of Sins* 2.11 (See *Later*, 198).

44. *An Unfinished Treatise Against Julian* 6.22 (*Later*, 197); *On the Reward and Remission* 2.11; *Enchiridion* 35.

45. *On Marriage and Concupiscence* 2.15. Cf. Kelly, *Doct.*, 364.

46. *On Grace and Free Will* 15; cf. *Against Two Letters of the Pelagians* 1.5 (*Later*, 203–4).

47. See *On Marriage and Concupiscence* 1.28, 29 (*Later*, 202–3); *Against Two Letters of the Pelagians* 1.27. Like Ambrose, Augustine found the primary expression of concupiscence in the sexual act. (See Volz, *FPEC*, 55; Lohse, *SHCD*, 113–14.) He too believed the virgin birth of Christ was necessary for Christ's perfect innocence. See Frend, *Rise*, 679, 695 (n. 191); Brown, *Augustine*, 388; Seeberg, *THD* 1:345–46.

48. See *To Simplicianus, on Various Questions* 1.2.16, 20; *On the Grace of Christ* 2.34 (*Later*, 204); *Enchiridion* 8, 9. On Augustine and predestination see Kelly, *Doct.*, 366ff.; González, *HCT* 2:44ff.; Seeberg, *THD* 1:350ff.; Battenhouse, *Companion*, 227ff.

CHAPTER 5

1. See Gustaf Aulén, *Christus Victor*, trans. A. G. Hebert (London: SPCK, 1931); Robert S. Paul, *The Atonement and the Sacraments* (New York: Abingdon, 1960); H. D. McDonald, *The Atonement of the Death of Christ* (Grand Rapids: Baker, 1985).

2. This discussion is adapted from Edward Schillebeeckx, *Christ*, trans. John Bowden (New York: Crossroad, 1981), 477ff.

3. See the extensive writings of Karl Barth in *CD* 4, parts 1–3. Cf. James Denney, *The Christian Doctrine of Reconciliation* (London: Hodder & Stoughton, 1918).

4. See *TDNT* 2:400–420; *IDB* 3:704–6; *ISBE* 3:731–33; Schillebeeckx, *Christ*, 484–85. A significant theological study is Arthur C. Cochrane, *The Mystery of Peace* (Elgin, Ill.: Brethren Press, 1986).

5. See *TDNT* 2:174–225; Markus Barth, *Justification*, trans. A. M. Woodruff III (Grand Rapids: Eerdmans, 1971).

6. See H. E. W. Turner, *The Patristic Doctrine of Redemption* (London: A. R. Mowbray, 1952), 33–34; *Didache* (10.2) in Richardson, *ECF*, 175; Thomas F. Torrance, *The Doctrine of Grace in the Apostolic Fathers* (Edinburgh: Oliver & Boyd, 1948), 46.

7. See *I Clem.* 59.2; 36.2 (*ECF*, 70, 60).

8. See *I Clem.* 1.2; 11.1; 15.1; 32.4; 15.2; 21.8.
9. *I Clem.* 33.7; cf. 16.17 (*ECF*, 59, 51–52).
10. Justin Martyr, *Dialogue with Trypho* 18.3. Cf. Kelly, *Doct.*, 169; Seeberg, *THD* 1:115; *I Apol.* 44. Justin spoke of "Christians before Christ," including Socrates and Abraham. See *I Apol.* 46 (*Early*, 60). He referred to baptism as "illumination" (*I Apol.* 61; *ECF*, 283).
11. *Dial. with Trypho* 85.1. Cf. Kelly, *Doct.*, 169. This view of the Logos set a rational foundation for salvation as illumination.
12. This countered gnostic fatalism. Christ as example spurred martyrs to be faithful unto death (cf. 1 Peter 2:21). Some believed their own sufferings, like Christ's, had a saving value. See Volz, *FPEC*, 64–65.
13. Irenaeus, *Ag. Her.* 5.1. See McDonald, *Atonement*, 126ff.
14. *Ag. Her.* 2.22.4. See Pelikan, *CT* 1:144; Kelly, *Doct.*, 170–74; Volz, *FPEC*, 66.
15. *Ag. Her.* 3.18.1, in Norris, *CC*, 49.
16. *Ag. Her.* 5 (preface).
17. See *Ag. Her.* 3.21.10; cf. 3.22.3. Tertullian also uses the Eve-Mary antithesis. See *On the Flesh of Christ* 17, in *Early*, 126–27.
18. *Ag. Her.* 5.21.2; 5.1, in Norris, *CC*, 58.
19. McDonald, *Atonement*, 155. Cf. Kelly, *Doct.*, 174–77; Pelikan, *CT* 1:147; who notes that "satisfaction" may derive from Roman private law (Tertullian was trained in law), where it refers to "the amends one made to another for failing to discharge an obligation, or from Roman public law, which enabled the term to be interpreted as a form of punishment."
20. See Tertullian, *On Penitence* 7.5–14; *Scorpiace* 7; *On the Resurrection* 8. See Tertullian on merit in Johann Heinz, *Justification and Merit: Luther vs. Catholicism* (Berrien Springs, Mich.: Andrews Univ. Press, 1984), 114–16.
21. Hilary of Poitiers was the first to use *satisfaction* for the death of Christ. He equated satisfaction with *sacrifice* and saw the cross as Christ's act of reparation to God on the behalf of sinners. See Pelikan, *CT* 1:147, citing *Expos. of the Psalms* 53.12–13.
22. See *On Modesty* 22.4; *Against the Jews* 13. Cf. Pelikan, *CT* 1:148; Volz, *FPEC*, 73.
23. *On Penitence* 2; 10; *Scorpiace* 6. Cf. Heinz, 115; Seeberg, *THD* 1:133–34.
24. Aulén calls the Christus Victor view the "classic view." Cf. Volz, *FPEC*, 68ff.; Turner, *Patristic Doctrine*, chap. 3.
25. Origen, *In Rom.* 5.1, in Turner, *Patristic Doctrine*, 51. Cf. *Against Celsus* 1.60; 6.45; Kelly, *Doct.*, 185.
26. *In Matt.* 16.8 (*Early*, 224). Cf. Kelly, *Doct.*, 185–86.
27. *On First Principles* 1.6.1; 3.6.3. Cf. Pelikan, *CT* 1:151.
28. See Pelikan, *CT* 1:155. Cf. William G. Rusch, "How the Eastern Fathers Understood What the Western Church Meant by Justification," in *Justification by Faith*, ed. H. George Anderson et al. (Minneapolis: Augsburg, 1985), 131–42. The Western church emphasized original sin and humanity's physical solidarity with Adam and participation in his sinful act. This view was largely absent in the East. Western legalism and the development of the penitential system, as well as the Pelagian controversy, all tended to orient the West toward justification while the East used a different framework.
29. Clement of Alexandria, *Exhortation to the Greeks* 1.8.4. See Pelikan, *CT* 1:155.
30. See Rusch, "Eastern Fathers," 135.
31. Ignatius of Antioch, *Letter to the Ephesians* 4.2; 9.2; *Letter to Polycarp* 6.1. See Rusch, "Eastern Fathers," 134.

32. See Irenaeus, *Ag. Her.* 5.1; 3.6.1; 3.19.1.
33. Clement of Alexandria, *The Tutor*, 1, 5, 26; *Carpets* 5, 10, 63. See Rusch, "Eastern Fathers," 137. Origen developed this idea when speaking of the transformation of Moses' face. See his *Comm. on John* 32, 27.
34. See Athanasius, *On the Incarnation* 54 (*Early*, 293). Cf. Volz, *FPEC*, 77, as well as Athanasius, *Against the Arians* 1.38; Kelly, *Doct.*, 378.
35. *Incarnation* 54; Rusch, "Early Fathers," 138.
36. See Gregory of Nazianzus, *Orations* 37.13–15; 38.8–10; Gregory of Nyssa, *Catechetical Orations* 37; Basil the Great, *Against Eunomius* 1.14; John of Damascus, *On the Orthodox Faith* 1.14; Rusch, "Eastern Fathers," 139; Kelly, *Doct.*, 380ff.
37. See Augustine, *Explanations on the Psalms* 49.2; *Sermons* 47, 117, 121, 166, 259; *City of God* 14.4.2. See Rusch, "Eastern Fathers," 141.
38. See Augustine, *The Spirit and the Letter* 26, 45; Anderson, *Justification*, 18 and n. 6.
39. Augustine, *Sermon* 174.2; 174.1, in Turner, *Patristic Doctrine*, 108.
40. *Enchiridion* 108 (*Later*, 225).
41. On Christ as mediator see *On the Trinity* 4.14, 19; Turner, *Patristic Doctrine*, 109–10; Kelly, *Doct.*, 390.
42. On Christ as example see *On the Instruction of the Unlearned* 4.8; *On the Trinity* 8.7; Turner, *Patristic Doctrine*, 111; Kelly, *Doct.*, 393.
43. On Christ as victor over Satan see *Trinity* 4.13, 16–19; McDonald, *Atonement*, 158–59; Kelly, *Doct.*, 391–92. In one sermon Augustine dramatically stated that the body of Christ was the bait by which Satan was caught like a mouse in a trap. See *Ser.* 263.1, in Kelly, *Doct.*, 391.
44. On Christ as the Savior from death see *Trinity* 4.12.15; *On the Manichaean Heresy* 14.6.7; McDonald, *Atonement*, 159–60; Kelly, *Doct.*, 393.
45. On Christ as a sacrifice see *Trinity* 4.15, 17, 19. Christ is both priest and victim. See *City of God* 10, 20; Turner, *Patristic Doctrine*, 109.
46. Pelagius, *Ad. Rom. exp.* 8.29. See González, *HCT* 2:31; Robert F. Evans, *Pelagius: Inquiries and Reappraisals* (New York: Seabury, 1968), 115ff.; Pelikan, *CT* 1:315ff.
47. Pelagius, *Expositiones XIII epistolarum Pauli*, in Evans, *Pelagius*, 119.
48. Augustine, *On the Grace of Christ and Original Sin* 2.34.
49. See *Enchir.* 32, 37, 117, 107, 105; *On Nature and Grace* 35; *Trinity* 15.37; *On the Spirit and the Letter* 5; *Epis.* 184. 4. *On Rebuke and Grace* 45.
50. *On the Spirit and the Letter* 45; cf. 51–52; Heick, *HCT* 2:203. The growth is an ever-becoming righteous in love. See *Epis.* 167.3, 13. See Heinz, 121ff.
51. *On Grace and Free Will* 33 (*Later*, 206). Cf. Kelly, *Doct.*, 367.
52. *On Rebuke and Grace* 29–34.
53. *On Grace and Free Will* 31 (cf. 17); *On the Spirit and the Letter* 52 (cf. 60), in *Later*, 207. Augustine does not mean that grace opposes freedom, for grace does not force one to make a decision against one's will. Rather, when the will is changed by God, it desires to do good. See González, *HCT* 2:45.
54. See *On Rebuke and Grace* 12–16; *Enchir.* 98–99. To the question of why God elects some to be saved and others not to be saved, the only answer of God according to Augustine is, "I so will." Humans cannot call God into account. See Heick, *HCT* 2:205; Pelikan, *CT* 1:298; Kelly, *Doct.*, 368–69.
55. *Coll.* 13.8, in González, *HCT* 2:56.
56. Augustine wrote his *On the Predestination of the Saints* and *On the Gift of Perseverance* against these theologians. See González, *HCT* 2:56–59; Lohse, *SHCD*, 122–27; Pelikan, *CT* 1:319–24. The term *semi-Pelagian* arose in the sixteenth century.

57. See J. Patout Burns, ed. and trans., *Theological Anthropology* (Philadelphia: Fortress, 1981), chap. 7, for the documents of the Synod of Orange.

58. Ibid., 119. Cf. Pelikan, *CT* 1:327–29; Seeberg, *THD* 1:380–82. The differences between the Augustinians and the semi-Pelagians can be likened to the split in Indian religion over the means of "salvation." J. S. Whale writes:

> The two parties were known as the monkey-school and the cat-school respectively. For, on the approach of danger the baby monkey climbs on to its mother's back, holds on and, as the mother leaps away to safety, is saved along with her: primarily through the mother monkey's act, of course, but also through the cooperation of her offspring. But when danger threatens a mother cat, she takes her kitten by the scruff of the neck and, willy-nilly, saves it. The kitten does nothing: it contributes nothing at all to the process of its salvation ("not by works, lest any kitten should boast"). (*The Protestant Tradition* [1955; rpt. Cambridge: University Press, 1959], 140–41)

For Whale this describes the differences between the medieval Schoolmen and the Reformers.

59. See Pelikan, *CT* 4, chap. 1; Anderson, *Justification*, 18; Heiko Oberman, *Forerunners of the Reformation* (Philadelphia: Fortress, 1981).

60. Some scholars place Luther's conversion in 1514; others put it in 1518. See Eric W. Gritsch, "The Origins of Lutheran Teaching on Justification," in Anderson, *Justification*, 163.

61. See Luther's "Sermon on Baptism," in *WA* 37:661.20–26.

62. See Eric W. Gritsch, *Martin—God's Court Jester* (Philadelphia: Fortress, 1983), 15.

63. See *WA* 54:185.17–20; 186.3–9; English translation in Pelikan, *LW* 34:336–37. Cf. Gritsch, "Origins," 164; *Martin*, 14.

64. See Gritsch, "Origins," 164. Luther strongly contrasted law and gospel. As a mirror, a hammer, and a mask the law shows the enormity of sin in order to drive us to the gospel. The law says no to all human enterprises for obtaining salvation. Only then can humans hear the yes in the gospel of Jesus Christ. See Seeberg, *THD* 2:246ff.; Gerhard Ebeling, *Luther*, trans. R. A. Wilson (Philadelphia: Fortress, 1970), chaps. 7, 8; Anderson, *Justification*, chap. 15.

65. See *WA* 56:39, passim; 2:490; *LW* 27:221; *WA* 39/1:46; *LW* 34:111; *WA* 39/1:98; *LW* 34:167. Luther also distinguished justification from fulfilling the law. See *WA* 39/1:443; Paul Althaus, *The Theology of Martin Luther*, trans. Robert C. Schultz (Philadelphia: Fortress, 1966), 226.

66. *WA* 39/1:83; *LW* 34:153. Cf. *WA* 39/1:97; *LW* 34:166; *WA* 40/1:229; *LW* 26:130; Althaus, *Theology of Luther*, 227. Luther frequently spoke of a "cheerful exchange" or a "wonderful exchange" of Christ's righteousness exchanged for human sin. See *WA* 7/25.34; *LW* 31:351; *WA* 10/3:356.21–30. Augustine had spoken of this "fortunate exchange" (*Conf.* 10.43.68–70). See Gritsch, *Martin*, 173; Heinz, 191, 211; Pelikan, *CT* 4:163.

67. *WA* 2:491; *LW* 27:222. This righteousness of Christ's is "outside" or "alien" to us. See *WA* 39/1:83; *LW* 34:153. Pelikan describes this as the "divine monergism" for which Luther argued against the medieval Scholastics. See *CT* 4:145.

68. *WA* 39/1:46; *LW* 34:110. See Althaus, *Theology of Luther*, 230. Luther referred to the will as *servum arbitrium*. See *WA* 56:398.11–12; 385:17–18; Seeberg, *THD* 2:242ff.; Ebeling, *Luther*, 216–18; Pelikan, *CT* 4:140ff. This bondage is the result of the sin of humans, whom he described as being "turned in upon themselves" (*in curvatus in se*). See *WA* 56:304.26, 356.5, passim; Heinz, 189; Heick, *HCT* 1:336.

69. WA 40/1:229; LW 26:130. Cf. Althaus, *Theology of Luther*, 230–31.
70. Luther, *Deutsche Bibel (DB)* 7, 10, 16–18, in Heinz, 24. On the Holy Spirit see WA 56:379.2–6.
71. WA 39/1:252; cf. 39/1:83; LW 34.152; WA 39/1:356; Althaus, *Theology of Luther*, 237. Luther can use the word *justification* for sanctification. See WA 2:495.2–3; WA 39/1:252.9–12.
72. See the formula in WA 56:70.272; LCC 15:127; 57:165; 2:496–97; LW 27:230; WA 56:268.27–28, 269.21–24, 272.17.
73. See WA 39/1:376; 6:216. Cf.WA 39/1:507; Althaus, *Theology of Luther*, 243.
74. See DB 6–10, in Heinz, 24; Gritsch, "Origins," 166; WA 39/1:283.18–19.
75. WA 12.282. See Althaus, *Theology of Luther*, 246, and similar citations in Pelikan, CT 4:147.
76. WA 10/3:225 in Althaus, *Theology of Luther*, 247. Cf. WA 40/1:577; LW 26:379; WA 39/1:1-2., 225.3–9; Heinz, 49. Heinz speaks of "good works" in Luther as following consecutively from justification (see pp. 410–11).
77. WA 40/3:352.2; Heinz, 13. Cf. *Expos. of Psalm 130:4* in WA 40/3:352.3; Gritsch, "Origins," 25. Valentin E. Löscher in 1718 said justification by faith was "the article on which the church stands and falls."
78. Like Augustine, Luther believed in predestination that led to assurance of salvation. See WA 43:460.2–13; WA 18.600ff.; Seeberg, THD 2:244–45, Althaus, *Theology of Luther*, chap. 20.
79. For Luther the idea of merit is guilty of "usurping the right that belongs to Christ alone. Only he delivers from sin and grants righteousness and eternal life." See WA 49/1:236–38; Pelikan, CT 4:146, 148; Heinz, chap. 2; Oberman, *Forerunners*, chap. 3. Cf. WA 18:769.26–27; LW 33:266; Heinz, 416.
80. See Anderson, *Justification*, 209–13; George H. Tavard, *Justification* (New York: Paulist, 1983), 71.
81. See H. J. Schroeder, *Canons and Decrees of the Council of Trent* (1941; rpt. St. Louis: Herder, 1955), 21–23.
82. Ibid., 42. Cf. Anderson, *Justification*, 220, where Carl Peters writes, "Human works of whatever kind are not of themselves enough; God's grace given through Jesus Christ is needed. This is the unmistakable meaning of the first canon of Session 6."
83. Luther as perceived by Roman Catholics is discussed in Tavard, *Justification*, chap. 5. Hans Küng has argued that Karl Barth's and Trent's doctrines of justification exhibit a "complete consensus"; see his *Justification* (1964; rpt. Philadelphia: Westminster, 1981). Heinz (322–26) sees some contemporary Catholic theologians trying to reinterpret Trent in order to forge a harmony with Luther's views. These efforts include a method of explanation that seeks a compromise (Auer, Ratzinger), a method of completion that would "further develop" Trent's formulations (Jedin, Schillebeeckx), and a method of correction that would revise Trent by arguing that Luther was not really understood by the council and thus not really condemned by it (Hasler, Pesch, Küng).
84. See Heinz, 407–16, who sees the two as having "two different interpretations of the gospel" based on whether in salvation humans are "receivers" (Protestant) or "contributors" (Roman Catholic). Cf. González, HCT 3:220–22; Lohse, SHCD, 193–96; Anderson, *Justification*, 230–40.
85. Recent Lutheran–Roman Catholic dialogues note areas of common concern as well as "different outlooks." Both sides are urged to "take seriously the concerns of the other and to strive to think jointly about the problems." See Anderson, *Justification*, 57.

CHAPTER 6

1. See Paul C. Empie et al., eds., *Teaching Authority & Infallibility in the Church* (Minneapolis: Augsburg, 1980), chaps. 10, 11 (hereafter cited as *Teaching*).
2. See *ISBE* 1:591ff.; *IDB* 1:498ff.; J. C. Turro and R. E. Brown, "Canonicity," in *The Jerome Biblical Commentary*, ed. R. E. Brown et al. (Englewood Cliffs, N.J.: Prentice-Hall, 1968), 515–34; F. F. Bruce, *Tradition: Old and New* (Grand Rapids: Zondervan, 1970).
3. James L. Kugel and Rowan A. Greer, *Early Biblical Interpretation* (Philadelphia: Westminster, 1986), chap. 1.
4. See Robert M. Grant, *A Short History of the Interpretation of the Bible* (1948; rpt. New York: Macmillan, 1966), passim; Kugel/Greer, 81ff., 126ff.; Kelly, *Doct.*, 69–79.
5. See R. P. C. Hanson, *Tradition in the Early Church* (Philadelphia: Westminster, 1962), chap. 1.
6. Kugel/Greer, 109. The Septuagint includes books that were not finally admitted into the Hebrew canon; they comprise the Old Testament Apocrypha. Irenaeus also included 1 Clement and the Shepherd of Hermas as Scripture. Cf. Volz, *FPEC*, 139.
7. See F. F. Bruce, "Tradition and the Canon of Scripture," in *The Authoritative Word: Essays on the Nature of Scripture*, ed. Donald K. McKim (Grand Rapids: Eerdmans, 1983), 72–74; *ISBE* 1:604; Lohse, *SHCD*, 2–8. Cf. Kugel/Greer, 110; Heick, *HCT* 1:84; Volz, *FPEC*, 141.
8. See James J. Megivern, ed., *Bible Interpretation* (Wilmington, N. C.: Consortium Books, 1978), 36–38, 48. Cf. Hanson, *Tradition*, chap. 5.
9. See Irenaeus, *Against Heresies* 1.10.2; 5.20.1; Tertullian, *Prescription Against Heretics* 21; *Against Marcion* 1.21; 4.5. Cf. Kelly, *Doct.*, 36.
10. For Irenaeus this tradition was given by the Holy Spirit, and there is no contradiction between the oral and written tradition since both go back to the Apostles. Thus "tradition came to be regarded as explaining Scripture, or at least certain difficult passages in it, as on the other hand, Scripture became the norm for tradition" (Lohse, *SHCD*, 32). Cf. Volz, *FPEC*, 145; Kelly, *Doct.*, 39.
11. Athanasius, *Against the Heathen* 1.
12. Cyril of Jerusalem, *Catechetical Lectures* 4.17. Cf. Kelly, *Doct.*, 42.
13. Vincent of Lérins, *Commonitory* 2.3 in Pelikan, *CT* 1:333. Vincent's watchword was "not new doctrines, but old ones in new terms." See Volz, *FPEC*, 149.
14. Hanson, *Tradition*, 54–59, gives examples from the early church. Biblical examples are Rom. 1:3–4; 4:24–25; 8:34; 1 Cor. 8:6; 1 Tim. 2:5; 3:16; 2 Tim. 2:8; 1 Peter 3:18. Cf. C. H. Dodd, *The Apostolic Preaching and Its Developments* (1936; rpt. London: Hodder & Stoughton, 1967); Vernon H. Neufeld, *The Earliest Christian Confessions* (Grand Rapids: Eerdmans, 1983). Kelly notes the most basic New Testament creed is "Jesus is Lord" (*kurios Iēsous*; *Creeds*, 14).
15. In Kelly, *Creeds*, 73.
16. See Kelly, *Creeds*, chap. 4. Rufinus began the tradition that the Apostles' Creed was composed by the Apostles. Cf. p. 101; chap. 13.
17. Irenaeus, *Ag. Her.* 1.1.20; Tertullian, *Apologeticus* 46.17. Cf. Hanson, *Tradition*, 77.
18. Origen, *Comm. on John* 13.16. Cf. *Comm. on I Cor. LXXXIV* for the phrase "the ecclesiastical rule." See Hanson, *Tradition*, 78–79.
19. *Comm. on Psalm 48.12*; *Comm. on Matthew 15.7*; cf. 10.14; *Comm. on Psalm 27.5*, where the doctrine of the Trinity is one of these foundation doctrines commu-

nicated through "the ecclesiastical preaching" (Gr. *kērygma; On First Principles* 3.1.1). See Kelly, *Doct.*, 43.

20. "The rule of faith" is a contemporary account of the preaching and teaching content of the faith. See Irenaeus, *Ag. Her.* 4.7.4; Hanson, *Tradition*, 93, 110–14.

21. C. H. Turner wrote that "the old creeds were creeds for catechumens, the new creed was a creed for bishops." See Kelly, *Creeds*, 205–11.

22. Ignatius, *To the Trallians* 3.1, in *ECF*, 99.

23. Irenaeus, *Ag. Her.* 3.33.8; Tertullian, *Prescription Against Heretics* 32; cf. 21, 36, 37; Heick, *HCT* 1:99.

24. See Irenaeus, *Ag. Her.* 3.3.1, 2, in *ECF*, 372. Cf. Volz, *FPEC*, 171–72; *Teaching*, 301, n. 37.

25. Gregory the Great, *Epistles* 5.37, in Pelikan, *CT* 1:352. Cf. Geoffrey Barraclough, *The Medieval Papacy* (Norwich, England: Harcourt, Brace & World, 1968); Walter Ullmann, *A Short History of the Papacy in the Middle Ages* (London: Methuen & Co., 1972). The term *pope* means "father."

26. Cyprian, *On the Unity of the Church* 4. See Pelikan, *CT* 1:119, 159; Kelly, *Doct.*, 205ff.

27. For interpretations of Matt. 16:18 see Kelly, *Doct.*, 406ff., 417ff; Pelikan, *CT* 2–5.

28. Innocent, *Epistle* 37.1. Cf. Henry Chadwick, *The Early Church* (Harmondsworth, England: Penguin, 1967), 240; *Teaching*, 21.

29. In Chadwick, *Early Church*, 244.

30. Nilus Doxopatres (fl. 1143) was a canonist and theologian. See his *Order of the Patriarchal Sees*, cited in Pelikan, *CT* 2:163.

31. See Pseudo Photius, *Against Those Who Say Rome Is the First See* 4. Cf. Theodore of Studios, *Orations* 9.10, in Pelikan, *CT* 2:169.

32. Leo, *Epistle* 11.

33. These are in George H. Tavard, *Holy Writ or Holy Church* (New York: Harper, 1959), 47–48.

34. Guido Terrini, *Question on the Infallible Magisterium of the Roman Pontiff*, in Pelikan, *CT* 4:107. Cf. *Teaching*, 23.

35. See Heiko Oberman, *The Harvest of Medieval Theology: Gabriel Biel and Late Medieval Nominalism* (1963; rpt. Grand Rapids: Eerdmans, 1967), 6; Oberman, *Forerunners of the Reformation* (1966; rpt. Philadelphia: Fortress, 1981), 54ff. Cf. Oberman, "Quo vadis? Tradition from Irenaeus to Humani Generis," *Scottish Journal of Theology* 16 (1963): 225–55.

36. See Oberman, *Harvest*, 367–69; *Forerunners*, 54. Irenaeus identified the transmission of truth with episcopal succession. See *Ag. Her.* 4.

37. See Oberman, *Harvest*, 369–71; *Forerunners*, 54–55. Basil the Great (c. 330–70) claimed the Christian owes equal respect and obedience to both written and unwritten ecclesiastical traditions. Augustine held to both Tradition I and II.

38. See Oberman, *Harvest*, 376–77; 373–75; *Forerunners*, 59–60.

39. See Oberman, *Forerunners*, 70–72. Cf. Pelikan, *CT* 4:120.

40. See Oberman, *Forerunners*, 72–73.

41. Jean de Gerson, *On the Spiritual Life of the Soul* 2, in Pelikan, *CT* 4:121.

42. In Eric W. Gritsch, *Martin—God's Court Jester* (Philadelphia: Fortress, 1983), 107.

43. Martin Luther, *Ninety-five Theses* 62, in *WA* 1:236. Cf. Pelikan, *CT* 4:128.

44. *WA* 38:208. Cf. Paul Althaus, *The Theology of Martin Luther*, trans. Robert C. Schultz (Philadelphia: Fortress 1966), 339.

45. *WA* 7:838.7. Cf. *LW* 32:112; Gritsch, *Martin*, 93.

46. *WA* 38:206. See Althaus, *Theology of Luther*, 338. Gritsch writes, "Luther con-

tended that Scripture interprets itself; Rome insisted that Scripture must be interpreted by the teaching office of the church, the *magisterium* of bishops headed by the bishop of Rome" (*Martin*, 108). Cf. Rogers and McKim, *AIB*, 76.

47. Cf. Rogers and McKim, *AIB*, 89–116; Donald K. McKim, "Calvin's View of Scripture," in *Readings in Calvin's Theology*, ed. Donald K. McKim (Grand Rapids: Baker, 1984), 43–68.

48. Cf. *Inst.* III.1.3ff.; 2.15, 33–36; McKim, "Calvin's View," 55–56.

49. See *Inst.* IV.5–11 as well as Calvin's *Acts of the Council of Trent with the Antidote* (1547).

50. See *Inst.* IV.8, 10–16. Cf. IV.9.

51. See Calvin, *On Scandals*; Pelikan, *CT* 4:211.

52. See Tavard, *Holy Writ*, chap. 13.

53. *Canons and Decrees of the Council of Trent*, trans. H. J. Schroeder (1941; rpt. St. Louis: Herder, 1955), 17. The Latin text is given on p. 296.

54. *Acts of the Council of Trent* 8.ix, 1551, in Pelikan, *CT* 4:277.

55. In Pelikan, *CT* 4:277. Cf. Tavard, *Holy Writ*, 202ff.; Dewey Beegle, *Scripture, Tradition, and Infallibility* (Grand Rapids: Eerdmans, 1973), 102–3; Robert Gnuse, *The Authority of the Bible* (New York: Paulist, 1985), 115.

56. This is the view of many contemporary Roman Catholics. See Avery Dulles, "The Authority of Scripture: A Catholic Perspective," in *Scripture in the Jewish and Christian Traditions*, ed. Frederick E. Greenspahn (Nashville: Abingdon, 1982), 35. Tavard writes that the source of all Christian truth and behavior is the gospel of Christ. The gospel comes by the power of the Holy Spirit who uses "two sets of vessels: Holy Scripture and traditions. In as far as they convey the same Gospel of Christ, in as far as they channel the original impetus whereby the Spirit moved the Apostles, both Scriptures and traditions are entitled to the same adhesion of faith. For faith reaches Christ and the Spirit whatever the medium used to contact us. . . . The touchstone of a Scripture as of a tradition is the Gospel, 'kept in the Catholic Church in a continuous succession'" (*Holy Writ*, 208).

57. See Peter Chirico, *Infallibility: The Crossroads of Doctrine* (Wilmington, Del.: Michael Glazier, 1983), xxxix, translating from *Enchiridion Symbolorum, Definitionum, et Declarationum de Rebus Fidei et Morum*, eds. H. Denzinger and A. Schonmetzer, 32d ed. (Freiburg: Herder, 1963), 3073–74 (hereafter cited as *DS*).

58. See Avery Dulles, "Infallibility: The Terminology," in *Teaching*, chap. 2; Chirico, 143ff. Cf. *Teaching*, 49. In *Infallible?* (trans. Edward Quinn [New York: Doubleday, 1971]), Hans Küng has questioned papal infallibility. Cf. *Teaching*, 159–68.

59. *DS*, 1826, 1831, in Lohse, *SHCD*, 210.

60. Robert S. Paul, *The Church in Search of Its Self* (Grand Rapids: Eerdmans, 1972), pts. 1 and 2.

61. See John Dillenberger, *Protestant Thought and Natural Science* (Nashville: Abingdon, 1960); Colin Gunton, *Enlightenment and Alienation* (Grand Rapids: Eerdmans, 1985); Henning Graf Reventlow, *The Authority of the Bible and the Rise of the Modern World*, trans. John Bowden (Philadelphia: Fortress, 1985).

CHAPTER 7

1. See Alexander Ganoczy, *An Introduction to Catholic Sacramental Theology*, trans. William Thomas and Anthony Sherman (New York: Paulist, 1984), chap. 3; Joseph Martos, *Doors to the Sacred: A Historical Introduction to Sacraments in the Catholic Church* (New York: Doubleday, 1982), pt. 2.

2. See Ganoczy, *Sacramental Theology*, 13–14. The public nature of the gospel contrasts with the "secrets" of the mystery cults. Cf. *TDNT* 2:803–13.

3. See Justin Martyr, *I Apology* 1.25, 27, 54; II Apology, 12; Ganoczy, *Sacramental Theology*, 15.

4. Tertullian, *To the Martyrs* 3.1; *On the Spectacles* 24.4; Cf. Ganoczy, *Sacramental Theology*, 18; Martos, *Doors*, 42.

5. See Martos, *Doors*, 42; K. R. Hagenbach, *A Text-Book of the History of Doctrines*, trans. C. W. Busch, rev. by Henry B. Smith, 2 vols. (New York: Sheldon & Co., 1868), 1:212.

6. See Augustine, *On Marriage and Concupiscence* 1.11; *On Baptism Against the Donatists* 1.2; Hagenbach, *Doctrines* 1:355; Seeberg, *THD* 1:321.

7. See Hagenbach, *Doctrines* 2:79, citing Aquinas, *ST* III:62.5, and Bonaventura, *Breviloquium* VI. Schleiermacher commented: "Thus the poor laity have no sacrament for ignorance, nor have the poor clergy a sacrament to counteract lust." On Eastern church sacraments see Ganoczy, *Sacramental Theology*, 52; Pelikan, *CT* 2.

8. See Augustine, *City of God* 10.5; Ganoczy, *Sacramental Theology*, 20.

9. Augustine, *On Christ. Doctrine* 3.9, 13. Cf. Ganoczy, *Sacramental Theology*, 21.

10. *Lett.* 138.7. Cf. Kelly, *Doct.*, 425.; *On the Instruction of the Unlearned* 26.50. In *Lett.* 138.1 he speaks of "a sign of a sacred thing"; Martos, *Doors*, 59; Cf. *Sermon* 272.

11. See *Lett.* 98.9.

12. *Homilies on the Gospel of John*, tract. 80, sec. 3 (*NPNF* 7:344); *The Teacher* 10.33. Cf. Ganoczy, *Sacramental Theology*, 21; Lohse, *SHCD*, 137.

13. See *Lett.* 98.9; Ganoczy, *Sacramental Theology*, 24. Augustine wrote of "the water, therefore, presenting the sacrament of grace outwardly, and the Spirit inwardly effecting the benefit of grace" (*Lett.* 98.2; *On Baptism* 5.21, 29). See Seeberg, *THD* 1:321, who writes that for Augustine "the outward observance of the sacrament and the inner work of grace do not always correspond."

14. See *On Baptism* 7.53, 102. Cf. Seeberg, *THD* 1:324.

15. *On Baptism* 7.19, 37; 4.1. Cf. Pelikan, *CT* 1:311. Augustine argued for two effects of baptism. One was the seal, which was permanent. The other was God's grace, which removed sin from the soul of the baptized. A Christian who sinned lost God's grace but not the seal. Those baptized into a heretical sect could not receive the grace of forgiveness because they were in a sinful state of separation from the church. After they repented, this sin could be forgiven. See Martos, *Doors*, 56; Kelly, *Doct.*, 428.

16. See Hugo, *On Sacs.* 1.9; cf. 1.12; Ganoczy, *Sacramental Theology*, 25; Seeberg, *THD* 2:61, 80; Hagenbach, *Doctrines* 2:76–81.

17. Peter Lombard, *Sentences* 4.1A in Seeberg, *THD* 2:80; Martos, *Doors*, 69.

18. Hugo, *On Sacs.* 1.9.2 in Seeberg, *THD* 2:80.

19. Aquinas, *ST* III:60.2; Cf. Seeberg, *THD* 2:125.

20. See *ST* III:60.8, 2. Cf. Ganoczy, *Sacramental Theology*, 27; Martos, *Doors*, 80ff.

21. See Aquinas, *Comm. on the Sentences* I:1.5; *ST* III:62.4. Cf. Ganoczy, *Sacramental Theology*, 27; Seeberg, *THD* 2:128–29. This was reaffirmed at the Council of Trent.

22. *ST* III:68.8; Cf. 64:8–10; Ganoczy, *Sacramental Theology*, 27. Cf. Hugo, *On Sacs.* 1.9.1; Seeberg, *THD* 2:126.

23. Lombard, *Sent.* 4:4B. See Seeberg, *THD* 2:80.

24. See *ST* III:62.6; Bonaventura, *Brevil.* IV. See Seeberg, *THD* 2:127. Ganoczy writes, "The Thomistic school spoke of a 'physical' effectiveness in which a

sacrament contains and transmits grace dynamically, as a canal does water. The basic idea behind this was, as for Thomas himself 'instrumental causality' (*ST* III:62.5; cf. *De Veritate* 27.4). The progression of grace could be traced by a linear schema: God ► Sacrament ► Individual" (*Sacramental Theology*, 33).

25. *ST* III:62.1. An alternative medieval understanding represented by Duns Scotus and the Franciscan school speaks of a "moral causality." For "because of its divine institution and promise, the sacrament is able, in its celebration, to move God, so that he gives his gracious support to the recipient. This grace, however, comes directly from God and not from a primary mediation of the sacrament. The sacrament works rather on God who in this way is reminded of his promise. Here we could present the schema: Sacrament ► God ► Individual" (Ganoczy, *Sacramental Theology*, 33–34, citing Duns Scotus [d. 1308]. Cf. Seeberg, *THD* 2:126ff.

26. Augustine, *Hom. on the Gospel of John* 80.3, in *NPNF*, 2d ser., 7:344.

27. Luther, *Small Catechism* 4:1. See Pelikan, *CT* 4:180. Luther requires the Word of God and an outward sign for a sacrament; baptism and the Lord's Supper are the only true sacraments of the New Testament churches. See *WA* 11:454. Cf. Martos, *Doors*, 110.

28. *Small Catechism* 6:8. See Pelikan, *CT* 4:180.

29. *WA* 2:686, 693. Cf. Seeberg, *THD* 2:282. On "promise" see Paul Althaus, *The Theology of Martin Luther*, trans. Robert C. Schultz (1966; rpt. Philadelphia: Fortress, 1979), 345–48.

30. *WA* 1:544, *LW* 31:106–7; *WA* 7:321, *LW* 32:15.; *WA* 38:231. Cf. Althaus, *Theology of Luther*, 349.

31. Zwingli, *Comm. on True and False Religion* 15. See Pelikan, *CT* 4:189; González, *HCT* 3:74; W. P. Stephens, *The Theology of Huldrych Zwingli* (Oxford: Clarendon, 1986), chap. 9.

32. See S. M. Jackson, *The Selected Works of Huldreich Zwingli*, 3 vols. (1901; rpt. Philadelphia, 1972), 3:180–81; Stephens, *Theology of Zwingli*, 183.

33. Zwingli, *Works*, 3:184, cited in González, *HCT* 3:74; Zwingli, *Works* 3:179, 182; Stephens, *Theology of Zwingli*, 184.

34. *An Account of the Faith* in Stephens, *Theology of Zwingli*, 186.

35. Zwingli, *Works* 2:258–59; Cf. 2:116–17. Stephens writes that "Zwingli's understanding of the sacraments moves from the earlier writings, where they are signs of the covenant with which God assures us, through a period where the emphasis is on them as signs with which we assure others that we are one with them in the church, to the later writings, where something of both these emphases is present" (*Theology of Zwingli*, 192).

36. Only those who receive the gift of faith (the elect) gain spiritual benefits from the sacraments. G. C. Berkouwer writes that for Calvin "the granting of salvation does not come separate from the sign and seal" but rather "it belongs to the essence of the sacrament that the signs are instrumentally (not abstractly) interpreted in the light of the correlation between faith and the sacrament." The two terms *signs* and *seals* "taken together make clear that the sacraments are symbols, but not symbols that stand by themselves" (*The Sacraments*, trans. Hugo Bekker [Grand Rapids: Eerdmans, 1969], 138–39).

37. *Canons and Decrees of the Council of Trent*, trans. H. J. Schroeder (1941; rpt. St. Louis: Herder, 1955), 51. Heick writes that "according to the teachings of the Thomists, grace is embedded in the sacraments. . . . According to the Scotists, an inward spiritual power runs parallel to the external act" (*HCT* 1:489).

38. In Schroeder, *Canons,* 52–53; Cf. Martos, *Doors,* 119.
39. Cornelius (Acts 10:48) is the exception to baptism preceeding the reception of the Holy Spirit.
40. *Didache* 9.5; 7.1–3 (*ECF,* 175, 174). Cf. Kelly, *Doct.,* 193–94.
41. *Ep. to Barnabas* 11.11; 16.7–8.
42. *1 Clem.* 46.6, in *ECF,* 46. Cf. Pelikan, *CT* 1:164.
43. Justin, *I Apol.* 61 (*ECF,* 282–83). Cf. Pelikan, *CT* 1:163ff.
44. Irenaeus, *Proof of the Apostolic Preaching* 41–42; *Ag. Her.* 3.17.2 in *Early,* 94.
45. See *On Baptism* 1.18; 12–15; *Ag. Marcion* 1.28. Cf. Pelikan, *CT* 1:163ff.; Kelly, *Doct.,* 209; Heick, *HCT* 1:216–17.
46. Clement, *Tutor* 1.6; 26.1–2. Cf. Pelikan, *CT* 1:164.
47. See Origen, *On First Principles* 1.3.2; 2.10.7; *Hom. in Exodus* 5.5; *In Luke* 22; 27; *In Rom.* 5.9. Cf. Kelly, *Doct.,* 208; Seeberg, *THD* 1:156.
48. Cyprian, *Lett.* 73.12; *To Donatus* 4; *On the Lord's Prayer* 23; etc. See Seeberg, *THD* 1:194.
49. Cyprian, *Lett.* 70.1; 72.1; 73.6, 21; etc. See Seeberg, *THD* 1:184, 194; Pelikan, *CT* 1:166, 291.
50. *Against the Two Ep. of the Pelagians* 3.3.5; *Ser.* 58.5.6. See Kelly, *Doct.,* 429; Pelikan, *CT* 1:304; Seeberg, *THD* 1:322.
51. See *On the Merits and the Remission of Sins* 2.31.50; *On Original Sin* 39.44; *On Nature and Grace* 53.61; Pelikan, *CT* 1:304. Cf. Martos, *Doors,* 175–76.
52. *On Baptism* 1.12, 18; 5.8, 9; 6.5, 7. See Seeberg, *THD* 1:320.
53. *On the Merits and Remission* 1.25 in *Later,* 243; *On Baptism* 4.31, 32, in *Later,* 243.
54. See *On the Mer. and Rem.* 1.10; 1.39; Kelly, *Doct.,* 432.
55. Lombard, *Sent.* 4.3; Hugo, *On the Sacs.* 2.6.2. Cf. Martos, *Doors,* 184; Seeberg, *THD* 2:130.
56. *On Simoniacs* 11 in Pelikan, *CT* 3:205; cf. 30–31.
57. *ST* III:69.2, 4. See Seeberg, *THD* 2:130; Martos, *Doors,* 187.
58. In Schroeder, *Canons,* 53–54. Cf. Martos, *Doors,* 194–95.
59. See Seeberg, *THD* 2:284, and *Small Catechism* (1529) 4:86. Exorcism is the first act in Luther's order of baptism. See Eric W. Gritsch, *Martin—God's Court Jester* (Philadelphia: Fortress, 1983), 179, 256, n. 8. Cf. Althaus, *Theology of Luther,* chap. 26.
60. *WA* 2:728; *LW* 35:30. Cf. Seeberg, *THD* 2:284; *WA* 2:732; *LW* 35:35–36; Althaus, *Theology of Luther,* 356; Heick, *HCT* 1:344.
61. See the citations in Stephens, *Theology of Zwingli,* 201, 120, 198–216. On Luther and the Anabaptists see Althaus, *Theology of Luther,* 370–74. Cf. John Calvin, *Treatises Against the Anabaptists and Against the Libertines,* ed. and trans. Benjamin Wirt Farley (Grand Rapids: Baker, 1982).
62. G. W. Bromiley, ed., *Zwingli and Bullinger* (Philadelphia: Westminster, 1953), 136. Cf. Stephens, *Theology of Zwingli,* 214ff.
63. This alludes to Zwingli's interpretation of *sacramentum* based on the classical use of the word as "nothing else than an initiatory ceremony or a pledging." Calvin rejects this approach. Cf. *Inst.* IV.14.13; 16.4.
64. See *Inst.* IV.15.22; 16.3ff. On "accommodation" see Donald K. McKim, "Calvin's View of Scripture," in *Reading in Calvin's Theology,* ed. Donald K. McKim (Grand Rapids: Baker, 1984), 54.
65. For Calvin and Zwingli infant baptism is equivalent to Old Testament circumcision as a sign of God's covenant now fulfilled in Christ. See *Inst.* IV.16; Berkouwer, *Sacraments,* chaps. 6, 8. Calvin did not believe that baptism frees

one from original sin, but through baptism, "believers are assured that this condemnation has been removed and withdrawn from them" (IV.15.10).

CHAPTER 8

1. *Didache* 9.5 in *ECF*, 175. On the agape or "love feast" see *IDB* 1:53–54; Dom Gregory Dix, *The Shape of the Liturgy* (1945; rpt. New York: Seabury, 1982), chap. 4; *The Study of Liturgy*, ed. Cheslyn Jones et al. (New York: Oxford Univ. Press, 1978), 147–69.
2. See Jones, *Liturgy*, 172–76, 147ff.; Alasdair I. C. Heron, *Table and Tradition* (Philadelphia: Westminster, 1983), 59–63; Dix, *Liturgy*, chap. 5.
3. Justin Martyr, *I Apology* 66 in *ECF*, 286. For an analysis cf. Arthur C. Cochrane, *Eating and Drinking with Jesus* (Philadelphia: Westminster, 1974), 119–22.
4. *Didache* 10.3 in *ECF*, 176.
5. Ignatius, *To the Smyrnaeans* 7.1 (*ECF*, 114).
6. Irenaeus, *Against Heresies* 4.18.5. Cf. 4.17.5; (*Early*, 96–97). Pelikan, *CT* 1:169.
7. Tertullian, *On the Resurrection of the Body* 8 in *ECF*, 148. Volz notes that "Tertullian recalled an instance where a mouse found the bread, but the bread was preserved from desecration by a ball of fire which snatched it away and consumed it" (*FPEC*, 108). Tertullian also spoke of the bread as "a figure" (*figura*) of Christ's body and once of "the bread by which He represents (*repraesentat*) His very body." But as Kelly notes, "The verb *repraesentare*, in Tertullian's vocabulary, retained its original significance of 'to make present.' All that his language really suggests is that, while accepting the equation of the elements with the body and blood, he remains conscious of the sacramental distinction between them" (*Doct.*, 212).
8. Cyprian, *On the Lord's Prayer* 18. Cf. Kelly, *Doct.*, 212.
9. Athanasius, *Frag. from a Sermon to the Baptized*, in Kelly, *Doct.*, 212.
10. Cyril of Jerusalem, *Catechetical Lectures* 22 (*Later*, 45).
11. *Cat. Lects.* 23.7 in *Later*, 46. Cf. Heron, *Table*, 65–66; Kelly, *Doct.*, 442–43.
12. Gregory of Nyssa, *Cat. Oration* 37, in *Later*, 165.
13. Chrysostom, *On the Betrayal of Judas* 1.6; *Hom. in Matthew* 82.5; Ambrose of Milan, *On the Mysteries* 52–54, in Kelly, *Doct.*, 446.
14. Clement of Alexandria, *Stromateis* 5.10, in *Early*, 181–82; *Paedagogus* 1.6 in *Early*, 181.
15. Origen, *In Matt.* 85, in *Early*, 250–51; cf. 11, 14; Seeberg, *THD* 1:156.
16. See Basil of Caesarea, *Letters* 8.4, in Kelly, *Doct.*, 442.
17. Augustine, *Serm.* 272. Cf. Kelly, *Doct.*, 447.
18. *On Baptism* 5.8, 9. Cf. 9.15; *Expl. on the Psalms* 98.9, in *Later*, 247. Cf. Pelikan, *CT* 1:305.
19. *Expos. on John* 26.18; 26.12. Cf. *City of God* 21.25; *On Christ. Doctrine* 3.24. Seeberg, *THD* 1:323; *Later*, 246; Cochrane, *Eating*, 123.
20. *Expos. on John* 25.12; 26.14, 15; *Serm.* 272; *City of God* 21.25.2; Cf. Pelikan, *CT* 1:305; Seeberg, *THD* 1:323.
21. Cyprian, *Epis.* 63. Cf. Kelly, *Doct.*, 214ff.
22. See Martos, *Doors*, 259ff.; Heron, *Table*, 80–87.
23. See González, *HCT* 2:117; Lohse, *SHCD*, 142ff.
24. On Berengar see Heick, *HCT* 1:272ff.; Pelikan, *CT* 3:186ff.
25. In Lohse, *SHCD*, 147.
26. *Ibid.*, 149.

27. Ibid., 153. See Pelikan, *CT* 3:203, on Pope Alexander's usage. Martos attributes the term to Hildebert of Tours early in the thirteenth century (*Doors*, 271).
28. Aquinas, *ST* III.76.7. Cf. Heron, *Table*, 96ff.; Martos, *Doors*, 275ff.
29. *Canons and Decrees of the Council of Trent*, trans. H. J. Schroeder (1941; rpt. St. Louis: Herder, 1955), 73, 75. The distinction between Christ's "natural mode" and his "sacramental presence" was made by Aquinas. See Martos, *Doors*, 273–75.
30. In Schroeder, *Canons*, 74.
31. The "significationist/transformationist" terminology comes from Ralph W. Quere, "Changes and Constants: Structure in Luther's Understanding of the Real Presence in the 1520's," *The Sixteenth Century Journal* 16/1 (1985): 46.
32. This analysis is drawn from Quere, "Luther," 47ff.
33. See *WA* 2:743.20–23; *LW* 35:51. Cf. Quere, "Luther," 48–55.
34. *WA* 6:360, 359; *LW* 35:88, 87. Cf. Quere, "Luther," 50–53.
35. *WA* 8:518.21; *LW* 36:176. Cf. Quere, "Luther," 53–54.
36. *WA* 11:433, 450.11–13; *LW* 36:278, 297. Cf. Althaus, *Theology of Luther*, 380; Quere, "Luther," 55–57.
37. *WA* 18:203.30–34. Cf. Quere, "Luther," 57–64.
38. *Large Catechism* V.28, in *The Book of Concord*, ed. and trans. Theodore G. Tappert et al. (Philadelphia: Fortress, 1959), 449. Cf. Quere, "Luther," 64ff.
39. *WA* 6:511; *LW* 36:35. See Althaus, *Theology of Luther*, 391ff. Luther's view has been called "consubstantiation," a concept that goes back to the early 1200s. Here "the substance of Christ was added to that of the material elements when the words of consecration were spoken" (see Martos, *Doors*, 270). Transubstantiation developed from the argument that two substances could not occupy the same space, but, as Althaus says for Luther, "Christ's body and blood are present in the untransformed bread and wine" (*Theology of Luther*, 376). Heron claims Luther pressed the christological formula so it "became much more than an *analogy*, rather an *explanation* of how Christ's body and blood could be really present" (*Table*, 118). On ubiquity see Pelikan, *CT* 4:158–61; Heron, *Table*, chap. 6.
40. See Pelikan, *CT* 4:200. Heron writes, "Luther affirms the *intention* of the doctrine of transubstantiation, but rejects it as an inadequate, indeed misconceived *explanation*" (*Table*, 112–13).
41. S. M. Jackson, *The Selected Works of Huldreich Zwingli*, 3 vols. (1972; rpt. Philadelphia, 1901), 3:200 in González, *HCT* 3:75.
42. *Works* 3:214, 205. Cf. Quere, "Luther," 60–63; Cochrane, *Eating*, 124–28 for Zwingli's views.
43. In 1524 Zwingli received a letter (written in 1521) from the Dutch humanist Cornelius Hoen, who argued that "is" means "signifies" in the words of institution. Zwingli called this insight the "pearl of great price." From then on, Zwingli focused on John 6 as his key. See W. P. Stephens, *The Theology of Huldrych Zwingli* (Oxford: Clarendon, 1986), 227ff. Cf. Heron, *Table*, 116; Seeberg, *THD* 2:320; Pelikan, *CT* 4:158–59. Zwingli said, "We must understand first of all that throughout the Bible there are to be found figures of speech, [which are] . . . to be understood in another sense." See Pelikan, *CT* 4:194.
44. In Pelikan, *CT* 4:195. Zwingli said, "The body of Christ is then eaten, when his death for us is believed." See Seeberg, *THD* 2:321. Luther agreed that in John 6 Christ is describing faith, but he concluded that the Lord's Supper is not the subject of the chapter. See *WA* 33:182; 33:259–60; Lohse, *SHCD*, 173; Seeberg, *THD* 2:323.

45. Zwingli, *A Clear Instruction About the Lord's Supper* 1, in Pelikan, *CT* 4:197. Zwingli said a physical eating of Christ's body is "abhorrent to sense" (ibid., 194).
46. Stephens writes, "Zwingli has no difficulty in affirming the spiritual presence of Christ, but that is quite different from his bodily presence. 'If this presence of the body is spiritual' in the sense that 'in our hearts we trust in Christ as having died for us,' then Zwingli can assert that there is no difference between him and his opponents" (*Theology of Zwingli*, 243). Heron notes that "for Luther, the decisive saying is, 'This is my body.' For Zwingli, it is, 'Do this in remembrance of me'" (*Table*, 116). Zwingli's views are often called "memorialism."
47. On Marburg see Stephens, *Theology of Zwingli*, 248–50; Heron, *Table*, 120–22.
48. Calvin, *Replies to Joachim Westphal* 2; 3. Cf. Pelikan, *CT* 4:186.
49. *Short Treatise on the Holy Supper* 5. See Pelikan, *CT* 4:186. Calvin called Zwingli's views "false and pernicious." See Brian Gerrish, "Gospel and Eucharist: John Calvin on the Lord's Supper," in *The Old Protestantism and the New* (Chicago: Univ. of Chicago Press, 1982), 107.
50. *Inst.* IV.17.1. Gerrish's seven propositions summarize Calvin's views: the Lord's Supper is a gift; the gift is Jesus Christ himself; the gift is given through the signs; the gift is given by the Holy Spirit; the gift is given to all who communicate; the benefit of the gift is received by faith; and the gift evokes gratitude ("Gospel and Eucharist," 112–15).
51. *Short Treatise on the Holy Supper* 2. See Pelikan, *CT* 4:191.
52. *Replies to Westphal* 2. See Pelikan, *CT* 4:192. "The sacred mystery of the Supper consists in two things: physical signs, which, thrust before our eyes, represent to us, acording to our feeble capacity, things invisible; and spiritual truth, which is at the same time represented and displayed through the symbols themselves" (*Inst.* IV.17.11).
53. *The Best Way of Achieving Concord*, in Pelikan, *CT* 4:192. Cf. *Inst.* IV.14. Gerrish writes, "The signs 'present' what they 'represent'; they are not bare or empty signs, but are joined with the reality they signify" ("Gospel and Eucharist," 113).
54. *Inst.* IV.17.6. For Calvin on faith see IV.2.
55. He also opposed the Anabaptists. See his *Treatises Against the Anabaptists and Against the Libertines* and Willem Balke, *Calvin and the Anabaptist Radicals*, trans. William Heynen (Grand Rapids: Ferdmans, 1981). On the presence of Christ see Joseph N. Tylenda, "Calvin and Christ's Presence in the Supper— True or Real," *Scottish Journal of Theology* 27 (1974): 65–75. Tylenda concludes, "Calvin would have preferred the word 'true' [in the sense of 'really present' and not as fallacious, imaginary or counterfeit presence] when referring to the presence of the Lord's body in the Supper," since "for Calvin, the Supper was the sacrament of taking, eating and drinking the flesh and blood of our redemption, not the sacrament of a presence" (pp. 73–74).

CHAPTER 9

1. *Eschatology*, based on the Gk. *eschaton*, refers to the "last things." See Geoffrey Wainwright, *Eucharist and Eschatology* (New York: Oxford Univ. Press, 1971).
2. *IDB* 3:19.
3. A. M. Hunter, *The Work and Words of Jesus*, rev. ed. (Philadelphia: Westminster, 1973), 90. Cf. *TDNT* 1:564ff.
4. *TDNT* 1:582. Joachim Jeremias notes that in the Old Testament, God's reign is not spatial or static. It is a dynamic concept meaning that "God is realizing the

ideal of the king of righteousness, constantly longed for, but never fulfilled on earth" (*New Testament Theology*, trans. John Bowden [New York: Scribner's, 1971], 98).

5. C. H. Dodd coined *realized eschatology* to stress the present coming of the kingdom. Eschatology is thus focused on what has happened in history. See *The Parables of the Kingdom* (London: Collins, 1961), chap. 2. Others speak of *inaugurated eschatology*. See Hunter, *Work and Words*, 94.

6. Eusebius, *Eccl. History* 3.39.11–12. See Pelikan, *CT* 1:124.

7. Irenaeus, *Against Heresies* 5.33.2, in *ECF*, 374–75.

8. *Ep. of Barnabas* 15. Cf. Kelly, *Doct.*, 462. Reward for righteousness and punishment for wickedness was perhaps the chief element of early eschatology. See Seeberg, *THD* 1:81.

9. Justin Martyr, *Dialogue with Trypho* 80.2. Cf. Kelly, *Doct.*, 466; Pelikan, *CT* 1:125.

10. *Ag. Her.* 5.31.2, in *ECF*, 98; 5.25.1. Cf. Kelly, *Doct.*, 467–68; Seeberg, *THD* 1:134; Pelikan, *CT* 1:128.

11. *Ag. Her.* 5.33.2, in *ECF*, 394.

12. *Ag. Marcion* 3.24, in *Early*, 164. Tertullian cites Gal. 4:26; Phil. 3:20; Ezek. 48:30ff.; Rev. 21:2ff.

13. *On the Resurrection of the Flesh* 26.11; *Ag. Marcion* 4.33.8.

14. In Kelly, *Doct.*, 469; Pelikan, *CT* 1:128.

15. Origen, *On First Principles* 2.11.2–3; Pelikan, *CT* 1:125. Cf. 2.10.3, in *Early*, 255. Origen's Neoplatonism is seen in his interpretation of "Thy kingdom come": the soul should let itself be ruled by God and should become obedient to God's spiritual law (*On Prayer* 25.1; Karl Barth, *The Christian Life*, trans. G. W. Bromiley [Grand Rapids: Eerdmans, 1981], 244). See Origen, *Sel. in Psalms* 144.13; *In John* 19, 12, 78; Kelly, *Doct.*, 470.

16. Origen, *In Matt.* 14.7 on Matthew 18:23. See *TDNT* 1:589. On Origen's eschatology see Kelly, *Doct.*, 470ff.; Pelikan, *CT* 1:151; Seeberg, *THD* 1:159–60. Origen believed in the "restoration of all things," including the wicked and Satan (Acts 3:21). See Heick, *HCT* 1:123.

17. In Seeberg, *THD* 1:197.

18. *Sermons* 131.6.6 in Seeberg, *THD* 1:326, n. 2.

19. *City of God*, trans. Henry Bettenson (Middlesex, England: Penguin, 1972), 20.9. Cf. *Ser.* 213.7; 214.11; Seeberg, *THD* 1:326. In *Ser.* 259 Augustine rejects the literal interpretation of the millennium and is thus regarded as the founder of "amillennialism" as opposed to "premillennialism" and "postmillennialism."

20. *City of God* 20.25; cf. 21.26.

21. *Ibid.*, 14.28.

22. *Ibid.*, 14.13.

23. *Ibid.*, 11.1; 1.35; cf. 18.47–50.

24. *Ibid.*, 13.16. Cf. *Expos. on the Ps.* 98.4. Augustine uses *church* as the empirical Catholic church, the mystical body of Christ, the bride of Christ, or the invisible church of the elect. See Eric G. Jay, *The Church: Its Changing Image through Twenty Centuries* (Atlanta: John Knox, 1978), 92.

25. See Hans Schwarz, *On the Way to the Future* (Minneapolis: Augsburg, 1972), 152–53.

26. While Eusebius did not actually use the term "millennium" (*Eccl. History*, 10, 4), he saw visible progress toward the kingdom of God.

27. Gregory the Great, *Hom. on the Gospels* 2.38.2; 32.6; *Moral Discourses on Job* 33.18.34. Cf. Seeberg, *THD* 2:25.

28. See Pelikan, *CT* 3:42ff.; Jay, *The Church*, 105–6.
29. To Philip Melanchthon on June 2, 1530, *Briefe* 5.346, in Thomas F. Torrance, *Kingdom and Church* (Fair Lawn, N.J.: Essential Books, 1956), 20.
30. In 1533, however, "Luther had to deal severely with Michel Stifel for calculating that the world would end at 8 a.m. on October 19, 1533!" (*Tischreden* 4.51.2 in Torrance, *Kingdom*, 20).
31. Torrance provides a number of Luther's terms (*Kingdom*, 23–24). Cf. Paul Althaus, *The Ethics of Martin Luther*, trans. Robert C. Schultz (Philadelphia: Fortress, 1972), chap. 4; Eric W. Gritsch, *Martin—God's Court Jester* (Philadelphia: Fortress, 1983), chap. 6; Gerhard Ebeling, *Luther: An Introduction to His Thought*, trans. R. A. Wilson (Philadelphia: Fortress, 1972), chap. 11.
32. *WA* 51:239.22–30 (1534–35), in Ebeling, *Luther*, 177.
33. *WA* 45:252; cf. 280, 292; 47:853. Cf. Torrance, *Kingdom*, 24; Althaus, *Ethics*, 54–56.
34. *Ser. for the Third of Advent*, on Matt. 11:2–10, in Torrance, *Kingdom*, 24. Cf. Althaus, *Ethics*, 56–59.
35. "To confuse the two kingdoms . . . is to usurp the Kingdom of God or to force God's hand—and that is the very mark of Antichrist" (*WA* 40/1:51, 175–78). See Torrance, *Kingdom*, 30.
36. See Ebeling, *Ethics*, 185. Althaus writes that "even though the two governments are different from and essentially independent of each other, they still need each other" (*Ethics*, 59).
37. See *WA* 40:8; 5:217; 30/1:189ff.; 17/1:193–94; 8:539–40; 11:235; 6:293ff.; 2:73; Torrance, *Kingdom*, 32.
38. On Calvin see Torrance, *Kingdom*, chap. 4; H. Quistorp, *Calvin's Doctrine of the Last Things* (London: Lutterworth, 1955); David E. Holwerda, "Eschatology and History: A Look at Calvin's Eschatological Vision," in *Readings in Calvin's Theology*, ed. Donald K. McKim (Grand Rapids: Baker, 1984), chap. 18.
39. *Comm. on First Corinthians*, trans. John W. Fraser, *Calvin's New Testament Commentaries*, ed. David W. and Thomas F. Torrance, 12 vols. (1960; rpt. Grand Rapids: Eerdmans, 1980—hereafter cited as *CNTC*), 9:314. Christ is the *medium* of salvation.
40. *Comm. on Acts*, "Dedicatory Epistle" (*CNTC* 6:3). Cf. Torrance, *Kingdom*, 115.
41. See *Comm. on Acts* 2:33 (*CNTC* 6:74); *Ser. on Acts* 1:9–11; *Comm. on Heb.* 7:17f. (*CNTC* 12:98); *Comm. on Matt.* 24:14 (*CNTC* 3:82–83); *Comm. on Matt.* 25:31 (*CNTC* 3:112–13). The kingdom of God is "the forgiveness of sins, salvation, life, and utterly everything that we obtain in Christ." See *Inst.* III.3.19.
42. See *Comm. on Gen. 17:7*; Holwerda, "Eschatology and History," 324; *Comm. on Acts 3:21* (*CNTC* 3:103).
43. *Inst.* III.20.42. Cf. *Comm. on Acts* 2:17 (*CNTC* 6:56–59); *Comm. on Heb.* 2:13 (*CNTC* 12:27–30); *Comm. on Acts* 1:3 (*CNTC* 6:24–25); Torrance, *Kingdom*, 116.
44. See *Inst.* III.7–10; IV.20.
45. *Inst.* III.25.5. Cf. Quistorp, *Last Things*, 158–62; Holwerda, "Eschatology and History," 327–30.
46. When commenting on the phrase "the dead shall rise" in 1 Cor. 15:52, Calvin writes, "Since it was already the last times, the saints were to expect that day every single hour." See *Comm. on I Cor. 15:52* (*CNTC* 9:344). Cf. Torrance, *Kingdom*, 118–19; *Comm. on Acts 2:17* (*CNTC* 6:56).
47. *Comm. on Heb. 9:26* (*CNTC* 12:26).
48. *Comm. on Matt. 24:29* (*CNTC* 3:93). Cf. *Inst.* III.20.42.
49. *Comm. on Matt. 6:10* (*CNTC* 1:208).

50. *Inst.* III.25.5. Cf. *Comm. on Matt. 6:10 (CNTC* 1:207), where Calvin writes that God is "reigning" over humans "when they subdue their flesh to His yoke, and their own desires are laid aside, so that they willingly bind and give themselves over to His rule." Cf. Torrance, *Kingdom,* 120ff.

51. See Peter Toon, *Puritans, the Millennium and Israel* (Cambridge: James Clarke, 1970); Christopher Hill, *The World Turned Upside Down* (New York: Viking, 1972); *Antichrist in 17th-Century England* (London: Oxford University Press, 1971).

52. See Karl Barth, *The Christian Life,* trans. G. W. Bromiley (Grand Rapids: Eerdmans, 1981), 243. Cf. his *Protestant Theology in the Nineteenth Century* (Valley Forge: Judson, 1973). On Schleiermacher's and Ritschl's views in relation to the church, see Jay, *The Church,* chap. 16.

53. Barth, *Life,* 237. Cf. Arthur C. Cochrane, *The Mystery of Peace* (Elgin, Ill.: Brethren Press, 1986).

54. See Barth's comments on Schleiermacher and Ritschl in *Protestant Theology,* chaps. 11, 29; his *Theology of Schleiermacher,* ed. Dietrich Ritschl, trans. G. W. Bromiley (Grand Rapids: Eerdmans, 1982); H. Martin Rumscheidt, *Revelation and Theology: An Analysis of the Barth–Harnack Correspondence of 1923* (New York: Cambridge University Press, 1972).

55. Barth, *Life,* 240.

56. *Ibid.,* 244.

57. *Ibid.,* 242.

58. This phrase was associated with J. C. Blumhardt (1805–80) and his son Christoph (1842–1919). It was a favorite of Barth's (see *Life,* 256–60).

CHAPTER 10

1. See Jürgen Moltmann, *The Trinity and the Kingdom,* trans. Margaret Kohl (San Francisco: Harper & Row, 1981); *The Crucified God,* trans. R. Wilson and J. Bowden (New York: Harper & Row, 1974); *Theology of Hope,* trans. J. W. Leitch (New York: Harper & Row, 1967).

2. Karl Rahner, *The Trinity* (New York: Herder & Herder, 1970), 106.

3. Marjorie Hewitt Suchocki, *God–Christ–Church: A Practical Guide to Process Theology* (New York: Crossroad, 1982), pt. 2; Charles Hartshorne, *The Divine Relativity* (New Haven: Yale Univ. Press, 1948).

4. Rosemary Ruether, *Sexism and God-Talk* (Boston: Beacon Press, 1983); Virginia Ramey Mollenkott, *The Divine Feminine* (New York: Crossroad, 1983); Joan Chamberlain Engelsman, *The Feminine Dimension of the Divine* (Philadelphia: Westminster, 1979).

5. Don Cupitt, "The Finality of Christ," *Theology* 78 (1975): 625.

6. John F. O'Grady, *Models of Jesus* (New York: Doubleday, 1982).

7. See Suchocki, *God–Christ–Church,* pt. 3; John Cobb, *Christ in a Pluralistic Age* (Philadelphia: Westminster, 1975); Patricia Wilson-Kastner, *Faith, Feminism, and the Christ* (Philadelphia: Fortress, 1983); Rosemary Ruether, *To Change the World: Christology and Cultural Criticism* (New York: Crossroad, 1981).

8. Wolfhart Pannenberg, *Jesus—God and Man,* trans. Duane A. Priebe (Philadelphia: Westminster, 1968); cf. Pannenberg, *Basic Questions in Theology* 1, trans. George H. Kehm (Philadelphia: Fortress, 1983).

9. Shubert M. Ogden, *Christ without Myth* (New York: Harper & Row, 1961).

10. John Hick, *God and the Universe of Faiths* (New York: St. Martin's, 1973).

11. Ibid., 152; John A. T. Robinson, *The Human Face of God* (Philadelphia: Westminster, 1973).
12. Hans Küng, *On Being a Christian*, trans. Edward Quinn (New York: Doubleday, 1976).
13. See Karl Rahner, "Anonymous Christians," in *Theological Investigations*, trans. Karl H. Kruger, 15 vols. (Baltimore: Helicon, 1969), 6:390–98; "Atheism and Implicit Christianity," *ibid.*, 9:145–65; "Anonymous Christianity and the Missionary Task of the Church," *ibid.*, 12:161–81.
14. See Eric G. Jay, *The Church: Its Changing Image through Twenty Centuries* (Atlanta: John Knox, 1980), 302, 439.
15. See Robert S. Paul, *The Church in Search of Its Self* (Grand Rapids: Eerdmans, 1972).
16. Dietrich Bonhoeffer, *Letters and Papers from Prison*, ed. Eberhard Bethge (New York: Macmillan, 1972), 382; Jay, *The Church*, 340.
17. See Barth, *CD*, IV/1; IV/2.
18. Paul Tillich, *Systematic Theology*, 3 vols. (Chicago: Univ. of Chicago Press, 1951, 1957, 1963), 3:162–63.
19. Hans Küng, *The Church* (Garden City, N.Y.: Doubleday, 1976), 11.
20. *Ibid.*, 169–77.
21. See Colin Gunton, *Enlightenment and Alienation* (Grand Rapids: Eerdmans, 1985); Diogenes Allen, *Philosophy for Understanding Theology* (Atlanta: John Knox, 1985).
22. In Linwood Urban, *A Short History of Christian Thought* (New York: Oxford Univ. Press, 1986), 146.
23. John Macquarrie, *In Search of Humanity* (New York: Crossroad, 1983); cf. the review by Donald K. McKim in *Review of Books and Religion* 12/10 (Sept.–Oct. 1984): 14–17, 32–33.
24. Wolfhart Pannenberg, *Anthropology in Theological Perspective*, trans. Matthew J. O'Connell (Philadelphia: Westminster, 1985), 20. Cf. his *What is Man?* (Philadelphia: Fortress, 1970).
25. See H. George Anderson et al., eds., *Justification by Faith* (Minneapolis: Augsburg, 1985), 16, 70–72.
26. Pannenberg, *Anthropology*, 311–12.
27. See Gustavo Gutiérrez, *A Theology of Liberation*, trans. and ed. Caridad Inda and John Eagleson (Maryknoll, N.Y.: Orbis, 1973); José Miguez Bonino, *Doing Theology in a Revolutionary Situation*, ed. William H. Lazareth (Philadelphia: Fortress, 1975).
28. Suchocki, *God–Christ–Church*, chap. 12.
29. Rosemary Ruether, "Feminist Interpretation: A Method of Correlation," in *Feminist Interpretation of the Bible*, ed. Letty M. Russell (Philadelphia: Westminster, 1985), 115; Phyllis Trible, "Postscript: Jottings on the Journey," *ibid.*, 149; Letty M. Russell, "Authority and the Challenge of Feminist Interpretation," *ibid.*, 138.
30. Robert Gnuse, *The Authority of the Bible: Theories of Inspiration, Revelation and the Canon of Scripture* (New York: Paulist, 1985), 114.
31. Article IX of *Dei Verbum*, in *The Documents of Vatican II*, ed. and trans. W. M. Abbott and J. Gallagher (New York: Guild, 1966). Cf. Avery Dulles, "Scripture: Recent Protestant and Catholic Views," in *The Authoritative Word: Essays on the Nature of Scripture*, ed. Donald K. McKim (Grand Rapids: Eerdmans, 1983), 246–51.

32. Paul J. Achtemeier, "How the Scriptures were Formed," in McKim, *Authoritative Word*, 14. Cf. David H. Kelsey, *The Uses of Scripture in Recent Theology* (Philadelphia: Fortress, 1975), 32–119.
33. Rogers and McKim, *AIB*, passim.
34. *A Guide to Contemporary Hermeneutics: Major Trends in Biblical Interpretation*, ed. Donald K. McKim (Grand Rapids: Eerdmans, 1986).
35. Edward Schillebeeckx, *Christ, the Sacrament of the Encounter with God* (New York: Sheed & Ward, 1963).
36. Karl Rahner, *Foundations of the Christian Faith* (New York: Seabury, 1978), chap. 8.
37. Alexandre Ganoczy, *An Introduction to Catholic Sacramental Theology*, trans. William Thomas and Anthony Sherman (New York: Paulist, 1984), 156.
38. Karl Barth, *The Church's Teaching About Baptism*, trans. Ernest A. Payne (London: SCM, 1948); *CD* IV/4. Cf. Geoffrey W. Bromiley, *Introduction to the Theology of Karl Barth* (Grand Rapids: Eerdmans, 1979), 239–43.
39. Moltmann, *Theology of Hope*, 329, 180.
40. Pannenberg, *Basic Questions* 1:74.
41. Wolfhart Pannenberg, *Theology and the Kingdom of God* (Philadelphia: Westminster, 1969), 56, 61, 75.
42. Charles Hartshorne, "Process Philosophy as a Resource for Christian Thought," in *Philosophical Resources for Christian Theology*, ed. Perry LeFevre (Nashville: Abingdon, 1968), 52.
43. Suchocki writes of the "double focus" of the kingdom of God, which she defines as "God's triumph of goodness over evil in the ultimacy of justice." The two dimensions of the one kingdom are the eternal and the temporal (*God–Christ–Church*, 174).
44. Gutiérrez speaks of liberation on three levels: political, historical, and theological in Jesus Christ. These levels may be distinguished but also constitute a basic unity in which all are present (*Theology of Liberation*, 177).

Selected Bibliography

In addition to the works listed in the Abbreviations and the references in the text, the following resources are useful.

CHAPTER 1

Bavinck, Herman. *The Doctrine of God*, translated by William Hendriksen. Grand Rapids: Baker, 1980.

Eichrodt, Walther. *Theology of the Old Testament*, translated by J. A. Baker. 2 vols. Philadelphia: Westminster, 1967.

Prestige, G. F. *God in Patristic Thought*. London: SPCK, 1952.

von Rad, Gerhard. *Old Testament Theology*, translated by D. M. G. Stalker. 2 vols. Edinburgh: Oliver and Boyd, 1962, 1965.

CHAPTER 2

Dunn, James D. G. *Christology in the Making*. Philadelphia: Westminster, 1980.

Marshall, I. H. *The Origins of New Testament Christology*. Downers Grove, Ill.: Inter-Varsity, 1976.

Moule, C. F. D. *The Origin of Christology*. New York: Cambridge University Press, 1977.

Wells, David F. *The Person of Christ*. Westchester, Ill.: Crossway, 1984.

CHAPTER 3

Berkouwer, G. C. *The Church*, translated by James E. Davison. Grand Rapids: Eerdmans, 1976.

Bultmann, Rudolf. *Theology of the New Testament*, translated by Kendrick Grobel. 2 vols. New York: Scribner's, 1951, 1955.

Dulles, Avery. *Models of the Church*. Garden City, N.Y.: Doubleday, 1974.

Frend, W. H. C. *Martyrdom and Persecution in the Early Church*. Garden City, N.Y.: Doubleday, 1967.

CHAPTER 4

Berkouwer, G. C. *Man: The Image of God,* translated by Dirk W. Jellema. Grand Rapids: Eerdmans, 1962.
Cunliffe-Jones, Hubert, and Benjamin Drewery, editors. *A History of Christian Doctrine.* Philadelphia: Fortress, 1980.
Hall, Douglas John. *Imaging God.* Grand Rapids: Eerdmans, 1986.
Hoekema, Anthony A. *Created in God's Image.* Grand Rapids: Eerdmans, 1986.

CHAPTER 5

Berkouwer, G. C. *Faith and Justification,* translated by Lewis B. Smedes. Grand Rapids: Eerdmans, 1968.
Moffatt, James. *Grace in the New Testament.* New York: Long & Smith, 1932.
Morris, Leon. *The Cross in the New Testament.* Exeter, England: Paternoster, 1967.
Toon, Peter. *Justification and Sanctification.* Westchester, Ill.: Crossway, 1983.

CHAPTER 6

Berkouwer, G. C. *Holy Scripture,* edited and translated by Jack B. Rogers. Grand Rapids: Eerdmans, 1975.
Dulles, Avery. *Models of Revelation.* Garden City, N.Y.: Doubleday, 1983.
McKim, Donald K. *What Christians Believe About the Bible.* Nashville: Nelson, 1985.
Ridderbos, Herman N. *Studies in Scripture and Its Authority.* Grand Rapids: Eerdmans, 1978.

CHAPTER 7

Beasley-Murray, G. R. *Baptism in the New Testament.* London: Macmillan, 1963.
Cullmann, Oscar. *Baptism in the New Testament.* London: SCM, 1956.
Flemington, W. F. *The New Testament Doctrine of Baptism.* London: SPCK, 1957.
Lampe, G. W. H. *The Seal of the Spirit.* London: Longmans, 1951.

CHAPTER 8

Gäbler, Ulrich. *Huldrych Zwingli: His Life and Work,* translated by Ruth C. L. Gritsch. Philadelphia: Fortress, 1986.
Jeremias, Joachim. *The Eucharistic Words of Jesus,* translated by Norman Perrin, 3d ed. London: SCM, 1966.
McDonnell, Kilian. *John Calvin, the Church, and the Eucharist.* Princeton: University Press, 1967.
Wallace, Ronald S. *Calvin's Doctrine of the Word and Sacrament.* Edinburgh: Oliver & Boyd, 1953.

CHAPTER 9

Berkouwer, G. C. *The Return of Christ,* translated by James Van Oosterom. Grand Rapids: Eerdmans, 1972.
Bright, John. *The Kingdom of God.* Nashville: Abingdon, 1953.
Gowan, Donald G. *The Eschatology of the Old Testament.* Philadelphia: Fortress, 1986.
Ridderbos, Herman. *The Coming of the Kingdom,* translated by H. de Jongste. Philadelphia: Presbyterian & Reformed, 1962.

CHAPTER 10

Bracken, Joseph A. *What Are They Saying About the Trinity?* New York: Paulist, 1979.

Drummond, Richard H. *Toward a New Age in Christian Theology.* Maryknoll, N.Y.: Orbis, 1985.

Hodgson, Peter C., and Robert H. King, editors. *Christian Theology: An Introduction to Its Traditions and Tasks,* revised and enlarged ed. Philadelphia: Fortress, 1985.

McKim, Donald K. "Hearkening to the Voices: What Women Theologians Are Saying." *The Reformed Journal* 35 (1985): 7–10.

Index